The McDonaldization of Society

An Investigation into the Changing Character of Contemporary Social Life

REVISED EDITION

Sociology of Work: Concepts and Cases by Carol Auster

Adventures in Social Research: Data Analysis Using SPSS for WINDOWS by Earl Babbie and Fred Halley

Race, Ethnicity, Gender, and Class: The Sociology of Group Conflict and Change by Joseph F. Healey

The Production of Reality: Essays and Readings in Social Psychology by Peter Kollock and Jodi O'Brien

Sociological Snapshots: Seeing Social Structure and Change in Everyday Life, 2nd. ed., by Jack Levin

Diversity in America by Vincent N. Parrillo

Expressing America: A Critique of the Global Credit Card Society by George Ritzer

Shifts in the Social Contract: Understanding Change in American Society by Beth Rubin

Sociology: Exploring the Architecture of Everyday Life by David M. Newman

Sociology: Exploring the Architecture of Everyday Life (Readings) by David M. Newman

Sociology for a New Century

A Pine Forge Press Series edited by Charles Ragin, Wendy Griswold, and Larry Griffin

How Societies Change by Daniel Chirot

Cultures and Societies in a Changing World by Wendy Griswold

Crime and Disrepute by John Hagan

Gods in the Global Village by Lester R. Kurtz

Constructing Social Research by Charles C. Ragin

Women and Men at Work by Barbara Reskin and Irene Padavic

Cities in a World Economy by Saskia Sassen

The McDonaldization
of Society

An Investigation into the Changing Character of Contemporary Social Life

REVISED EDITION

George Ritzer
University of Maryland

PINE FORGE PRESS
Thousand Oaks, California ◆ London ◆ New Delhi

For information, address:

 Pine Forge Press
A Sage Publications Company
2455 Teller Road
Thousand Oaks, California 91320
(805) 499-4224
E-mail: sales@pfp.sagepub.com

Sage Publications Ltd.
6 Bonhill Street
London EC2A 4PU
United Kingdom

Sage Publications India Pvt. Ltd.
M-32 Market
Greater Kailash I
New Delhi 110 048 India

Production: Greg Hubit Bookworks
Typesetter: Vividh Media Productions, Inc.
Text and Cover Design: Lisa S. Mirski
Production Manager: Rebecca Holland

Printed in the United States of America

96 97 98 99 10 9 8 7 6 5 4 3 2 1

Library of Congress Cataloging-in-Publication Data
Ritzer, George
    The McDonaldization of Society: an investigation into the
changing character of contemporary social life / George Ritzer. —
Rev. ed.
        p.   cm
    Includes bibliographical references (p. 205–238) and index.
        ISBN 0-8039-9076-6 (alk. paper). — ISBN 0-8039-9077-4 (pbk.
alk. paper)
        1. Social structure—United States.   2. United States—Social
conditions—1980-   3. Management—Social aspects—United
States.   4. Fast food restaurants—Social aspects—United States.
5. Rationalization (Psychology)   I. Title.
HM131.R58   1995
306'.0973—dc20   95-16950
                                                            CIP

To Alan Ritzer, who helped open my eyes to McDonaldization, and to Paul O'Connell, whose gentleness and Shavian wit were inspirations for this book.

About the Author

George Ritzer is an acknowledged expert in the field of social theory and sociology of work and has served as Chair of the American Sociological Association's Sections on Theoretical Sociology and Organizations and Occupations. A Distinguished Scholar-Teacher at the University of Maryland, Professor Ritzer has been honored with that institution's Teaching Excellence award. Two of his most recent books are *Expressing America: A Critique of the Global Credit Card Society* (Pine Forge Press) and *Sociology: Experiencing Changing Societies* (6th edition) with Kenneth Kammeyer and Norman Yetman. McGraw-Hill will soon publish his forthcoming book, *Postmodern Social Theory*.

About the Publisher

Pine Forge Press is a new educational publisher, dedicated to publishing innovative books and software throughout the social sciences. On this and any other of our publications, we welcome your comments and suggestions.

Please call or write us at

Pine Forge Press
A Sage Publications Company
2455 Teller Road
Thousand Oaks, CA 91320
(805) 499-4224
internet: sales@pfp.sagepub.com

Contents

Preface to the Revised Edition

While it may only be in part traceable to the first edition of this book, uses of the term *McDonaldization*, as well as interest in the phenomenon it describes, are on the increase:

- A recent newspaper article is entitled "'McDonaldization' of Maryland Banking: Can Nations Bank Meet the State's Diverse Needs?"
- In a recent "Zippy" cartoon by Bill Griffith on the future of Cuba, one character utters the line, "Will th' tourism they're so actively encouraging eventually bring with it th' dreaded McDonaldization of their culture? Will they be able to resist its shiny allure?"
- Within academia, scholars in a variety of fields have found the concept useful.
- In sociology, the idea has been widely employed in scholarly work, is an entry in at least one dictionary of sociology, and has quickly become a staple in textbooks introducing students to the discipline.
- At least seven translations (German, Italian, Portuguese, Spanish, Korean, Czech, and Hungarian) of *The McDonaldization of Society* have been published or are under contract and in preparation.

This diverse and high level of interest is one reason for this revision. The other is that while only three years have elapsed since the first edition of this book was published, the process of McDonaldization continues to accelerate dramatically. It is difficult to keep up with the numerous developments. I have done my best to keep readers abreast of these changes, but I am certain that many readers will have examples of their own that are not covered in these pages. (In anticipation of another revision, and in an effort to de-McDonaldize the relationship between author and reader, I would appreciate receiving such examples, with documentation if possible, by e-mail [Ritzer@bss1.umd.edu] or "snail mail" to the University of Maryland.)

In addition to many minor changes, additions, and refinements, there are several major changes in this edition that are worthy of special note. Most important, a new chapter (9) has been added: "Frontiers of McDonaldization: Birth, Death, and Beyond." I attempt to show that McDonaldization is not only expanding in any number of obvious ways (geographically, for example), but also expanding to encompass the birth process (and before) and the death process (and beyond). If birth and death can be McDonaldized, is anything safe from the process? In addition, based largely on Zygmunt Bauman's excellent book, *Modernity and the Holocaust*, I have added a section on the Holocaust to the chapter on the precursors of McDonaldization. I argue that the Holocaust was driven by bureaucratization and was anticipated by Max Weber's theory of rationalization. I have also restructured some of the discussion to highlight general points about McDonaldization and its fundamental dimensions. Finally, rather than just add new blocks of material, I have, to a large extent, rewritten the text to make the themes and issues even clearer and more accessible. Thus, I offer a substantial revision, although the basic structure and thrust of the argument remain the same as those of the first edition.

I have received a wealth of valuable comments toward improving the book and would like to thank the following for their help:

Mary Rogers, *University of West Florida*
Cynthia Woolever, *Midway College*
Stephen Kulis, *Arizona State University*
Jim Mannon, *DePauw University*
Kathleen F. Slevin, *William & Mary College*
Stephen N. Butler, *Earlham College*
Michael L. Sanow, *Towson State University*
James R. McIntosh, *Lehigh University*
J. C. Smith, *University of Wisconsin, Oshkosh*
Caleb Rosado, *Humboldt State University*
Fred Pampel, *University of Colorado, Boulder*
James T. Ault, III, *Creighton University*
Dan Cover, *Furman University*
Stephen P. Legeay, *Shaw University*
Lillian Daughaday, *Murray State University*
Jeana M. Abromeit, *Alverno College*
Aliza Kolker, *George Mason University*
Harry R. Moody, *Hunter College*

I would also like to thank the developmental editor Rebecca Smith, the copyeditor Molly Roth, and the Pine Forge Press staff, principally production manager Rebecca Holland and president Steve Rutter, for their help with this revision. Also to be thanked are my assistants Heidi Jones, Rachel Landsberg, and, especially, Allan Liska. A number of undergraduate students made contributions to this edition, but I would especially like to thank Melissa Therrien. Jeremy Ritzer once again endured the difficulties of working with his father and reading his father's work to do the index. Finally, I would like to thank the forces behind McDonaldization for providing me with so many new and dramatic examples of the process they are so intent on extending to new domains and regions of the world.

Preface to the First Edition

I have been thinking about the process of rationalization for many years. It has long been believed that bureaucracy represents the ultimate form of rationalization. However, it gradually began to dawn on me that something new was on the horizon, something destined to replace the bureaucratic structure as the model for rationalization. That "something" turned out to be the fast-food restaurant, most notably McDonald's, which revolutionized not only the restaurant business, but also American society and, ultimately, the world.

As a New Yorker, I came late to McDonald's because, during my teenage years (the 1950s), the fast-food restaurant had not yet invaded large cities to any great degree. I can remember the first time I ever saw a McDonald's. It was on an automobile trip to Massachusetts in 1958, and, for some reason, it left an indelible mark on my memory. Retrospectively, I think I realized, at least subliminally, that those golden arches represented something new and important.

About a decade later, and by this time a professional sociologist, I lived in New Orleans. When my brother Alan Ritzer, a lifelong New Yorker, came to visit, we went to McDonald's, his first exposure to the fast-food restaurant. He, too, was struck by the significance of this phenomenon and of the problems it posed for society.

Through the 1970s I developed my theoretical orientation, which was heavily influenced by the work of the German social theorist Max Weber and his views about the rationalization process. He viewed bureaucracy as the paradigm case of rationality. Although Weber recognized the advantages of rationalization, he was most animated by its dangers, especially the possibility of what he called an "iron cage" of rationality. Weber felt that rational systems were inhuman and dehumanizing. He dreaded the possibility, indeed the likelihood, that an increasing number of sectors of society would become rationalized; he felt that society would ultimately become a seamless web of rational institutions. Once rational systems proliferated to that extent, we would be faced with an iron cage of rationality: there could be no escape, no exit.

By the early 1980s, I began to put Weber's theory of rationalization together with my concern with the growth of the fast-food restaurant. By this time, McDonald's was far more ubiquitous, and its clones in the fast-food business, as well as in many other social settings, were spreading throughout society. Alarmed by this trend, in 1983 I wrote an essay entitled, "The McDonaldization of Society."

With the latter essay out of my system, I moved on to other things, including other applications of Weberian theory. During a speech I gave in 1990, I touched on McDonaldization in the context of a far broader discussion of the applications of Weberian theory to the modern world. I thought that the most important part of the talk was an effort to explain the rise of Japanese industry, and the decline of American industry, in terms of rationalization. However, when it came time for open discussion, the audience only wanted to talk about McDonaldization. This was clearly an idea with which people resonated. Over the years, I had received similar reactions from students whenever I lectured on McDonaldization. In fact, as McDonaldization became more and more ubiquitous, the level of interest in the phenomenon, and in the problems it generated, increased dramatically.

It seemed clear to me that it was time to write a book on the issue. In the decade since I had written my essay, fast-food restaurants had proliferated to the degree that they were virtually everywhere. Also, many other businesses had been organized along the lines developed by McDonald's. Almost all social institutions (for example, education, sports, politics, and religion) were adapting McDonald's principles to their operations. And McDonaldization was spreading around the world—fast-food croissanteries in Paris (of all places), Kentucky Fried Chicken in Beijing, McDonald's in Beijing and Moscow.

In fact, in May 1992, just as this book [first edition] was going to press, I was in Moscow lecturing at the Russian Academy of Sciences. Stunned by the many changes taking place in that society, I was particularly drawn to the spread of McDonaldization. There, in the heart of Moscow, stood the new McDonald's. Muscovites were and still are attracted to it in droves for a variety of reasons, not the least of which is the fact that it is the symbol of the rationalization of America and its coveted market economy. The rationality of McDonald's stands in stark contrast to the irrationalities of the remnants of communism. Long lines and long waits (so much for *fast* food) are common, but one sunny Saturday in May the line stretched as far as the eye could see. In fact, teenagers were offering, in exchange for a few rubles, to get you a "Beeg Mek" in no more than ten or fifteen minutes. Seemingly oblivious to its potential problems, Russians (and most others) are in a headlong rush toward McDonaldization.

This book is essentially a work in social criticism. McDonald's clearly has many advantages, and they will be mentioned throughout the book. However, McDonald's and its many clones have plenty of opportunity, and spend huge sums of money, to tell you about their good points. This book seeks to give the public discourse a little balance by focusing on the problems created, and the dangers posed, by McDonaldization.

As a theoretically based work in social criticism, this book is part of a historical tradition in the social sciences in which social theory is used to critique society and thereby to provide the base for its betterment. This tradition animated Weber as well as other social theorists such as Georg Simmel, Emile Durkheim, Karl Marx, C. Wright Mills, and Jurgen Habermas.

I should point out that I bear no particular animus toward McDonald's. It is no better or worse than other fast-food restaurants and other manifestations of the rationalization process. I have labeled the process of concern here "McDonaldization" because McDonald's was, and is, the most important manifestation of this process. Besides, it has a better ring to it than some of the alternatives—"Burger Kingization," "Seven Elevenization," "Fuddruckerization," "H & R Blockization," "Kinder Care-ization," "Jiffy Lube-ization," or "Nutri/Systemization."

As the preceding list makes clear, a wide array of social phenomena are linked in this book under the heading of McDonaldization. Some have been directly affected by the principles of the fast-food restaurant, whereas in other cases the effect is more indirect. Some have all the basic dimensions of McDonaldization, but others only one or two. In any case, in my view they all are part of what Weber called the rationalization process, or to make Weber more timely, McDonaldization.

The major themes of this book, especially the critiques of the irrationalities of McDonaldization, are likely to be highly controversial. My experience in lecturing on this theme is that audiences generally support McDonaldization and feel protective toward it. Critiques of McDonaldization inevitably spawn heated debate in the lecture hall. It is hoped that this book will spark a similar debate in a larger arena. The generation of such debate, as well as the insights to be derived from it, is the essence not only of good teaching but also of good sociology. Whether or not the reader agrees with my conclusions, I will have succeeded in achieving my goal if the reader has been provoked into rethinking this significant aspect of everyday life.

This book is written to be accessible to a wide readership. However, it is firmly based on one of the strongest social theories, Weber's theory of rationalization. It is also an "empirical" study, albeit highly informal. The "data" are drawn from a wide range of available sources and deal with the full range of social phenomena that fall under the heading of McDonaldization. However, although it is theory-based and relies on "data," this is not written as a dry theoretical and empirical study; it is not weighted down by the requirements of scholarly monographs. Rather, it is designed to be a book that can be read by many people and inform them of a wide-ranging social development that is occurring all around them. More important, it is written as a warning that the seductions and attractions of McDonaldization should not blind us to its many dangers.

I would like to thank Gladys Martinez, Brian Hoffman, JoAnn DeFiore, and Steve Lankenau for their invaluable help as graduate research assistants on this book. I also want to thank a number of my undergraduate students for many valuable insights into the McDonaldization of society. Their generation is even more enmeshed in our McDonaldized society than mine, and if present trends continue, their children will be still more ensnared. Among these students are Alyson J. Blewett, Carolyn Eddy, Melissa Fireman, Jennifer Gilbert, Wendy Grachik, Tremelle I. Howard, Paula Hutter, Anna Kennedy, Andrew Paradise, Mark C. Polk, Tim Prewitt, Sean Savio, Jamie Schapiro, Keri Sferra, Caroline Smith, Paul Tewksbury, Constance H. Ward, and most notably, Dora Giemza. Also to be thanked are several colleagues, including Conrad Kottak, Larry Mintz, Linda Moghadam, Stan Presser, and, as usual, Ken Kammeyer. Among the reviewers to be thanked are John Walsh, Peter Kollock, Wolf Heydebrand, Marshall Fishwick, Gary Alan Fine, and Robin Leidner, whose comments and critiques were invaluable in shaping this book.

I would like to thank especially Steve Rutter, publisher and president of Pine Forge Press, for believing in this book and for using it as Pine Forge's first publication. Finally, I need to thank Paul Dreyfus for his diligence as a copy editor, and Jeremy Ritzer for his skills as indexer.

I hope that this book offers readers some new insights into the society they are constructing. If they are as alarmed as I am by the dangers posed by McDonaldization, perhaps they can do what Weber thought virtually impossible—act to reverse the trend toward McDonaldization. Although I do not think such a reversal is possible, or even necessarily desirable, I do think that there are steps that people can take to ameliorate the problems, to humanize a McDonaldized society. It is hoped that this book will not only inform, but also serve as a warning, and perhaps most important, point the reader in directions that can help make the "iron cage of McDonaldization" a more human setting in which to work and live.

1

An Introduction
to
McDonaldization

Ray Kroc, the genius behind the franchising of McDonald's restaurants, was a man with big ideas and grand ambitions. But even Kroc could not have anticipated the astounding impact of his creation. McDonald's is one of the most influential developments in twentieth-century America. Its reverberations extend far beyond the confines of the United States and the fast-food business. It has influenced a wide range of undertakings, indeed the way of life, of a significant portion of the world. And that impact is likely to expand at an accelerating rate.[1]*

However, this is *not* a book about McDonald's, or even the fast-food business, although both will be discussed frequently throughout these pages. Rather, McDonald's serves here as the major example, the "paradigm," of a wide-ranging process I call *McDonaldization*, that is,

> *the process by which the principles of the fast-food restaurant are coming to dominate more and more sectors of American society as well as of the rest of the world.*

As you will see, McDonaldization affects not only the restaurant business, but also education, work, health care, travel, leisure, dieting, politics, the family, and virtually every other aspect of society. McDonaldization has shown every sign of being an inexorable process by sweeping through seemingly impervious institutions and parts of the world.

McDonald's success is apparent: in 1993 its total sales reached $23.6 billion with profits of almost $1.1 billion.[2] The average U.S. outlet has total sales of approximately $1.6 million in a year.[3] Many entrepreneurs envy such sales and profits and seek to emulate McDonald's success. McDonald's, which first began franchising in 1955, opened its 12,000th outlet on

---

* Citations may be found at the back of the book, beginning on page 205.

March 22, 1991. By the end of 1993, McDonald's had almost 14,000 restaurants worldwide.

The impact of McDonaldization, which McDonald's has played a central role in spawning, has been manifested in many ways:

- The McDonald's model has been adopted not only by other budget-minded hamburger franchises such as Burger King and Wendy's, but also by a wide array of other low-priced fast-food businesses. Subway, begun in 1965 and now with nearly 10,000 outlets, is considered the fastest-growing of these businesses, which include Pizza Hut, Sbarro's, Taco Bell, Popeye's, and Charley Chan's. Sales in so-called "quick service" restaurants in the United States rose to $81 billion by the end of 1993, almost a third of total sales for the entire food-service industry.[4] In 1994, for the first time, sales in fast-food restaurants exceeded those in traditional full-service restaurants, and the gap between them is projected to grow.[5]

- The McDonald's model has also been extended to "casual dining," that is, more "upscale," higher-priced restaurants with fuller menus. For example, Outback Steakhouse and Sizzler sell steaks, Fuddrucker's offers "gourmet" burgers, Chi-Chi's and Chili's sell Mexican food, The Olive Garden proffers Italian food, and Red Lobster purveys . . . you guessed it.

- McDonald's is making increasing inroads around the world.[6] In 1991, for the first time, McDonald's opened more restaurants abroad than in the United States.[7] As we move toward the next century, McDonald's expects to build twice as many restaurants each year overseas than it does in the United States. By the end of 1993, over one-third of McDonald's restaurants were overseas; at the beginning of 1995, about half of McDonald's profits came from its overseas operations. McDonald's has even recently opened a restaurant in Mecca, Saudi Arabia.[8]

- Other nations have developed their own variants of this American institution. The large number of fast-food croissanteries in Paris, a city whose love for fine cuisine might lead you to think it would prove immune to fast food, exemplifies this trend. India has a chain of fast-food restaurants, Nirula's, which sells mutton burgers (about 80% of Indians are Hindus, who eat no beef) as well as local Indian cuisine.[9] Perhaps the most unlikely spot for an indigenous fast food restaurant, war-ravaged Beirut of 1984, witnessed the opening of Juicy Burger, with a rainbow instead of golden arches and J.B. the Clown for Ronald McDonald. Its owners hoped that it would become the "McDonald's of the Arab world."[10]

- Other countries with their own McDonaldized institutions have begun to export them to the United States. For example, the Body Shop is an ecologically sensitive British cosmetics chain with 893 shops in early 1993, 120 of which were in the United States, with 40 more scheduled to open that year.[11] Furthermore, American firms are now opening copies of this British chain, such as The Limited, Inc.'s, Bath and Body Works.

- As indicated by the example of the Body Shop, other types of business are increasingly adapting the principles of the fast-food business to their needs. Said the vice chairman of Toys Я Us, "We want to be thought of as a sort of McDonald's of toys."[12] The founder of Kidsports Fun and Fitness Club echoed this desire: "I want to be the McDonald's of the kids' fun and fitness business."[13] Other chains with similar ambitions include Jiffy-Lube, AAMCO Transmissions, Midas Muffler & Brake Shops, Hair Plus, H & R Block, Pearle Vision Centers, Kampgrounds of America (KOA), Kinder Care (dubbed "Kentucky Fried Children"[14]), Jenny Craig, Home Depot, Barnes & Noble, Petstuff, and Wal-Mart (the nation's largest retailer with about 2,500 stores and almost $55 billion in sales.[15])

- Almost 10% of America's stores are franchises, which currently account for 40% of the nation's retail sales. It is estimated that by the turn of the century, about 25% of the stores in the United States will be chains, by then accounting for a whopping two-thirds of retail business.[16] About 80% of McDonald's restaurants are franchises.[17]

McDonald's as "Americana"

McDonald's and its many clones have become ubiquitous and immediately recognizable symbols throughout the United States as well as much of the rest of the world. For example, when plans were afoot to raze Ray Kroc's first McDonald's restaurant, hundreds of letters poured into McDonald's headquarters, including the following:

> Please don't tear it down! . . . Your company's name is a household word, not only in the United States of America, but all over the world. To destroy this major artifact of contemporary culture would, indeed, destroy part of the faith the people of the world have in your company.[18]

In the end, the restaurant was not only saved, but turned into a museum! A McDonald's executive explained the move: "McDonald's . . . is really a part of Americana." Similarly, when Pizza Hut opened in Moscow in 1990, a Russian student said, "It's a piece of America."[19] Reflecting on the growth of fast-food restaurants in Brazil, the president of Pepsico (of which Pizza Hut is part) of Brazil said that his nation "is experiencing a passion for things American."[20]

McDonald's truly has come to occupy a central place in popular culture.[21] It can be a big event when a new McDonald's opens in a small town. Said one Maryland high-school student at such an event, "Nothing this exciting ever happens in Dale City."[22] Newspapers avidly cover developments in the fast-food business. Fast-food restaurants also play symbolic roles on television programs and in the movies. A skit on the television show *Saturday Night Live* satirized specialty chains by detailing the hardships of a franchise that sells nothing but Scotch tape. In the movie *Coming to America*, Eddie Murphy plays an African prince whose introduction to America includes a job at "McDowell's," a thinly disguised McDonald's. Michael Douglas, in *Falling Down*, vents his rage against the modern world in a fast-food restaurant dominated by mindless rules designed to frustrate customers. *Moscow on the Hudson* has Robin Williams, newly arrived from Russia, obtain a job at McDonald's. H. G. Wells, a central character in the movie *Time After Time*, finds himself transported to the modern world of a McDonald's, where he tries to order the tea he was accustomed to drinking in Victorian England. In *Sleeper*, Woody Allen awakens in the future only to encounter a McDonald's. Finally, *Tin Men*, ends with the heroes driving off into a future represented by a huge golden arch looming in the distance.

Many people identify strongly with McDonald's; in fact to some it has become a sacred institution.[23] At the opening of the McDonald's in Moscow, one journalist described the franchise as the "ultimate icon of Americana," while a worker spoke of it "as if it were the Cathedral in Chartres . . a place to experience 'celestial joy.'"[24] Kowinski argues that shopping malls, which almost always encompass fast-food restaurants, are the modern "cathedrals of consumption" to which people go to practice their "consumer religion."[25] Similarly, a visit to another central element of McDonaldized society, Walt Disney World,[26] has been described as "the middle-class hajj, the compulsory visit to the sunbaked holy city."[27]

McDonald's has achieved its exalted position because virtually all Americans, and many others, have passed through its golden arches on innumerable occasions. Furthermore, most of us have been bombarded by commercials extolling McDonald's virtues, commercials that are tailored to different audiences. Some play to young children watching Saturday-morning cartoons. Others solicit young adults watching prime-time programs.

Still others coax grandparents to take their grandchildren to McDonald's. In addition, these commercials change as the chain introduces new foods (such as breakfast burritos), creates new contests, and ties its products to things such as new motion pictures. These ever-present commercials, combined with the fact that people cannot drive very far without having a McDonald's pop into view, have served to embed McDonald's deep in popular consciousness. A poll of school-age children showed that 96% of them could identify Ronald McDonald, second only to Santa Claus in name recognition.[28]

Over the years, McDonald's has appealed to people in many ways. The restaurants themselves are depicted as spick-and-span, the food is said to be fresh and nutritious, the employees are shown to be young and eager, the managers appear gentle and caring, and the dining experience itself seems fun-filled. People are even led to believe that they contribute, at least indirectly, to charities such as the Ronald McDonald Houses for sick children.

The Long Arm of McDonaldization

McDonald's has strived to continually extend its reach within American society and beyond. As the company's chairman said, "Our goal: to totally dominate the quick service restaurant industry worldwide. . . . I want McDonald's to be more than a leader. I want McDonald's to dominate."[29]

McDonald's began as a phenomenon of suburbs and medium sized towns, but in recent years it has moved into big cities and smaller towns[30], in the United States and beyond, that supposedly could not support such a restaurant. You can now find fast-food outlets in New York's Times Square as well as on the Champs Elysees in Paris. Soon after it opened in 1992, the McDonald's in Moscow sold almost 30,000 hamburgers a day and employed a staff of 1,200 young people working two to a cash register.[31] McDonald's plans to open many more restaurants in the former Soviet Union and in the vast new territory in Eastern Europe that has now been laid bare to the invasion of fast-food restaurants. In early 1992, Beijing witnessed the opening of the world's largest McDonald's, with 700 seats, 29 cash registers, and nearly 1,000 employees. On its first day of business, it set a new one-day record for McDonald's by serving about 40,000 customers.[32]

Small satellite, express, or remote outlets, opened in areas that cannot support full-scale fast-food restaurants, are expanding rapidly. They have begun to appear in small store fronts in large cities and in nontraditional settings such as department stores, service stations, and even schools. These satellites typically offer only limited menus and may rely on larger outlets for food storage and preparation.[33] McDonald's is considering opening express outlets in museums, office buildings, and corporate cafeterias.

No longer content to dominate the strips that surround many college campuses, fast-food restaurants have moved onto many of those campuses. The first fast-food restaurant opened at the University of Cincinnati in 1973. Today, college cafeterias often look like shopping-mall food courts. In conjunction with a variety of "branded partners" (for example, Pizza Hut and Subway), Marriott now supplies food to almost 500 colleges and universities.[34] The apparent approval of college administrations puts fast-food restaurants in a position to further influence the younger generation.

More recently, another expansion has occurred: People no longer need to leave the highway to obtain fast food quickly and easily. Fast food is now available at convenient rest stops along the highway. After "refueling," we can proceed with our trip, which is likely to end in another community that has about the same density and mix of fast-food restaurants as the locale we left behind. Fast food is also increasingly available in service stations,[35] hotels,[36] railway stations, airports, and even on the trays for in-flight meals. The following advertisement appeared in the *Washington Post* and the *New York Times* a few years ago: "Where else at 35,000 feet can you get a McDonald's meal like this for your kids? Only on United's Orlando flights." Now, McDonald's so-called "Friendly Skies Meals" are generally available to children on Delta flights. Similarly, in December 1994, Delta began to offer Blimpie sandwiches on its North American flights,[37] and Continental now offers Subway sandwiches. How much longer before McDonaldized meals will be available on all flights everywhere by every carrier? In fact, on an increasing number of flights, prepackaged "snacks" have already replaced hot main courses.

In other sectors of society, the influence of fast-food restaurants has been subtler, but no less profound. Though McDonald's and other fast-food restaurants have begun to appear in high schools and trade schools,[38] few lower-grade schools as yet have in-house fast food restaurants. However, many have had to alter school cafeteria menus and procedures to make fast food readily available.[39] Apples, yogurt, and milk may go straight into the trash can, but hamburgers, fries, and shakes are devoured. Furthermore, fast-food chains are now trying to market their products in school cafeterias.[40] The attempt to hook school-age children on fast food reached something of a peak in Illinois where McDonald's operated a program called, "*A for Cheeseburger.*" Students who received *A*'s on their report cards received a free cheeseburger, thereby linking success in school with rewards from McDonald's.[41]

The military has also been pressed to offer fast food on both bases and ships. Despite the criticisms by physicians and nutritionists, fast-food outlets increasingly turn up *inside* hospitals. Though no homes yet have a McDonald's of their own, meals at home often resemble those available in fast-food restaurants. Frozen, microwavable, and prepared foods, which bear a striking resemblance to meals available at fast-food restaurants, often find their way to the dinner table. Then there is also home delivery of fast foods, especially pizza, as revolutionized by Domino's.

McDonald's is such a powerful model that many businesses have nicknames beginning with *Mc*. Examples include "McDentists" and "McDoctors," for drive-in clinics designed to deal quickly and efficiently with minor dental and medical problems;[42] "McChild" Care Centers, for child care centers such as Kinder-Care; "McStables," for the nationwide racehorse-training operation of Wayne Lucas; and "McPaper," for the newspaper *USA TODAY*.[43]

However, it is worth noting that McDonald's is not always crazy about this proliferation. Take the case of *We Be Sushi*, a San Francisco chain with three outlets. A note appears on the back of the menu explaining why the chain was not named "McSushi":

> The original name was *McSushi*. Our sign was up and we were ready to go. But before we could open our doors we received a very formal letter from the lawyers of, you guessed it, McDonald's. It seems that McDonald's has cornered the market on every McFood name possible from McBagle (sic) to McTaco. They explained that the use of the name McSushi would dilute the image of McDonald's.[44]

As powerful as it is, McDonald's has not been alone in pressing the fast-food model on American society and the rest of the world. Other fast-food giants, such as Burger King and Kentucky Fried Chicken, have played a key role, as have innumerable other businesses built on the principles of the fast-food restaurant.

Even the derivatives of McDonald's and the fast-food industry in turn exert their own influence. For example, the success of *USA TODAY* has led many newspapers across the nation to adopt, for example, shorter stories and color weather maps. As one *USA TODAY* editor put it, "The same newspaper editors who call us McPaper have been stealing our McNuggets."[45] The influence of *USA TODAY* is blatantly manifested in

The Boca Raton News, a Knight-Ridder newspaper. This newspaper is described as "a sort of smorgasbord of snippets, a newspaper that slices and dices the news into even smaller portions than does *USA TODAY*, spicing it with color graphics and fun facts and cute features like 'Today's Hero' and 'Critter Watch'."[46] As in *USA TODAY*, stories in *The Boca Raton News* usually do not jump from one page to another; they start and finish on the same page. To meet this need, long, complex stories often have to be reduced to a few paragraphs. Much of a story's context, and much of what the principals have to say, is severely cut back or omitted entirely. With its emphasis on light news and color graphics, the main function of the newspaper seems to be entertainment. Even the *New York Times* has undergone changes (for example, the use of color) as a result of the success of *USA TODAY*.

The expansion deep into the newspaper business suggests that McDonaldization may be inexorable and may therefore come to insinuate itself into every aspect of society and people's private lives. In the movie *Sleeper*, Woody Allen not only created a futuristic world in which McDonald's was an important and highly visible element, but he also envisioned a society in which even sex underwent the process of McDonaldization. The denizens of his future world were able to enter a machine called an "orgasmatron," which allowed them to experience an orgasm without going through the muss and fuss of sexual intercourse.

Sex actually has, like virtually every other sector of society, undergone a process of McDonaldization. "Dial-a-porn" allows people to have intimate, sexually explicit, even obscene conversations with people they have never met and probably never will meet.[47] There is great specialization here: Dialing numbers such as 555-FOXX will lead to a very different phone message than dialing 555-SEXY. Those who answer the phones mindlessly and repetitively follow "scripts" that have them say such things as, "Sorry, tiger, but your Dream Girl has to go . . . Call right back and ask for me."[48] Escort services advertise a wide range of available sex partners. People can see highly specialized pornographic movies (heterosexual, homosexual, sex with children, and sex with animals) at urban multiplexes and can rent them from local video stores for viewing in the comfort of their living rooms. Various technologies (vibrators, for example) enhance the ability of people to have sex on their own without the bother of having to deal with a human partner. In New York City, an official called a three-story pornographic center "the McDonald's of sex" because of its "cookie-cutter cleanliness and compliance with the law."[49] These examples suggest that no aspect of people's lives is immune to McDonaldization.

The Dimensions of McDonaldization

Why has the McDonald's model proven so irresistible? Four alluring dimensions lie at the heart of the success of this model and, more generally, of McDonaldization. In short, McDonald's has succeeded because it offers consumers, workers, and managers efficiency, calculability, predictability, and control.[50]

First, McDonald's offers *efficiency*, or the optimum method for getting from one point to another. For consumers, this means that McDonald's offers the best available way to get from being hungry to being full. (Similarly, Woody Allen's orgasmatron offered an efficient method for getting people from quiescence to sexual gratification.) Other institutions, fashioned on the McDonald's model, offer similar efficiency in losing weight, lubricating cars, getting new glasses or contacts, or completing income-tax forms. In a society where both parents are likely to work, or where there may be only a single parent, efficiently satisfying the hunger and many other needs of people is very attractive. In a society where people rush, usually by car, from one spot to another, the efficiency of a fast-food meal, perhaps even without leaving their cars by wending their way along the drive-through lane, often proves impossible to resist. The fast-food model offers people, or at least appears to offer them, an efficient method for satisfying many needs.

Like their customers, workers in McDonaldized systems function efficiently. They are trained to work this way by managers, who watch over them closely to make sure they do. Organizational rules and regulations also help ensure highly efficient work.

Second, McDonald's offers *calculability*, or an emphasis on the quantitative aspects of products sold (portion size, cost) and service offered (the time it takes to get the product). Quantity has become equivalent to quality; a lot of something, or the quick delivery of it, means it must be good. As two observers of contemporary American culture put it, "As a culture, we tend to believe deeply that in general 'bigger is better.'"[51] Thus, people order the *Quarter Pounder*, the *Big* Mac, the *large* fries. More recently, there is the lure of the "double this" (for instance, Burger King's "Double Whopper With Cheese") and the "triple that." People can quantify these things and feel that they are getting a lot of food for what appears to be a nominal sum of money. This calculation does not take into account an important point: the extraordinary profitability of fast-food outlets and other chains, which indicates that the owners, not the consumers, get the best deal.

People also tend to calculate how much time it will take to drive to McDonald's, be served the food, eat it, and return home; then, they compare that interval to the time required to prepare food at home. They often conclude, rightly or wrongly, that a trip to the fast-food restaurant will take less time than eating at home. This sort of calculation particularly supports home-delivery franchises such as Domino's, as well as other chains that emphasize time saving. A notable example of time saving in another sort of chain is Lens Crafters, which promises people, "Glasses fast, glasses in one hour."

Some McDonaldized institutions combine the emphases on time and money. Domino's promises pizza delivery in half an hour, or the pizza is free. Pizza Hut will serve a personal pan pizza in five minutes, or it, too, will be free.

Workers at McDonaldized systems also tend to emphasize the quantitative rather than the qualitative aspects of their work. Since the quality of the work is allowed to vary little, workers focus on such things as how quickly tasks can be accomplished. In a situation analogous to that of the customer, workers are expected to do a lot of work, very quickly, for low pay.

Third, McDonald's offers *predictability*, the assurance that their products and services will be the same over time and in all locales. The Egg McMuffin in New York will be, for all intents and purposes, identical to those in Chicago and Los Angeles. Also, those eaten next week or next year will be identical to those eaten today. There is great comfort in knowing that McDonald's offers no surprises. People know that the next Egg McMuffin they eat will taste about the same as the others they have eaten; it will not be awful, but it will not be exceptionally delicious, either. The success of the McDonald's model suggests that many people have come to prefer a world in which there are few surprises.

The workers in McDonaldized systems also behave in predictable ways. They follow corporate rules as well as the dictates of their managers. In many cases, not only what they do, but also what they say, is highly predictable. McDonaldized organizations often have scripts that employees are supposed to memorize and follow whenever the occasion arises.[52] This scripted behavior helps create highly predictable interactions between workers and customers. While customers do not follow scripts, they tend to develop simple recipes for dealing with the employees of McDonaldized systems.[53] As Robin Leidner argues,

> McDonald's pioneered the routinization of interactive service work
> and remains an exemplar of extreme standardization. Innovation is
> not discouraged . . . at least among managers and franchisees. Ironi-
> cally, though, 'the object is to look for new, innovative ways to create

an experience that is exactly the same no matter what McDonald's you walk into, no matter where it is in the world.'[54]

Fourth, *control*, especially through the *substitution of nonhuman for human technology*, is exerted over the people who enter the world of McDonald's. A *human technology* (a screwdriver, for example) is controlled by people; a *nonhuman technology* (the assembly line, for instance) controls people. The people who eat in fast-food restaurants are controlled, albeit (usually) subtly. Lines, limited menus, few options, and uncomfortable seats all lead diners to do what management wishes them to do—eat quickly and leave. Further, the drive-through (in some cases walk-through) window leads diners to leave before they eat. In the Domino's model, customers never come in the first place.

The people who work in McDonaldized organizations are also controlled to a high degree, usually more blatantly and directly than customers. They are trained to do a limited number of things in precisely the way they are told to do them. The technologies used and the way the organization is set up reinforce this control. Managers and inspectors make sure that workers toe the line.

McDonald's also controls employees by threatening to use, and ultimately using, nonhuman technology to replace human workers. No matter how well they are programmed and controlled, workers can foul up the system's operation. A slow worker can make the preparation and delivery of a Big Mac inefficient. A worker who refuses to follow the rules might leave the pickles or special sauce off a hamburger, thereby making for unpredictability. And a distracted worker can put too few fries in the box, making an order of large fries seem skimpy. For these and other reasons, McDonald's has felt compelled to steadily replace human beings with nonhuman technologies, such as the soft-drink dispenser that shuts itself off when the glass is full, the french-fry machine that rings and lifts itself out of the oil when the fries are crisp, the preprogrammed cash register that eliminates the need for the cashier to calculate prices and amounts, and, perhaps at some future time, the robot capable of making hamburgers.[55] This technology increases the corporation's control over workers. Thus, McDonald's can assure customers that their employees and service will be consistent.

The Advantages of McDonaldization

This discussion of four of the fundamental characteristics of McDonaldization makes it clear that there are good, solid reasons why McDonald's has succeeded so phenomenally and why the process of McDonaldization is moving ahead so dramatically. As a result, people such as the economic columnist, Robert Samuelson, strongly support McDonald's. Samuelson confesses to "openly worship McDonald's," and he thinks of it as "the greatest restaurant chain in history." However, even Samuelson recognizes that there are those who "can't stand the food and regard McDonald's as the embodiment of all that is vulgar in American mass culture."[56]

McDonaldization has undoubtedly led to positive changes.[57] Here are a few specific examples:

- There is a far greater availability of goods and services than before; their availability depends less on time or geographic location.

- This wider range of goods and services is available to a much larger portion of the population.

- People are able to get what they want or need almost instantaneously.

- It is far more convenient to get what they want or need.

- Goods and services are of a far more uniform quality; at least some people get even better goods and services than before McDonaldization.

- Far more economical alternatives to high-priced, customized goods and services are widely available; therefore, people can afford things they could not previously afford.

- Fast, efficient goods and services are available to a population that is working longer hours and has fewer hours to spare.

- In a rapidly changing, unfamiliar, and seemingly hostile world, there is comfort in the comparatively stable, familiar, and safe environment of a McDonaldized system.

- Because of quantification, consumers can more easily compare competing products.

- People can do things, such as obtain money or a bank balance in the middle of the night, that were impossible before.

- It is now safer to do things (for example, diet) in a carefully regulated and controlled system.

- People are more likely to be treated similarly, no matter what their race, gender, or social class.

- Organizational and technological innovations are more quickly and easily diffused through networks of identical operators.

- The products of one culture are more easily diffused to others.

More specifically, McDonald's itself offers many praiseworthy programs, such as its Ronald McDonald Houses, which permit parents to stay with children undergoing treatment for serious medical problems; job-training programs for teenagers; programs to help keep its employees in school; efforts to hire and train the handicapped; the McMasters program, aimed at hiring senior citizens; and an enviable record of hiring and promoting minorities.[58]

A Critique of McDonaldization: The Irrationality of Rationality

Though McDonaldization offers powerful advantages, it has a downside. Efficiency, predictability, calculability, and control through nonhuman technology can be thought of as the basic components of a *rational* system.[59] However, rational systems inevitably spawn irrationalities. The downside of McDonaldization will be dealt with most systematically under the heading of the *irrationality of rationality*; in fact, paradoxically, the irrationality of rationality can be thought of as the fifth dimension of McDonaldization. The basic idea here is that rational systems inevitably spawn irrational consequences. Another way of saying this is that rational systems serve to deny human reason; rational systems are often unreasonable.

For example, McDonaldization has produced a wide array of adverse effects on the environment. Take just one example: the need to grow uniform potatoes to create those predictable french fries that people have come to expect from fast-food restaurants. It turns out that the need to grow such potatoes has adversely affected the ecology of the Pacific Northwest. The huge farms that now produce such potatoes rely on the extensive use of chemicals. The need to produce a perfect fry means that much of the potato is wasted, with the remnants either fed to cattle or used for fertilizer. However, the underground water supply is now showing high levels of nitrates that may be traceable to the fertilizer and animal wastes.[60] There are, of course, many other ecological problems associated with the McDonaldization of society—the forests felled to produce paper, the damage caused by polystyrene and other materials, the enormous amount of food needed to produce feed cattle, and so on.

Another unreasonable effect of the fast-food restaurant is that it is often a dehumanizing setting in which to eat or work. Customers lining up for a burger or waiting in the drive-through line and workers preparing the food often feel as though they are part of an assembly line. Hardly amenable to eating, assembly lines have been shown to be inhuman settings in which to work.

Of course, the criticisms of the irrationality of the fast-food restaurant will be extended to all facets of the McDonaldizing world. For example, at the opening of Euro Disney, a French politician said that it will "bombard France with uprooted creations that are to culture what fast food is to gastronomy."[61] This clearly indicates an abhorrence of McDonaldization, whatever guise it may take.

As you have seen, there *are* great gains to be made from McDonaldization. However, this book will focus on the great costs and enormous risks of McDonaldization. McDonald's and the other purveyors of the fast-food model spend billions of dollars each year outlining the benefits of their system. However, the critics of the system have few outlets for their ideas. There are, for example, no commercials between Saturday-morning cartoons warning children of the dangers associated with fast-food restaurants.

A legitimate question may be raised about this critique of McDonaldization: Is it animated by a romanticization of the past and an impossible desire to return to a world that no longer exists? Some critics do base their critiques on the idea that there was a time when life was slower and less efficient, and offered more surprises; when people were freer; and when one was more likely to deal with a human being than a robot or a computer.[62] Although they have a point, these critics have undoubtedly exaggerated the positive aspects of a world without McDonald's, and they have certainly tended to forget the liabilities associated with such a world. As an example of the latter, take the following case of a visit to a pizzeria in Havana, Cuba:

> The pizza's not much to rave about—they scrimp on tomato sauce, and the dough is mushy.
>
> It was about 7:30 P.M., and as usual the place was standing-room-only, with people two deep jostling for a stool to come open and a waiting line spilling out onto the sidewalk.
>
> The menu is similarly Spartan. . . . To drink, there is tap water. That's it—no toppings, no soda, no beer, no coffee, no salt, no pepper. And no special orders.
>
> A very few people are eating. Most are waiting. . . . Fingers are drumming, flies are buzzing, the clock is ticking. The waiter wears a watch around his belt loop, but he hardly needs it; time is evidently not his chief concern. After a while, tempers begin to fray.

But right now, it's 8:45 P.M. at the pizzeria, I've been waiting an hour and a quarter for two small pies.[63]

Few would prefer such irrational systems to the rationalized elements of society. More important, critics who revere the past do not seem to realize that we are not returning to such a world. In fact, fast-food restaurants have begun to appear in Havana.[64] The increase in the number of people, the acceleration of technological change, the increasing pace of life—all this and more make it impossible to go back to the nonrationalized world, if it ever existed, of home-cooked meals, traditional restaurant dinners, high-quality foods, meals loaded with surprises, and restaurants populated only by chefs free to fully express their creativity.

While one basis for a critique of McDonaldization is the past, another is the future.[65] The future in this sense is defined as human potential, unfettered by the constraints of McDonaldized systems. This critique holds that people have the potential to be far more thoughtful, skillful, creative, and well-rounded than they are now. If the world were less McDonaldized, people would be better able to live up to their human potential. This critique is based not on what people were like in the past, but on what they could be like in the future, if only the constraints of McDonaldized systems were eliminated, or at least eased substantially. The criticisms put forth in this book reflect the latter, future-oriented perspective rather than a romanticized past and a desire to return to it.

Conclusion

This chapter should have given you a sense not only of the advantages and disadvantages of McDonaldization but also of the range of phenomena that will be discussed throughout this book. In fact, such a wide range of phenomena can be linked to McDonaldization that you may be led to wonder, What isn't McDonaldized? Is McDonaldization the equivalent of modernity? Is everything contemporary McDonaldized?

While much of the world has been McDonaldized, at least three aspects of contemporary society have largely escaped McDonaldization. First, there are those aspects traceable to an earlier, "premodern" age. A good example is the mom-and-pop grocery store. Second, new businesses have sprung up, at least in part, as a reaction against McDonaldization. For instance, people fed up with McDonaldized motel rooms in Holiday Inns or Motel 6's can instead stay in a bed-and-breakfast, which offers a room in a private home with personalized attention and a homemade breakfast from the proprietor. Finally, some analysts believe that the world has moved into a new, "postmodern" age and that aspects of postmodern society are less rational than before. Thus, for example, in a postmodern society, "modern" high-rise housing projects make way for smaller, more livable communities. Thus, although it is ubiquitous, McDonaldization is *not* simply another term for contemporary society. There is more to the contemporary world than McDonaldization.

Furthermore, McDonaldization is *not* an all-or-nothing process. There are degrees of McDonaldization. Fast-food restaurants, for example, have been heavily McDonaldized, universities moderately McDonaldized, and the mom-and-pop grocers mentioned earlier only slightly McDonaldized. It is difficult to think of social phenomena that have escaped McDonaldization totally, but there may be a local enterprise in Fiji yet untouched by this process.

Overall, this book argues that McDonald's represents a monumentally important development and that the process that it has helped spawn, McDonaldization, is engulfing more and more sectors of society and areas of the world. Though it has yielded a number of benefits to society, it also entails a considerable number of costs and risks.

Because this is a work in the social sciences, broadly defined, it is not enough merely to assert that McDonaldization is spreading throughout society. This text must present *evidence* for that assertion. After a discussion of the precursors to McDonaldization in chapter 2, chapters 3–6 provide that evidence in the context of a discussion of four of the basic dimensions of rationalization—efficiency, calculability, predictability, and greater control through the replacement of human by nonhuman technology. Numerous examples in each chapter show the degree to which McDonaldization has penetrated society and how that process continues at an accelerating rate. In chapter 7, the fifth and paradoxical element of rationalization—the irrationality of rationality—is explored. Though much of the book criticizes McDonaldization, this chapter presents the critique most clearly and directly, discussing a variety of irrationalities, the most important of which is the dehumanization associated with progressive rationalization. Chapter 8 discusses the inevitability of McDonaldization. This is followed by a discussion, in chapter 9, of the way McDonaldization has pushed its frontiers to encompass not just life, but birth (and before) and death (and beyond). In the final chapter, some practical steps are offered to allow those who are bothered, if not enraged, by the process to survive in an increasingly McDonaldized world.

2

McDonaldization and Its Precursors

From the Iron Cage to the Fast-Food Factory

M cDonaldization did not emerge in a vacuum; it was preceded by a series of developments that not only anticipated it but also gave McDonald's many of the basic characteristics touched on in Chapter 1.[1] In this chapter you will look briefly at a few of these developments. First, you will examine the notion of bureaucracy and Max Weber's theories about it as well as the larger process of rationalization. Next, you will read a discussion of the Nazi Holocaust, a highly rationalized method of mass killing that can be viewed as the logical extreme of Weber's fears about rationalization and bureaucratization. Then, you will look at scientific management as it was invented at the turn of the century by F.W. Taylor, Henry Ford's assembly line, the mass-produced suburban houses of Levittown, the shopping mall, and the original McDonald's. These are not only of historical interest; most continue to be important to this day.

Bureaucratization: Making Life More Rational

A *bureaucracy* is a large-scale organization composed of a hierarchy of offices. In these offices, people have certain responsibilities and must act in accord with rules, written regulations, and means of compulsion exercised by those who occupy higher-level positions. The bureaucracy is largely a creation of the modern Western world. Though earlier societies had organizational structures, they were not nearly as effective as the bureaucracy. For example, in traditional societies, officials performed their tasks on the basis of a personal loyalty to their leader. These officials were subject to personal whim rather than impersonal rules. Their offices lacked clearly defined spheres of competence, there was no clear hierarchy of positions, and officials did not have to obtain technical training to gain a position.

Ultimately, the bureaucracy differs from earlier methods of organizing work because it has a formal structure that, among other things, allows for greater efficiency. Institutionalized rules and regulations lead, even force, those employed in the bureaucracy to choose the best means to arrive at their ends. A given task is broken up into a variety of components, with each office responsible for a distinct portion of the larger task. Incumbents of each office handle their part of the task (usually following preset rules and regulations), often in a predetermined sequence. When each of the incumbents has, in order, handled the required part, the task is completed. Furthermore, in handling the task in this way, the bureaucracy has used what its past history has shown to be the optimum means to the desired end.

The roots of modern thinking on bureaucracy lie in the work of the turn-of-the-century German sociologist Max Weber.[2] His ideas on bureaucracy are embedded in his broader theory of the rationalization process. In the latter, Weber described how the Occident managed to become increasingly rational—that is, dominated by efficiency, predictability, calculability, and nonhuman technologies that control people. He also examined why the rest of the world largely failed to rationalize. As you can see, McDonaldization is an extension of Weber's theory of rationalization. For Weber, the model of rationalization was the bureaucracy; for me, the fast-food restaurant is the paradigm of McDonaldization.

Weber demonstrated in his research that the modern Western world had produced a distinctive kind of rationality. Various types of rationality had existed in all societies at one time or another, but none had produced the type that Weber called *formal rationality*. This is the sort of rationality I refer to when I discuss McDonaldization or the rationalization process in general.

What is formal rationality? According to Weber, formal rationality means that the search by people for the optimum means to a given end is shaped by rules, regulations, and larger social structures. Individuals are not left to their own devices in searching for the best means of attaining a given objective. Weber identified this as a major development in the history of the world: Previously, people had been left to discover such mechanisms on their own or with vague and general guidance from larger value systems (religion, for example).[3] After the development of formal rationality, they could use rules to help them decide what to do. More strongly, people existed in social structures that dictated what they should do. In effect, people no longer had to discover for themselves the optimum means to an end; rather, optimum means had already been discovered and were institutionalized in rules, regulations, and structures. People simply had to follow them. An important aspect of formal rationality, then, is that it allows individuals little choice of means to ends. Since the choice of means is guided or even determined, virtually everyone can (or must) make the same, optimal choice.

Weber praised the bureaucracy, his paradigm of formal rationality, for its many advantages over other mechanisms that help people discover and implement optimum means to ends. The most important advantages are the four basic dimensions of rationalization (and McDonaldization).

First, Weber viewed the bureaucracy as the most *efficient* structure for handling large numbers of tasks requiring a great deal of paperwork. As an example, Weber might have used the Internal Revenue Service, for no other structure could handle millions of tax returns so well.

efficiency

Second, bureaucracies emphasize calculability, or the quantification of as many things as possible. Reducing performance to a series of quantifiable tasks helps people gauge success. For example, an IRS agent is expected to process a certain number of tax returns each day. Handling less than the required number of cases is unsatisfactory performance; handling more is excellence.

calculability

The quantitative approach presents a problem: little or no concern for the actual quality of work. Employees are expected to finish a task with little attention paid to how well it is handled. For instance, IRS agents may manage large numbers of cases and, as a result, receive positive evaluations from their superiors. Yet they may actually handle the cases poorly, costing the government thousands, or even millions, of dollars in uncollected revenue. Or, the agents may handle cases so quickly that taxpayers may be angered by the way the agents treat them.

Third, because of their well-entrenched rules and regulations, bureaucracies also operate in a highly *predictable* manner. Incumbents of a given office know with great assurance how the incumbents of other offices will behave. They know what they will be provided with and when they will receive it. Outsiders who receive the services the bureaucracies dispense know with a high degree of confidence what they will receive and when they will receive it. Again, to use an example Weber might have used, the millions of recipients of checks from the Social Security Administration know precisely when they will receive their checks and exactly how much money they will receive.

predictability

Finally, bureaucracies emphasize *control over people through the replacement of human with nonhuman technology*. As you will recall, nonhuman technologies (machines and rules, for example) tend to control people, while

nonhuman technology

human technologies (hammers and pens, for example) tend to be controlled by people. Indeed, the bureaucracy itself may be seen as one huge nonhuman technology. Its nearly automatic functioning may be seen as an effort to replace human judgment with the dictates of rules, regulations, and structures. Employees are controlled by the division of labor, which allocates to each office a limited number of well-defined tasks. Incumbents must do those tasks, and no others, in the manner prescribed by the organization. They may not, in most cases, devise idiosyncratic ways of doing those tasks. Furthermore, by making few, if any, judgments, people begin to resemble human robots or computers. Having reduced people to this status, it is then possible to think about actually replacing human beings with machines. This has already occurred to some extent: in many settings, computers have taken over bureaucratic tasks once performed by humans. One can imagine that once the technology has been developed and priced reasonably, robots will begin replacing humans in the office.

Similarly, the bureaucracy's clients are also controlled. They may receive only certain services and not others from the organization. For example, the Internal Revenue Service can offer people advice on their tax returns, but not on their marriages. People may receive those services in a certain way only. For example, people can only receive welfare payments by check, not cash.

Thus, the bureaucracy, like the fast-food restaurant, is well-defined by four basic components of formal rationality: efficiency, predictability, quantification, and control through the substitution of nonhuman for human technology.

The bureaucracy also suffers from the *irrationality of rationality*. Like the fast-food restaurant, it is a dehumanizing place in which to work and by which to be serviced. As Ronald Takaki put it, these rationalized settings are places in which "the self was placed in confinement, its emotions controlled, and its spirit subdued."[4] In other words, they are settings in which people cannot behave as human beings, where people are dehumanized.

But the irrationalities of bureaucracies hardly stop there. Instead of remaining efficient, bureaucracies can become increasingly inefficient because of "red tape" and the other pathologies associated with them. Bureaucracies often become unpredictable as employees grow unclear about what they are supposed to do and clients do not get the services they expect. The emphasis on quantification often leads to large amounts of poor-quality work. Because of these and other inadequacies, bureaucracies begin to lose control over those who work within and are served by them. Anger at the nonhuman technologies that can replace them often lead people to undercut or sabotage the operation of these technologies. All in all, what were designed as highly rational operations often end up quite irrational.

Although Weber was concerned about the irrationalities of formally rationalized systems such as bureaucracies, he was even more animated by what he called the "iron cage of rationality." In Weber's view, bureaucracies are cages in the sense that people are trapped in them, their basic humanity denied. Weber feared most that these systems would grow more and more rational and that rational principles would come to dominate an accelerating number of sectors of society. Weber anticipated a society of people locked into a series of rational structures, who could move only from one rational system to another. Thus, people would move from rationalized educational institutions to rationalized work places, from rationalized recreational settings to rationalized homes. Society would become nothing more than a seamless web of rationalized structures; there would be no escape.

A good example of what Weber feared is found in the contemporary rationalization of recreational activities. Recreation can be thought of as a way to escape the rationalization of daily routines. However, over the years these escape routes have themselves become rationalized, embodying the same principles as bureaucracies and fast-food restaurants. Of the many examples of the rationalization of recreation,[5] take today's vacations. For those who wish to visit Europe, a package tour rationalizes the process. People can efficiently see, in a rigidly controlled manner, many sights while traveling in conveyances, staying in hotels, and eating in fast-food restaurants just like those at home. For those who wish to escape to the Caribbean, there are resorts such as Club Med that offer many routinized activities and where one can stay in predictable settings without ever venturing out into the unpredictability of native life on a Caribbean island. For those who wish to flee back to nature within the United States, rationalized campgrounds offer little or no contact with the unpredictabilities of nature. People can even remain within their RVs and enjoy all of the comforts of home—TV, VCR, Nintendo, CD player. These and legion other examples show that the escape routes from rationality have, to a large degree, become rationalized. With little or no way out, people do live to a large extent in the iron cage of rationality.

The fast-food restaurant can also be seen as part of a bureaucratic system; in fact, huge conglomerates now own many of the fast-food chains. Further, the fast-food restaurant has employed the rational principles pioneered by the bureaucracy. McDonald's has combined bureaucratic and other principles to help create McDonaldization.

The Holocaust: The End-Product Was Death

Weber wrote about rationalization and bureaucratization in the early 1900s. It can be argued that his worst fears about these processes were realized in the Nazi Holocaust that began within a few decades of his death in 1920.

Zygmunt Bauman contends that "the Holocaust may serve as a paradigm of modern bureaucratic rationality."[6] Like the bureaucracy, the Holocaust was a distinctive product of Western civilization. Further, Bauman argues that the Holocaust was not an aberration, but "in keeping with everything we know about our civilization, its guiding spirit, its priorities, its immanent vision of the world."[7] That is, the Holocaust required the rationality of the modern world. It could not have occurred in premodern, less rationalized societies. In fact, the pogroms that occurred in such societies were too primitive, too inefficient to murder systematically the millions of people killed in the Holocaust.

The Holocaust can be seen as an example of modern social engineering in which the goal was the production of a perfectly rational society. To the Nazis, this perfect society was free of Jews (as well as gypsies, gays, lesbians, and the disabled). Bauman sees an analogy here to gardening. Just as a perfect garden is free of weeds, so a perfect Nazi society was one that was *Judenfrei*. Using a medical analogy, Hitler also defined the Jews as a "virus," a disease that had to be eliminated from Nazi society.

The Holocaust had all of the basic characteristics of rationalization (and McDonaldization). First, it was an efficient mechanism for the destruction of massive numbers of human beings. For example, early experiments showed that bullets were inefficient; the Nazis eventually settled on gas as the most efficient means of destroying people. The Nazis also found it efficient to use members of the Jewish community to perform a variety of tasks (for example, choosing the next group of victims) that they otherwise would have had to perform themselves.[8] Many Jews cooperated because it seemed like the "rational" thing to do (they might be able to save others, or themselves) in such a rationalized system.

Second, the Holocaust emphasized calculability, for instance, how many people could be killed in the shortest period of time. Bauman offers the following further examples:

> For railway managers, the only meaningful articulation of their object is in terms of tonnes per kilometre. They do not deal with humans, sheep, or barbed wire; they only deal with cargo, and this means an entity consisting entirely of measurements and devoid of quality. For

most bureaucrats, even such a category as cargo would mean too strict a quality-bound restriction. They deal only with the financial effects of their actions. Their object is money.[9]

There was certainly little attention paid to the quality of the life, or even of the death, of the Jews as they marched inexorably to the gas chambers.

In another quantitative sense, the Holocaust has the dubious distinction of being seen as the most extreme of mass exterminations:

> Like everything else done in the modern-rational, planned, scientifically informed, expert, efficiently managed, co-ordinated-way, the Holocaust left behind and put to shame all its alleged pre-modern equivalents, exposing them as primitive, wasteful and ineffective by comparison. Like everything else in our modern society, the Holocaust was an accomplishment in every respect superior. . . . It towers high above the past genocidal episodes."[10]

Third, there was an effort to make mass murder predictable. Thus, the whole process had an assembly-line quality about it. Trains snaked their way toward the concentration camps, victims lined up and followed a set series of steps. Once the process was complete, camp workers produced stacks of dead bodies for systematic disposal.

Finally, the victims were controlled by a huge nonhuman technology including the camps, the train system, the crematoria, and the bureaucracy that managed the entire process. Here is how Feingold describes some elements of this nonhuman technology:

> [Auschwitz] was also a mundane extension of the modern factory system. Rather than producing goods, the raw material was human beings and the end-product was death, so many units per day marked carefully on the manager's production charts. The chimneys, the very symbol of the modern factory system, poured forth acrid smoke produced by burning human flesh. The brilliantly organized railroad grid of modern Europe carried a new kind of raw material to the factories. It did so in the same manner as with other cargo. . . . Engineers designed the crematoria; managers designed the system of bureaucracy that worked with a zest and efficiency. . . . What we witnessed was nothing less than a massive scheme of social engineering.[11]

Needless to say, the Holocaust represented the ultimate in the irrationality of rationality—more specifically, the ultimate in dehumanization. After all, what could be more dehumanizing than murdering millions of people in such a mechanical way? Further, for the murders to have occurred in the first place, the victims had to be dehumanized, that is, "reduced to a set of quantitative measures."[12] Bauman concludes, "German bureaucratic machinery was put in the service of a goal incomprehensible in its irrationality."[13]

Discussing the Holocaust in the context of precursors of McDonaldization may seem extreme to some readers. Clearly, the fast-food restaurant *cannot* be discussed in the same breath as the Holocaust. There has been no more heinous crime in the history of humankind. Yet, there are strong reasons to discuss the Holocaust in this context. First, the Holocaust was based on the principles of formal rationality, relying extensively on the paradigm of that type of rationality—the bureaucracy. Second, the Holocaust was also linked, as we have seen, to the factory system, discussed in the next two sections. Finally, the spread of formal rationality today in McDonaldization supports Bauman's view that something like the Holocaust could happen again.

Scientific Management: Finding the One Best Way

The development of scientific management was an important precursor to McDonaldization. In fact, Weber at times mentions scientific management in his discussion of the rationalization process. Scientific management was created by Frederick W. Taylor, whose ideas played a key role in shaping the work world throughout the twentieth century.[14] Taylor developed a series of principles designed to rationalize work and was hired by a number of large organizations (for example, Bethlehem Steel) to implement those ideas, mostly in their factories.

Struck by the lack of efficiency in the work world, Taylor developed principles to make work more efficient. In *time-and-motion* studies, he examined workers he regarded as already reasonably efficient so he could discover the best way to do a job. He broke tasks down into minute components and attempted to discover the "one best way" of doing each of them. When he felt he had discovered the best way to do a job, he selected workers and taught them to perform the work in exactly the way he prescribed.

Overall, scientific management produced a nonhuman technology that exerted great control over workers. Employers found that when workers followed Taylor's methods, they worked much more efficiently, everyone performed the same steps (that is, their work exhibited predictability), and they produced a great deal more while their pay had to be increased only slightly (calculability). Thus, Taylor's methods meant increased profits to those enterprises that adopted them.

Like all rational systems, scientific management had its irrationalities. Above all, it was a dehumanizing system in which people were considered expendable and treated as such. Furthermore, because workers did only one or a few tasks, most of their skills and abilities remained unused. This had disastrous consequences, and by the 1980s American industry found itself outstripped by Japanese industry, which had found a way not only to be formally rational, but also to use the abilities of its workers more fully.[15]

Although people no longer hear a great deal about Taylor and scientific management, his ideas continue to shape the way that work, especially manual work, is performed. The fast-food restaurant has, at least implicitly, used scientific management to organize the way its employees work.[16] Labor in the fast-food restaurant is highly rationalized, geared to discover the most efficient way to grill a hamburger, fry chicken, or serve a meal. McDonald's did not invent these ideas, but rather brought them together with the principles of the bureaucracy and of the assembly line, thus contributing to the creation of McDonaldization.

The Assembly Line: Producing Robot-Like Workers

Like modern bureaucracy and scientific management, the assembly line came into existence at the dawn of the twentieth century. Pioneered in the bureaucratized automobile industry, the ideas of scientific management helped shape it. Henry Ford generally receives credit for its invention, although it had precursors in other industries (such as meat packing) and was mainly a product of Ford engineers (see chapter 3).[17] The automatic assembly line represented a remarkable step forward in the rationalization of production and became widely used throughout manufacturing. Like bureaucracy and the fast-food restaurant, even the Holocaust, the automobile assembly line beautifully illustrates the basic elements of formal rationality.

First, it is efficient. A large number of highly specialized, unskilled workers assembling cars along a moving conveyor belt is more efficient than putting a group of skilled workers in a room and asking them to build a car.

What each worker on the line does, such as putting a hubcap on each passing car, is highly predictable and leads to identical end products. The assembly line permits the quantification of many elements of the production process and maximizes the number of cars produced.

The assembly line is also a nonhuman technology that permits maximum *control* over workers, who must do certain tasks at specific points during the production process. It is immediately obvious when a worker fails to perform the required tasks. There would, for example, be a missing hubcap as the car moves down the line. The limited time allotted for each job allows little or no room for innovative ways of doing a specific task. Fewer, less-skilled people are able to produce cars. Furthermore, the specialization of each task permits the replacement of human workers with robots. The routine repetitive tasks required on the line are just the kind of work that robots were created to handle. Once tasks have been simplified so that they can be handled by "human robots," the stage is set for the replacement of human by nonhuman robots. Today, mechanical robots handle more and more assembly line tasks.

As has been well detailed by many observers, the assembly line carries with it much irrationality. It clearly offers a dehumanizing setting in which to work. Human beings, equipped with a wide array of skills and abilities, are asked to perform a limited number of highly simplified tasks over and over. Instead of expressing their human abilities on the job, people are forced to deny their humanity and to act like robots. People cannot express themselves in their work. This is but one of many ways the assembly line operates irrationally.

Despite its flaws, the assembly line had a profound influence on the development of the fast-food restaurant. The most obvious example of this is the conveyor belt used by Burger King to cook its hamburgers. Less obvious is the fact that much of the work in the fast-food restaurant is performed in assembly-line fashion with tasks broken down into their simplest components. For example, "making a hamburger" means grilling the burgers, putting them on the rolls, smearing on the "special sauce," laying on the lettuce and tomato, and wrapping the fully dressed burgers. Even customers must face a kind of assembly line, the drive-through window being the most obvious example. As one observer notes, "The basic elements of the factory have obviously been introduced to the fast-food phenomenon . . . [with] the advent of the feeding machine."[18]

It is worth noting here that in addition to being a precursor, the automobile assembly line laid the groundwork for McDonaldization in another way. The mass-production of affordable automobiles gave many people ready access to automobiles, which in turn led to the immense expansion of the highway system and the tourist industry that grew up alongside it.[19] Restaurants, hotels, campgrounds, gas stations, and the like arose and served as the precursors to many of the franchises that lie at the base of the McDonaldized society.

General Motors, especially Alfred Sloan, further rationalized the automobile industry's bureaucratic structure. Sloan is famous for GM's multidivisional system, in which the central office handled long-range decisions while the divisions made the day-to-day decisions.[20] This innovation proved so successful in its day that the other automobile companies as well as many other corporations adopted it.

Levittown: Putting up Houses "Boom, Boom, Boom"

The availability of the automobile helped make possible not only the fast-food restaurant, but also the development of suburbia, especially the mass-produced suburban houses pioneered by Levitt & Sons, founded by Abraham Levitt. Between 1947 and 1951, this company built 17,447 homes on former New York potato fields, thereby creating Levittown, Long Island, and an instant community of 75,000 people.[21] The first houses in Levittown, Pennsylvania went on sale in 1958. In addition to highly rationalized homes, this Levittown was a planned community from inception to completion. The expansion of such suburban communities helped provide the population base for the development of the fast-food restaurant. With their need for and access to automobiles, suburban dwellers were, and are, a natural constituency for the fast-food restaurant.

Levitt & Sons thought of their building sites as large factories based on assembly-line technology. As William Levitt, one of the sons, put it,

> What it amounted to was a reversal of the Detroit assembly line.... There, the car moved while the workers stayed at their stations. In the case of our houses, it was the workers who moved, doing the same jobs at different locations. To the best of my knowledge, no one had ever done that before.[22]

The workers performed specialized tasks, much like their compatriots on the automobile assembly line. Said Alfred Levitt, another one of the sons, "The same man does the same thing every day, despite the psychologists. It is boring; it is bad; but the reward of the green stuff seems to alleviate the boredom of the work."[23] Thus, the Levitts rationalized the work of the construction laborer much as Ford had done with the automobile worker, with much the same attitude toward the worker.

The housing site as well as the work was rationalized. In and around the locale, the Levitts constructed warehouses; woodworking shops; plumbing shops; and a sand, gravel, and cement plant. Thus, instead of buying these services and their resulting products from others and then shipping them to the construction site, the products and services were on-site and controlled by the Levitts. Where possible, the Levitts also used prefabricated products. However, they deemed making an entirely prefabricated house less efficient than a partially prefabricated one.

The actual construction of each house followed a series of rigidly defined and rationalized steps. For example, in constructing the wall framework, the workers did no measuring or cutting; each piece had been cut to fit. A wall siding consisted of $73\frac{1}{2}$ large sheets of Colorbestos, replacing the former requirement of 570 small shingles. All houses were painted under high pressure, using the same two-tone paint—green on ivory. As a result, "Once the groundwork is down, houses go up boom, boom, boom."[24] The result, of course, was a large number of nearly identical houses produced quickly at low cost.

The emphasis on quantitative factors went beyond the physical construction of the house. For example, to sell the houses, instead of emphasizing the total cost of the house, real estate agents focused their pitches on the size of the down payment and monthly payments. The agents believed that the kinds of buyers attracted to Levittown were far more interested in such immediate numbers than the apparently more remote issue of the asking price of a house. Advertisements for Levittown houses stressed "the size and value of the house."[25] In other words, Levittown, like its many successors in the march toward increased rationalization, emphasized the most house for the least money. (Once aimed at low-priced homes, the principles developed by Levitt, and more generally of McDonaldization, have been applied to high-priced homes; architects now speak of "McMansions."[26]) Similarly, today's fast-food restaurants often tell people, explicitly and implicitly, that they offer consumers the most meal for the lowest cost.

There have been many critics of life in identical houses in highly rationalized communities. An early critique renamed suburbia, "Disturbia," describing the suburban home as a "split level trap."[27] However, you can also look positively at suburban rationalization. For example, many residents of Levittown have customized their homes so that they no longer look as homogenous as before. People now see "the Levitt box disguised as a Tudor Manor, a Swiss chalet, a Pennsylvania Dutch barn.[28] Other observers have found much of merit in Levittown and suburbia. Herbert Gans, for example, concluded his study of a third Levittown built in New Jersey by arguing that "whatever its imperfections, Levittown is a good place to live."[29] Whether or not it is a "good" place to live, Levittown is certainly a rationalized place in which to live, and its principles lie at the base of much of modern suburbia.

Shopping Centers: Malling America

Another component of rationalized society, one whose development was fueled by the rise of automobiles and suburban housing, was the fully enclosed shopping mall.[30] The modern mall had precursors in the Galleria Vittorio Emanuele in Milan, Italy (completed in 1877) and the first planned outdoor shopping center in the United States (built in 1916). The original fully enclosed shopping mall, however, was Southdale Center in Edina, Minnesota, which opened in 1956, not long after the opening of Ray Kroc's first McDonald's. Today, there are tens of thousands of malls in the United States visited by hundreds of millions of shoppers each month. The United States's largest shopping mall to date opened in 1992 down the road from Edina, in Bloomington, Minnesota. It included 4 department stores, 400 specialty shops (many of them parts of chains), and an amusement park.[31]

Shopping malls and McDonaldized chains complement one another beautifully. On the one hand, the malls provide a predictable, uniform, and profitable venue for such chains. When a new mall is built, the chains line up to gain entry. On the other hand, most malls would have much unrented space and not be able to exist were it not for the chains. Simultaneous products of the fast-moving automobile age, malls and chains feed off each other, furthering McDonaldization.

Ironically, malls today have become a kind of community center for both young and old. Many elderly people now use malls as places to both exercise and socialize. Because some parents now take their children to malls to "play," malls are providing play rooms, free video games, and free movies.[32] Like many other contributors to the McDonaldization of society, malls strive to engage customers from cradle to grave.

William Kowinski argues that the mall "was the culmination of all the American dreams, both decent and demented; the fulfillment, the model of the postwar paradise."[33] One could give priority to the mall, as Kowinski does, and discuss the "malling of America." However, in my view, the fast-food restaurant is a far more powerful and influential force. Like the mall, however, McDonaldization can be seen as both "decent and demented."

McDonald's: Creating the "Fast-Food Factory"

Ray Kroc, the creator of the McDonald's empire, is usually credited with developing its rational principles. However, the basic McDonald's approach was created by two brothers, Mac and Dick McDonald.[34] The McDonald brothers opened their first restaurant in Pasadena, California, in 1937. They based the restaurant on the principles of high speed, large volume, and low price. To avoid chaos, they offered customers a highly circumscribed menu. Instead of personalized service and traditional cooking techniques, the McDonald brothers used assembly-line procedures for cooking and serving food. In place of trained cooks, the brothers' "limited menu allowed them to break down food preparation into simple, repetitive tasks that could be learned quickly even by those stepping into a commercial kitchen for the first time."[35] They pioneered the use of specialized restaurant workers such as "grill men," "shake men," "fry men," and "dressers" (those who put the "extras" on burgers and who wrapped them). They developed regulations dictating what workers should do and even what they should say. In these and other ways, the McDonald brothers took the lead in the development of the rationalized "fast-food factory."[36]

Kroc invented neither the McDonald's principles nor the idea of a franchise. The Singer Sewing Machine company pioneered franchising after the Civil War, and automobile manufacturers and soft-drink companies used it by the turn of the twentieth century. By the 1930s, it had found its way into retail industries such as Western Auto, Rexall Pharmacy, and the IGA food markets.

Furthermore, there had been many efforts to franchise food service before Kroc arrived on the scene in the early 1950s. The first food service franchises, the A&W Root Beer stands, made their debut in 1924. Howard Johnson began franchising ice cream and other food in 1935. The first Dairy Queen opened in 1944; efforts to franchise it nationally led to a chain of about 2,500 outlets by 1948. Other well-known food franchises predated McDonald's. Big Boy started in the late 1930s, and Burger King (then InstaBurger) and Kentucky Fried Chicken began in 1954. Thus, Kroc's first McDonald's, which opened on April 15, 1955, was a relative latecomer to the franchising business in general, and the food-franchise business in particular. But I am getting a bit ahead of the story.

In 1954, when Ray Kroc first visited it, McDonald's was but a single drive-in hamburger stand in San Bernardino, California. The basic menu, the approach, and even some of the techniques that McDonald's is famous for today had already been created by the McDonald brothers. Though by 1954 it was a local sensation, the McDonald brothers were content to keep it that way; they were doing very well and had few grand ambitions in spite of a few tentative steps toward franchising. With plenty of ambition for all of them, Kroc became their franchising agent and went on to build the McDonald's empire of franchises, thereby giving impetus to McDonaldization. At first, Kroc worked in partnership with the McDonald brothers, but after he bought them out in 1961 for $2.7 million, he was free to build the business as he wished.

Again, Kroc invented little that was new. Basically, he took the specific products and techniques of the McDonald brothers and combined them with the principles of other franchises (food-service and others), bureaucracies, scientific management, and the assembly line. Kroc's genius was in bringing all these well-known ideas and techniques to bear on the fast-food business and adding his ambition to turn it, through franchising, into a national, then international, business. *McDonald's and McDonaldization, then, do not represent something new, but rather the culmination of a series of rationalization processes that had been occurring throughout the twentieth century.*

Kroc's major innovation lay in the way he franchised McDonald's. For one thing, he did not permit regional franchises in which a single franchisee received control over all the outlets to be opened in a given area. Other franchisers had foundered because regional franchisees had grown too powerful and subverted the basic principles of the company. Kroc maximized central control, and thereby uniformity throughout the system, by granting franchises one at a time and rarely granting more than one franchise to a specific individual. Another of Kroc's innovations was to set the fee for a franchise at a rock-bottom $950. Other franchisers had set very high initial fees and made most of their money from them. As a result, they tended to lose interest in the continued viability of the franchisees. At McDonald's, profits did not come from high initial fees, but from the 1.9% of store sales it demanded of its franchisees. Thus, the success of Kroc and his organization depended on the prosperity of the franchisees. This mutual interest was Kroc's greatest contribution to the franchise business and a key factor in the success of McDonald's and its franchisees, many of whom became millionaires in their own right.

McDonald's achieved a balance between centralized control and the independence of franchisees. Though Kroc imposed and enforced a uniform system, he encouraged the franchisees to come up with innovations that could enhance not only their operations but also those of the system as a whole. Take the case of product innovations. Kroc himself was not a great product innovator. One of his most notorious flops was the Hulaburger, a slice of grilled pineapple between two pieces of cheese wrapped in a toasted bun. Successful creations, such as the fish sandwich, the Egg McMuffin, and, more generally, McDonald's breakfast meals, came from franchisees.

While not a major innovator, Kroc spearheaded a series of developments that further rationalized the fast-food business. For one thing, he (unwittingly) served as preacher (and cheerleader) for the principles of rationalization as he lectured "about uniformity, about a standardized menu, one size portions, same prices, same quality in every store."[37] This uniformity allowed McDonald's to differentiate itself from its competitors, whose food was typically inconsistent. McDonald's also led the field by imposing a limited menu (at first, ten items), creating tough standards for the fat content of hamburgers, converting to frozen hamburgers and french fries, using inspectors to check on uniformity and conformity, forming in 1961 the first full-time training center in the business called Hamburger University (which offered a "degree" in "Hamburgerology"), and publishing in 1958 an operations manual that detailed how to run a franchise.[38] This manual laid down many of the rational principles for operating a fast-food restaurant:

> It told operators *exactly* how to draw milk shakes, grill hamburgers, and fry potatoes. It specified *precise* cooking times for all products and temperature settings for all equipment. It fixed *standard* portions on every food item, down to the *quarter ounce* of onions placed on each hamburger patty and the *thirty-two slices per pound* of cheese. It specified that french fries be cut at *nine thirty-seconds of an inch* thick. And it defined quality *controls* that were unique to food service, including the disposal of meat and potato products that were held more than *ten minutes* in a serving bin.
>
> . . . Grill men . . . *were instructed* to put hamburgers down on the grill moving from left to right, creating *six rows of six* patties each. And because the first two rows were farthest from the heating element, they were *instructed* (and still are) to flip the third row first, then the fourth, fifth, and sixth before flipping the first two.[39] [Italics added.]

Conclusion

McDonaldization did not occur in a historical vacuum; it had important precursors that remain important to this day. These precursors provided the principles—of the assembly line, scientific management, and bureaucracy—on which fast-food restaurant chains were built. Furthermore, they provided the ground these chains needed to thrive—large numbers of factory workers and bureaucrats who worked great distances from their suburban dwellings, who possessed automobiles to transport them not only to and from work but also to and from the fast-food restaurants they increasingly needed and desired, and who visited the shopping malls that would house many fast-food restaurants and their rationalized derivatives.

While bureaucracies and other precursors are still important, I believe the fast-food restaurant has become the model of rationality. Just as Weber fretted over the emerging iron cage of rationality, I foresee a similar iron cage being created by the increasing ubiquity of the fast-food model. Weber was particularly upset by the irrationality of rationality, a concern that also lies at the heart of this book. Thus, this book is an effort to bring Weber's theory, developed at the turn of the twentieth century, to bear on developments that are accelerating as the twenty-first century draws near.

Although the fast-food restaurant adopts elements of its predecessors, it also represents a quantum leap in the process of rationalization. While McDonaldization is a logical extension of rationalization, McDonaldization is also a sufficiently more extreme form of rationalization to legitimize the use of a distinct label to describe the most contemporary aspects of the rationalization process.

Given this historical backdrop, the next five chapters discuss the basic dimensions of McDonaldization—efficiency, calculability (or quantification), predictability, increased control through substitution of nonhuman for human technology, and the seemingly inevitable by-product of rational systems—the irrationality of rationality. These chapters aim both to further define these dimensions and to illustrate, through the use of many examples, the way each appears in an increasingly wide array of social settings throughout the world. Besides the fast-food industry, higher education, health care, and the work place will be singled out for detailed treatment. The examples marshaled throughout the next five chapters serve as evidence to support the assertion that McDonaldization is sweeping through society.

3

Efficiency

Driving Through the Magic Kingdom Munching on Finger Food

McDonaldization implies a search for maximum efficiency in increasingly numerous and diverse social settings. *Efficiency* means choosing the optimum means to a given end. Let me clarify this definition. First, the truly optimum means to an end is rarely found. Rather, optimum in this definition implies the attempt to find and use the *best possible* means. According to the economist, Herbert Simon, people and organizations rarely maximize.[1] However, the drive for efficiency implies the search for a far better means to an end than would be employed under ordinary circumstances. Second, the generality of the terms *means and ends* makes it clear that efficiency can be applied to innumerable means and ends. In other words, there can be a search for optimum means within settings that involve a large number of disparate ends. This means that the drive for efficiency can and does occur within a wide variety of social settings.

In a McDonaldized society, people rarely search for the best means to an end on their own. Rather, they rely on the optimum means that have been previously discovered and institutionalized in a variety of social settings. Thus, the best means may be part of a technology, written into an organization's rules and regulations, or taught to employees during the process of occupational socialization. It would be inefficient if people always had to discover for themselves the optimum means to ends.

Efficiency is clearly advantageous to consumers, who can obtain what they need more quickly with less effort. Similarly, workers can perform their tasks more rapidly and easily. Managers and owners gain because work gets done and because customers are served more efficiently. But, as is always the case, irrationalities such as surprising inefficiencies and the dehumanization of customers and workers crop up.

The Fast-Food Industry: We Do It All for Them

Although the fast-food restaurant did not create the yearning for efficiency, it has helped turn it into a nearly universal desire. Many sectors of society have had to change in order to operate in the efficient manner demanded by those accustomed to life in the fast lane of the fast-food restaurant. However, when you look at the manifestations of efficiency in an array of social institutions later in this chapter, bear in mind that many of these instances cannot be traced directly to the influence of the fast-food restaurant. Some of them even predate and helped shape the fast-food restaurant. Nonetheless, they play a part in the preoccupation with efficiency that McDonald's has fueled.

In the early 1950s, the dawn of the era of the fast-food restaurant, the major alternative to fast food was the home-cooked meal made mostly from ingredients previously purchased at various markets. This was clearly more efficient than earlier methods, such as hunting game and gathering fruits and vegetables before cooking. By the 1950s, few Americans still relied on hunting or gardening for the ingredients for their meals; local stores and the burgeoning supermarkets were more efficient sites for obtaining food.

The efficiency of home cooking had also increased with the development of refrigerators, freezers, and gas and electric stoves. Cookbooks also made a major contribution to efficient home cooking. Instead of inventing a dish every time it was prepared, the cook could follow a recipe each time and thus more efficiently produce the dish.

But the home-cooked meal was, and still is, a relatively inefficient way to eat. It requires going to the market, preparing the ingredients, cooking the food, eating it, and cleaning up afterward. The restaurant has long been a more efficient alternative in terms of effort.

But restaurants can also be inefficient—it may take several hours to go to a restaurant, consume a meal, and then return home. The desire for more efficient restaurants led to the rise of some of the ancestors of the fast-food restaurants—diners, cafeterias, and early drive-through or drive-in restaurants. The modern fast-food restaurant was the next step toward more efficient food consumption. Increasing efficiency has been largely a matter of streamlining various processes, simplifying products, and having the customer do work formerly done by paid employees.

Streamlining the Process

Above all else, Ray Kroc was impressed by the efficiency of the McDonald brothers' operation, as well as the enormous profit potential of such a system applied at a large number of sites. Here is how Kroc described his initial reactions to the McDonald's system:

> I was fascinated by the simplicity and effectiveness of the system.
> . . . each step in producing the limited menu was stripped down to its essence and accomplished with a minimum of effort. They sold hamburgers and cheeseburgers only. The burgers were . . . all fried the same way.[2]

But Kroc's obsession with efficiency predated his discovery of McDonald's and was manifest during his earlier career, which involved the sale of blenders to restaurants. What disturbed him in many of these restaurants was their lack of efficiency:

> There was inefficiency, waste, and temperamental cooks, sloppy service and food whose [sic] quality was never consistent. What was needed was a simple product that moved from start to completion in a streamlined path.[3]

Kroc toyed with other alternatives for increasing the efficiency of the restaurant meal before settling on the McDonald's hamburger as a model of efficiency:

> He had contemplated hot dogs, then rejected the idea. There were too many kinds of hot dogs—hot dogs with cereal and flour, the all-meat hot dog which is all kinds of meat, the all-beef hot dog, the kosher hot dog. And along with the different varieties, there were all sorts of different ways of cooking hot dogs. They could be boiled, broiled, rotisseried, charcoaled, and on and on. Hamburgers, on the other hand, were simplicity itself. The condiments were added to the hamburger, not built in. And there was only one way to prepare the hamburger—to grill it.[4]

Kroc and his associates experimented with each component of the hamburger to increase the efficiency of producing and serving it. For example, they started with only partially sliced buns that arrived in cardboard boxes. The griddle workers had to spend time opening the boxes, separating the buns, slicing them in half, and discarding the leftover paper and cardboard.

Eventually, they found that buns sliced completely in half could be used more efficiently. In addition, buns were made efficient by having them separated and shipped in reusable boxes. The meat patty received similar attention. For example, the paper between the patties had to have just the right amount of wax so that the patties would readily slide off the paper and onto the grill. Kroc made it clear that he aimed at greater efficiency:

> The purpose of all these refinements, and we never lost sight of it, was to make our griddle man's job easier to do quickly and well. And the other considerations of cost cutting, inventory control, and so forth were important to be sure, but they were secondary to the critical detail of what happened there at the smoking griddle. This was the vital passage of our *assembly-line*, and the product had to flow through it smoothly or the whole plant would falter.[5] [Italics added.]

Today, fast food restaurants prepare their menu items on a kind of assembly line involving a number of people in specialized operations (for example, the burger "dresser"). The ultimate application of the assembly line to the fast-food process is Burger King's conveyor belt: A raw, frozen hamburger placed on one end moves slowly via the conveyor under a flame and emerges in ninety-four seconds on the other end fully cooked. Similar techniques are employed at Dunkin' Donuts, Kentucky Fried Chicken (if you want spicy Cajun fried chicken you must wheel on down the road to Popeye's), Taco Bell, and Pizza Hut. A newer and even more specialized fast-food outlet, Cinnabon, has perfected the techniques to mass produce and serve cinnamon buns.

Getting diners into and out of the fast-food restaurant has also been streamlined. As three observers put it, McDonald's has done "everything to speed the way from secretion to excretion."[6] Parking lots adjacent to the restaurant offer readily available parking spots. It's a short walk to the counter, and although there is sometimes a line, food is usually quickly ordered, obtained, and paid for. The highly limited menu makes the diner's choice easy, in contrast to the many choices available in other restaurants. With the food obtained, it is but a few steps to a table and the beginning of the "dining experience." Because there is little inducement to linger, the diners generally gather the leftover paper, styrofoam, and plastic, discard them in a nearby trash receptacle, and get back in their cars to drive to the next (often McDonaldized) activity.

Not too many years ago, those in charge of fast-food restaurants discovered that the drive-through window made this whole process far more efficient. McDonald's opened its first drive-through in 1975 in Oklahoma City; within four years, almost half its restaurants had one. Instead of the "laborious" and "inefficient" process of parking the car, walking to the counter, waiting in line, ordering, paying, carrying the food to the table, eating, and disposing of the remnants, the drive-through window offered diners the option of driving to the window (perhaps waiting in a line of cars), ordering, paying, and driving off with the meal. You could eat while driving if you wanted to be even more efficient. The drive-through window is also efficient for the fast-food restaurant. As more and more people use the drive-through window, fewer parking spaces, tables, and employees are needed. Further, consumers take their debris with them as they drive away, thereby eliminating the need for additional trash receptacles and employees to empty those receptacles periodically.

A big area of growth for McDonald's today is smaller, cheaper, and even more efficient restaurants. About half the size of traditional McDonald's outlets, they have an average of fifty-five instead of eighty seats, more efficient technology, and more drive-through windows.[7] Similarly, McDonald's (and other fast-food restaurants) are building "satellites," or express locations, in such settings as Wal-Marts and service stations.

Modern technology offers further advances in streamlining the handling of customers in the fast-food restaurant. Here is a description of some of the progress in efficiency offered by Taco Bell in one of its California outlets:

> Inside, diners in a hurry for tacos and burritos can punch up their own orders on a touch-screen computer. Outside, drive-through customers see a video monitor flash back a list of their orders to avoid mistakes. They then can pay using a pneumatic-tube like those many banks employ for drive-up transactions. Their food, and their change, is waiting for them when they pull forward to the pickup window. And if the line of cars grows too long, a Taco Bell worker will wade in with a wireless keyboard to take orders.[8]

Simplifying the Product

Another efficient aspect of the fast-food restaurant is the nature of the food served. Complex foods based on sophisticated recipes are, needless to say, not the norm at fast-food restaurants. The staples of the industry are foods that require relatively few ingredients and are simple to prepare, serve, and eat.

In fact, fast-food restaurants generally serve finger food, food that can be eaten without utensils. Hamburgers, french fries, fried chicken, slices of pizza, tacos—the staples of the fast-food business—are all finger foods. Many innovations over the years have greatly increased the number and types of finger foods available. The Egg McMuffin is an entire breakfast—egg, Canadian bacon, English muffin—combined into a handy sandwich. It is far more efficient to devour such a sandwich than to sit down with knife and fork and eat a plate full of eggs, bacon, and toast. The creation of the Chicken McNugget, perhaps the ultimate finger food, reflects the fact that chicken is pretty inefficient as far as McDonald's is concerned. Bones, gristle, and skin of the chicken—barriers to efficient consumption—have all been eliminated in the Chicken McNugget. Customers can pop the bite-size morsels of fried chicken right into their mouths even as they drive. Were they able to, the mass purveyors of chicken, for example, Perdue, would breed a more efficiently consumed chicken free of bones, gristle, and skin.[9] McDonald's also offers an apple pie that, because it is completely encased in dough, can be munched like a sandwich.

The limited number of available choices and options also contributes to efficiency in the fast-food restaurant. McDonald's does not serve egg rolls (at least not yet), and Taco Bell does not offer fried chicken. In spite of what they tell people, fast-food restaurants are far from not only full-serve restaurants but also the old cafeterias that offered a vast array of foods.

Pity the consumer who has a special request in the fast-food restaurant. The fast-food advertisement, "We do it your way," implies that these chains happily accommodate special requests. However, because much of their efficiency stems from the fact that they virtually always do it one way—*their* way, the last thing that fast-food restaurants want to do is do it your way. The typical hamburger is usually so thin that it can only be cooked one way—well done. Bigger burgers (the McDonald's Quarter-Pounder, for example) can be prepared rare, but the fast-food restaurant prefers, for the sake of efficiency (and perhaps for health reasons), that they all be cooked one way. Customers with the temerity to ask for a rare burger or well-browned fries are likely to cool their heels for a long time waiting for such "exotica." Few customers are willing to do this because it defeats one of the main advantages of going to a fast-food restaurant—efficiency. The limited number of menu items also allows for highly efficient ordering of supplies and food delivery. In sum, what Henry Ford once said about cars has been extended to hamburgers, "Any customer can have a car painted any color that he wants so long as it is black."[10]

Putting Customers to Work

Two scholars have recently described how fast-food customers do unpaid labor:

> A few years ago, the fast food chain McDonald's came up with the slogan "We do it all for you." In reality, at McDonald's, we do it all for them. We stand in line, take the food to the table, dispose of the waste, and stack our trays. As labor costs rise and technology develops, the consumer often does more and more of the work.[11]

The salad bar is a classic example of putting the consumer to work. The customer "buys" an empty plate and then ambles over to the salad bar to load up on the array of vegetables and other foods available that day. Quickly seeing the merit in this, many supermarkets have now installed their own salad bars with a more elaborate array of alternative foods available to the consumer. The salad lover can now work as a salad chef at lunch hour in the fast-food restaurant and then do it all over again in the evening at the supermarket. All this is very efficient from the perspective of the fast-food restaurant and the supermarket, since they need only a small number of employees to keep the various compartments well stocked.

In a number of fast-food restaurants, including Roy Rogers (owned by Hardee's), consumers are expected to take a naked burger to the "fixin' bar" to add such things as lettuce, tomatoes, and onions. In such cases, they end up logging a few minutes a week as sandwich makers. In a more recent innovation at Burger King and other franchises, people must fill their own cups with ice and soft drinks, thereby spending a few moments as "soda jerks." In some ultramodern fast-food restaurants such as Taco Bell, people must punch in their own orders on computer screens. In these and other ways, the fast-food restaurant has grown more efficient by putting customers to work.

However, what is efficient for fast-food restaurants is often inefficient for consumers. For example, it is efficient for the fast-food restaurant to have consumers wait in line, but waiting in line is inefficient for consumers. So, too, it is efficient for fast-food restaurants to have the diner do much of the work done by employees in a traditional restaurant, but is this efficient to the consumer? Is it efficient to order your own food rather than having a waiter do it? Or to bus your own paper, plastic, and styrofoam rather than having a busperson do it?

Higher Education: Just Fill in the Box

In the educational system, specifically the university (now being dubbed "McUniversity"[12]), you can find many examples of the pressure for greater efficiency. One is the machine-graded, multiple-choice examination. In a much earlier era, students were examined individually by their professors. This may have been a good way to find out what students knew, but it was highly labor-intensive and inefficient. Later, the essay examination became very popular. While grading a set of essays was more efficient than giving individual oral examinations, it was still relatively inefficient and time-consuming. Enter the multiple-choice examination, the grading of which was a snap. In fact, graduate assistants could grade it, making it even more efficient for the professor. Now there are computer-graded examinations that maximize efficiency for both professors and graduate assistants. They even offer advantages to students, such as making it easier to study and limiting the effect of the subjective views of the grader on the grading process.

The multiple-choice examination still left the professor saddled with the inefficient task of composing the necessary sets of questions. Furthermore, at least some of the questions had to be changed each semester because new students were likely to gain possession of old exams. The solution: Textbook companies provided professors with books (free of charge) full of multiple-choice questions to accompany textbooks required for use in large classes. However, the professor still had to retype the questions or have them retyped. Recently, publishers have begun to provide these sets of questions on computer disks. Now all the professor needs to do is select the desired questions and let the printer do the rest. With these great advances in efficiency, professors now can choose to have very little to do with the entire examination process, from question composition to grading.

Publishers have provided other services to make teaching more efficient for those professors who adopt their textbooks. With the adoption of a textbook, a professor may receive many materials with which to fill class hours—lecture outlines, computer simulations, discussion questions, videotapes, movies, even ideas for guest lecturers and student projects. Professors who choose to use all these devices need do little or nothing on their own for their classes. A highly efficient means of teaching, this approach frees up time for other much more valued activities (by professors, but not students) such as writing and research.

Finally, worth noting is the development of a relatively new type of "service" on college campuses. For a nominal fee, students are provided with lecture notes, from instructors, teaching assistants, and top-notch students, for their courses. No more inefficient note-taking; in fact, no more inefficient class attendance. Students are free to pursue more valuable activities such as poring over arcane journals in the graduate library or watching the "soaps."

Health Care: Docs-in-a-Box

People might assume that modern medicine is immune to this drive for efficiency, and rationalization more generally.[13] However, medicine has moved toward greater efficiency and rationality. In fact, there have been instances of what may be termed "assembly-line medicine." One example is Dr. Denton Cooley (his "fetish is efficiency"), who gained worldwide fame for performing delicate open-heart surgery in a "heart surgery factory" that operated "with the precision of an assembly-line."[14] Even more striking is the following description of the Moscow Research Institute of Eye Microsurgery:

> In many ways the scene resembles any modern factory. A conveyor glides silently past five work stations, periodically stopping, then starting again. Each station is staffed by an attendant in a sterile mask and smock. The workers have just three minutes to complete their tasks before the conveyor moves on; they turn out 20 finished pieces in an hour.
>
> Nearly everything else about the assembly line, however, is highly unusual: the workers are eye surgeons, and the conveyor carries human beings on stretchers. This is . . . where the production methods of Henry Ford are applied to the practice of medicine . . . a "medical factory for the production of people with good eyesight."[15]

Such assembly lines are not yet the norm in medicine, yet one can imagine that they will grow increasingly common in the coming years.

Perhaps the best example of the increasing efficiency of medical practice in the United States and of the pervasive influence of McDonaldization is the growth of walk-in/walk-out surgical or emergency centers. These so-called "McDoctors" or "Docs-in-a-Box" serve patients who want medical problems handled with maximum efficiency. Each center handles only a limited number of minor problems, but with great dispatch. Although the patient with a laceration cannot be stitched as efficiently as a customer in search of a hamburger can be served, many of the same principles shape the two operations. For instance, it is more efficient for the patient to walk in without an appointment than to make an appointment with a regular physician and wait until that time arrives. For a minor emergency, such as a slight laceration, walking through a "McDoctors" is more efficient than working your way through the labyrinth of a large hospital's emergency room. Hospitals are set up to handle serious problems for which efficiency is not (yet) the norm, although some hospitals already employ specialized emergency-room physicians and teams of medical personnel. From the organization's point of view, a "McDoctors" can be run more efficiently than a hospital emergency room. "Docs-in-the-Box" can also be more efficient than private doctors' offices because they are not structured to permit the kind of personal (and therefore inefficient) attention patients expect from their private physicians.

Many factors impel the medical profession toward becoming more efficient, or more systematically finding the optimum means to the end of providing medical services.

◆   One factor key to increasing efficiency within medicine is the rise of investor-owned corporations (for example, Humana Inc. and Hospital Corporation of America) interested in medicine as a profit-making venture. In their efforts to maximize profits, these institutions and their professional managers seek to make operations as efficient as possible. Because of the need to be competitive, the emphasis on efficiency in such organizations is likely to carry over into nonprofit medical organizations.

◆   Pressure from the federal government and third-party payers, such as insurance companies (for example, Blue Cross–Blue Shield), to reduce costs is forcing medicine to streamline its activities. There is great pressure to do fewer things (for example, to eliminate unnecessary tests and surgical procedures) and do those things faster. In addition, more procedures occur on an outpatient basis. Thus, instead of hospitalizing a patient a day or two for a few tests or a minor surgical procedure, increasingly, tests or procedures are being performed during brief day trips to the hospital. The federal government, through Medicare, introduced the prospective payment and DRG (Diagnostic Related Groups) programs in 1983, in which a set amount is reimbursed to hospitals for a given medical diagnosis, no matter how long the patient is hospitalized. This replaces the system wherein the government paid whatever "reasonable" amount it was billed. The result is that instead of a leisurely stay in a hospital and a lengthy course of treatment, patients must face streamlined operations. Because the amounts paid are fixed, it behooves medical personnel to get patients in and out of hospitals as efficiently as possible. Many states and private insurers have developed prospective payment systems of their own.[16]

♦ An increase in competition has also forced medicine to become more efficient. This competition received impetus from a 1975 Supreme Court decision that declared physicians are subject to the Sherman Antitrust Act, and from a succeeding series of successful antitrust suits filed by the Federal Trade Commission against the medical profession's anticompetitive practices. The American Medical Association (AMA) had long sought to restrict competition through its code of ethics. The successful antitrust suits have led to a reduction in these restrictions, an increase in competition, and, as a result, pressure on physicians to seek ways of becoming more efficient. The support of competition by the Reagan administration in the 1980s also contributed to this change. Still another factor fueling increased medical competition, and therefore greater efficiency, is the increasing number of physicians. This substantial growth in the medical profession was encouraged, at least in part, by the Health Professions Educational Assistance Act of 1963.

♦ Still another factor is the expansion of medical bureaucracies with their inherent interest in efficiency. Hospitals, medical conglomerates, chains, health maintenance organizations (HMOs), third-party payers, and the government are all, or can be, huge bureaucratic systems. These, as all bureaucracies, are constructed for the efficient handling of large quantities of work. Physicians are likely to be pushed in the direction of greater efficiency to the degree that they are employed or affected by these bureaucracies.

♦ Beyond bureaucracies, many modern medical technologies have served to make the practice of medicine more efficient. For instance, laser technology has greatly increased the efficiency of delicate eye operations.

♦ Finally, there are consumers, accustomed to efficiently organized McDonaldized systems, who demand, among other things, that their trips to clinics or HMOs offer one-stop visits that include lab work, needed drugs, and consultations with physicians.

The Workplace: Just-in-Time, Not Just-in-Case

The emphasis on efficiency permeates many work settings. This emphasis comes in part from Taylor's ideas on scientific management. In fact, his followers came to be known as "efficiency experts." Taylor was animated by the belief that the United States suffered from "inefficiency in almost all our daily acts" and that there was a need for "greater national efficiency." His "time and motion" studies were designed to replace what Taylor called the inefficient "rule of thumb" methods that dominated work in his day with what he thought of as the "one best way"—that is, the optimum means to the end of doing a job.[17]

Taylor outlined a series of steps to be followed in time and motion studies:

1. Find a number of workers, preferably in diverse work settings, who are particularly skillful at the work in question.

2. Make a careful study of the elementary movements (as well as the tools and implements) employed by these people in their work.

3. Time each of these elementary steps carefully with the aim of discovering the most efficient way of accomplishing each step.

4. Make the work efficient by eliminating inefficient steps such as "all false movements, slow movements, and useless movements."

5. Finally, after all unnecessary movements have been eliminated, combine the most efficient movements (and tools) to create the famous "one best way" of doing a job.[18]

Although one hears little these days of Taylor, efficiency experts, and "time and motion" studies, their impact is strongly felt in a McDonaldized society. For instance, hamburger chains strive to discover and implement the "one best way" to grill hamburgers, cook french fries, prepare shakes, process customers, and the rest. The most efficient ways of handling a variety of tasks have been codified in training manuals and taught to managers who, in turn, teach them to new employees. The design of the fast-food restaurant and its various technologies have been put in place to aid in the attainment of the most efficient means to the end of feeding large numbers of people. Similar technologies have been developed to promote efficiency in factories, offices, and retail outlets of every description.

Turning to just one of these workplaces, the automobile industry, Henry Ford invented the automobile assembly line mainly because he wanted to save time, energy, and money (that is, to be more efficient). This way, he could increase car sales and the profitability of the Ford Motor Company. As mentioned earlier, Ford got the idea for the automobile assembly line from the overhead trolley system used at the time by Chicago meat packers to butcher cattle. As the steer was propelled along on the trolley system, a line of highly specialized butchers performed specific tasks, so that by the end of the line, the steer had been completely butchered. This system was clearly more efficient than having a single meat cutter handle all these tasks.

On the basis of this experience and his knowledge of the automobile business, Ford developed a set of principles for the construction of an automobile assembly line, principles that to this day stand as models of efficiency:

- Workers are not to take any unnecessary steps; work-related movements are reduced to an absolute minimum.

- Parts needed in the assembly process are to travel the least possible distance.

- Mechanical (rather than human) means are to be used to move the car (and parts) from one step in the assembly process to the next. (At first, gravity was used, but later electrical conveyor belts were employed.)

- Complex sets of movements are eliminated and the worker does "as nearly as possible only one thing with one movement."[19]

The introduction of the assembly line allowed for a massive increase in the efficiency of automobile manufacturing. As a result of its pioneering efforts, the Ford Motor Company could quickly increase productivity, lower costs, and therefore increase its sales and profitability. Other automobile companies soon adopted the assembly line, and many other industries embraced the model whole or in part.

The Japanese adopted American assembly-line technology after World War II and then made their own distinctive contributions to heightened efficiency. For example, the Japanese "just-in-time" system replaced the American "just-in-case" system. Both systems refer to the supply of needed parts to a manufacturing operation. In the American system, parts are stored in the plant until, or in case, they are needed. This leads to inefficiencies such as the purchase and storage (at great cost) of parts that will not be needed for quite some time. To counter these inefficiencies, the Japanese developed the "just-in-time" system: needed parts arrive at the assembly line just as they are to be placed in the car or whatever object is being manufactured. This eliminates inefficiencies by, in effect, including all the Japanese company's suppliers in the assembly-line process.

Other Settings: Move It Along

Though there is more than one way to make operations efficient, efficiency remains the common theme of various components of the McDonaldized world. As you will see, efficiency takes many forms in the wide array of rationalized settings.

Streamlining the Process

Consider the drive to streamline the process. Banks, for example, have instituted the drive-through window to increase the efficiency of banking for both consumers and bankers. Many photo processors have become drive-up kiosks that merely receive the film and then send it off to a central location for development.

I've participated in an excellent example of streamlining in higher education—custom publishing.[20] In a customized textbook, the publisher recruits a wide range of authors to write chapters on specific topics. The professor interested in adopting the book for class use receives a list of the available chapters. The professor may choose any subset of the chapters, which can be put together in the order the professor wishes. A customized book is produced, and the number required for the professor's class is printed. This development has been made possible by the advent of new computer technology as well as ultra-high-speed printers.

Customized textbooks are more efficient than regular textbooks in at least three ways. First, having many experts write a single chapter each requires just weeks or months of work; having one author write them all can take years. Second, because it will contain only those chapters that will actually be used, a customized book is more likely to have fewer chapters, to be more streamlined, than a traditional textbook. Third, the chapters can be mixed and matched in various ways to produce texts for many different courses; subsets of the same collection of chapters can be used in different courses.

Another example of efficiency in publishing is the advent of books-on-tape. Instead of doing nothing else while reading, people can now engage in other activities—driving, walking, jogging, or watching a sports event on TV with the sound off—while listening to a book.

Even religion has been streamlined through such things as drive-in churches and televised religious programs.[21] In 1985 the Vatican announced that Catholics could receive indulgences through the Pope's annual Christmas benediction on TV or radio. ("Indulgences are a release by way of devotional practices from certain forms of punishment resulting from sin.") Before this development Catholics had to engage in the far less efficient activity of going to Rome for the Christmas benediction and manifesting the "proper intention and attitude" to receive their indulgences in person.[22]

Simplifying the Product

Many products other than fast food have been simplified in the name of efficiency. For example, many businesses have adopted the idea of offering the consumer a limited number of choices and options. AAMCO Transmissions works mainly on transmissions and Midas Muffler largely restricts itself to the installation of mufflers. H&R Block does simple tax returns. Because it does not offer the full array of tax and financial services available from a CPA, it is undoubtedly not the best place to have complicated tax returns completed. "McDentists" may be relied on for simple dental procedures, but people would be ill-advised to have root canals done there. Pearle Vision Centers offer eye examinations, but people should go to an eye doctor for any major vision problem.

Many books-on-tape have appeared in abridged form. Gone are the "wasted" hours listening to "insignificant" parts of novels. With liberal cutting, *War and Peace* can be heard in one sitting.

Similarly, most "serious" newspapers (for example, the *New York Times* and the *Washington Post*) are relatively inefficient to read. This is especially true of stories that begin on page one and then carry over to additional pages. *USA TODAY* eliminated this inefficient presentation by keeping whole stories on the same page, in other words, by offering "News McNuggets." This was accomplished by ruthlessly editing stories to dramatically simplify and reduce narrative content (no words wasted), leaving a series of relatively bare facts. In this, *USA TODAY* was anticipated by the various digests, most notably the still popular *Reader's Digest*. The original aim of *Reader's Digest* was to offer magazine articles that "could be written to please the reader, to give him the nub of the matter in the new fast-moving world of the 1920s, instead of being written at length and with literary embellishments to please the author or the editor."[23] Other precursors to *USA TODAY* are magazines such as *Time*, *Newsweek*, and *Business Week*. The simplified character of the latter compared with the *Wall Street Journal* was stressed by two observers: "The message is that busy executives don't have time to read in depth so don't waste time reading the *Wall Street Journal* every day when one quick bite of *Business Week* once a week is sufficient to give you a step ahead of the competition."[24]

Putting Customers to Work

Many types of organizations insist that their customers do unpaid work. The advent of the automated teller machine (ATM) in the banking industry allows everyone to work, for at least a few moments, as unpaid bank tellers (and often pay fees for the privilege). Recently, to encourage the use of ATMs, some banks have begun charging a fee for the use of human tellers.[25]

Phone companies now make people put in a few minutes a day as operators. Instead of asking a long-distance operator to make calls, people are urged to dial such calls themselves, thereby requiring them to keep lengthy lists of phone numbers and area codes. Instead of simply dialing "0" to make a collect long-distance call, people must now remember lengthy 800 numbers to save money. Another such effort by the phone companies involves having people look up numbers in the phone book rather than call an operator for information. To discourage people from using the operator for such information, there is now likely to be a fairly hefty charge for the service. In the state of Washington, consumers can now install their own telephones simply by plugging them in the jacks, dialing 811, and answering a series of questions posed by a computer by punching digits on the phone.[26]

In some doctors' offices, patients must now weigh themselves and take their own temperatures. Instead of being interviewed by the government census taker, people usually receive a questionnaire in the mail to fill out on their own. In calling many businesses these days, instead of dealing with a human operator, people must follow a series of instructions from a computer by pushing a bewildering array of numbers and codes before they get, they hope, to the desired extension.[27] Here is the way one humorist describes such a "conversation" and the work involved for the caller:

> The party you are trying to reach—Thomas Watson—is unavailable at this time. To leave a message, please wait for the beep. To review your message, press 7. To change your message after reviewing it, press 4. To add to your message, press 5. To reach another party, press the star sign and enter the four-digit extension. To listen to Muzak, press 23. To transfer out of phone mail in what I promise you will be a futile effort to reach a human, press 0— because we treat you like one.[28]

The postal service has people do some of its work by pressing them to use increasingly long zip codes. Because the automated technologies used to sort mail break down when an address is not clearly written on the envelope, the postal service now asks people to type addresses on envelopes.[29]

Many of these examples may seem trivial. Clearly, it is not highly burdensome to write a zip code on an envelope or to look up a telephone number. But the totality of these various activities indicates a wide-ranging development. The modern consumer spends an increasingly significant amount of time and energy doing unpaid labor for a number of different organizations.

Now, here is a close look at four areas where efficiency has become more firmly entrenched: home cooking, shopping, entertainment, and sports.

Home Cooking (and Related Phenomena)

Given the efficiency of the fast-food restaurant, the home kitchen has had to grow more efficient or face total extinction. Had the kitchen not grown more efficient, a comedian could have envisioned a time when the kitchen would have been replaced by a large, comfortable telephone lounge used for calling Domino's for pizza delivery.

One key to the salvation of the kitchen is the microwave oven.[30] Far more efficient than conventional ovens for preparing a meal, the microwave has streamlined the process of cooking. Microwaves are usually faster than other ovens, and people can also prepare a wider array of foods in them. Perhaps most important, they spawned a number of microwavable foods (including soup, pizza, hamburgers, fried chicken, french fries, and popcorn) that permit the efficient preparation of the fare people usually find in fast-food restaurants. For example, one of the first microwavable foods produced by Hormel was an array of biscuit-based breakfast sandwiches "popularized in recent years by many of the fast-food chains," most notably McDonald's and its Egg McMuffin.[31] Banquet rushed to market with microwavable chicken breast nuggets. In fact, many food companies now employ people who continually scout fast-food restaurants for new ideas. As one executive put it, "Instead of having a breakfast sandwich at McDonald's, you can pick one up from the freezer of your grocery store."[32] Indeed, the efficiency of "homemade" fast foods at least in some ways *seems* to be greater than that afforded by the fast-food restaurant. Instead of getting into the car, driving to the restaurant, and returning home, people need only pop the desired foods in the microwave. On the other side, the efficiency of the microwaved meal suffers because it requires a prior trip to the market.

Furthermore, people ordinarily do not precisely calculate efficiency. Instead, a general perception develops that some things are efficient (for example, a fast-food restaurant, a microwaved dinner) and others are not (such as a multicourse dinner at a traditional restaurant or a home-cooked meal using a conventional oven). People in a McDonaldized society tend toward activities in the efficient category and away from those deemed inefficient, but they differentiate little among those things thought to be efficient. This partially accounts for the fact that, in spite of its greater efficiency, the home-cooked microwave meal has not cut appreciably into the business done by fast-food restaurants. In fact, such meals may contribute to the overall attraction of fast-food restaurants and the kinds of food they serve. That is because microwaved meals are part of McDonaldization and also contribute to its spread.

Another reason efficiency in the kitchen has not damaged the fast-food business is that fast food offers many advantages over the "home-cooked" microwaved dinner. For one, people can have dinner out rather than just another meal at home. For another, as Stan Luxenberg has pointed out in *Roadside Empires*, McDonald's offers more than an efficient meal; it offers fun—brightly lit, colorful, and attractive settings, garish packaging, special inducements to children, giveaways, contests—in short, it offers a carnival-like atmosphere in which to buy and consume fast food.[33] Thus, faced with the choice of an efficient meal at home or one in a fast-food restaurant, many people will choose the latter.

The microwave oven, as well as the range of products it has spawned, is but one of many contributors to the increasing efficiency of home cooking. Others include the electric beater, various food processors, and the freezer.

The widespread availability of the home freezer led to the expanded production of frozen foods. The most "efficient" frozen food is the "TV dinner." People can stock their freezers with an array of such dinners (for example, Chinese, Italian, and Mexican dinners as well a wide variety of "American" cooking) and readily bring them out and pop them into the oven, sometimes even the microwave. The large freezer has also permitted other efficiencies, such as a few trips to the market for enormous purchases rather than many trips for small ones. People can readily extract a wide range of ingredients when needed. Finally, freezers allow people to cook large portions that can then be divided up, frozen, and defrosted periodically for dinner.

However, even meals from the freezer have become comparatively inefficient with the advent of microwavable meals that can be stored on the shelves of one's pantry. Still another recent competitor for the most efficient meal at home is the fully cooked meal consumers may now buy at the supermarket. People can merely stop at the market on the way home and purchase all the courses of a meal, which they "prepare" by unwrapping the packages, no cooking required.

Supermarkets have long been loaded with other kinds of products that increase efficiency for those who want to "cook" at home. Instead of starting from scratch, the cook can use prepackaged mixes to make an array of

"homemade" foods—cakes, pies, pancakes, and waffles. No need to end-
lessly stir hot cereal; simply pour boiling water over the contents of a
premeasured packet. People no longer need to cook pudding from scratch,
or even use the more efficient instant mixes; they can now purchase pudding, already made, in the dairy cases of their supermarkets. All these can
be seen as streamlined products, as can microwavable and frozen dinners.

The McDonaldization of food preparation and consumption has also
reached the booming diet industry. Diet books promising all sorts of short-
cuts to weight loss are often at the top of the best-seller lists. Losing weight
is normally difficult and time-consuming, hence the lure of diet books that
promise to make weight loss easier and quicker, that is, more efficient.

For those on a diet, and many people are on more or less perpetual
diets, the preparation of low-calorie food has been streamlined. Instead of
cooking diet foods from scratch, they may now purchase an array of prepared diet foods in frozen and/or microwavable form. For those who do
not wish to go through the inefficient process of eating these diet meals,
there are products even more streamlined such as diet shakes (Slim-Fast,
for example) that can be "prepared" and consumed in a matter of seconds.

The issue of dieting points outside the home to the growth of diet centers such as Jenny Craig and Nutri/System.[34] Nutri/System sells dieters, at
substantial cost, prepackaged freeze-dried food. In what is close to the ultimate in streamlined cooking, all the dieter need do is add water. Freeze-
dried foods are also efficient for Nutri/System, because they can be efficiently
packaged, transported, and stored. Furthermore, the dieter's periodic visits
to a Nutri/System center are efficiently organized. A counselor is allotted
ten minutes with each client. During that brief time, the counselor takes
the client's weight, blood pressure, and measurements, asks routine questions, fills out a chart, and devotes whatever time is left to "problem solv-
ing." If the session extends beyond the allotted ten minutes and other clients
are waiting, the receptionist will buzz the counselor's room. Counselors
learn their techniques at Nutri/System University where, after a week of
training (no inefficient years of matriculation here), they earn certification
and an NSU diploma.

Shopping

Shopping has also grown more efficient. The department store obviously is
a more efficient place in which to shop than a series of specialty shops dis-
persed throughout the city or suburbs. The shopping mall increases efficiency by bringing a wide range of department stores and specialty shops

under one roof. Kowinski describes the mall as "an extremely efficient and effective selling machine."[35] It is cost-efficient for retailers because it is the collection of shops and department stores ("mall synergy") that brings in throngs of people. And it is efficient for consumers because in one stop they can visit numerous shops, have lunch at a "food court" (likely populated by many fast-food chains), see a movie, have a drink, and go to an exercise or diet center.

The drive for shopping efficiency did not end with the malls. Seven-Eleven and its clones have become drive-up, if not drive-through, minimarkets. For those who need only a few items, it is far more efficient (albeit more costly) to pull up to a highly streamlined Seven-Eleven than to run to a supermarket. No need to park in a large lot, obtain a cart, wheel through myriad aisles in search of needed items, wait in lines at the checkout and then tote purchases back to a sometimes distant car. At Seven-Eleven, consumers can park right in front and quickly find an array of goods, however thin and generally overpriced—bread, milk, cigarettes, aspirin—even videos and several "efficient" self-serve items such as hot coffee, hot dogs, microwaved sandwiches, cold soda, and Slurpees. Like the fast-food restaurant, which offers a highly circumscribed menu, Seven-Eleven has sought to cram its shops with a limited array of commonly sought goods. Seven-Eleven's efficiency stems from the fact that it ordinarily sells only one brand of each item, with many items unobtainable. For greater selection, the consumer must go to the inefficient (at least if you are shopping for a few items) supermarket.[36]

In recent years, catalogues (e.g., L.L. Bean, Lands' End) have become more popular. They enable people to shop from the comfort of their homes. Still more efficient, though it may lead to many hours in front of the TV, is home-television shopping. A range of products are paraded before viewers, who can purchase them simply by phoning in and conveniently charging their purchases. The latest advance in home shopping is the "scanfone," an at-home phone machine that includes "a pen-sized bar-code scanner, a credit card magnetic-strip reader, and a key pad." The customer merely "scans items from a bar-coded catalogue and also scans delivery dates and payment methods. The orders are then electronically relayed to the various stores, businesses, and banks involved."[37] Some mall operators fear that they will ultimately be put out of business because of the greater efficiency of shopping at home.

Shopping also offers many examples of imposing work on the consumer. The old-time grocery store, where the clerk retrieved the needed items, has been replaced by the supermarket, where a shopper may put in several hours a week "working" as a grocery clerk seeking out wanted (and unwanted) items during lengthy treks down seemingly interminable aisles. Having obtained the groceries, the shopper then unloads the food at the checkout and, in some cases, even bags the groceries.

Virtually gone are gas station attendants who fill gas tanks, check the oil, and clean windows; people now put in a few minutes a week as unpaid attendants. Furthermore, instead of paying a readily available attendant, people must trek into the station, or up to the kiosk, to pay for the gas. Indeed, in many stations people must pay first, return to pump their gas, and if they haven't pumped as much gas as they expected, trek back to the kiosk to get their change. In the latest "advance" in this realm, customers put their credit cards into a slot and pump the gas; their account is automatically charged for the gas pumped; and, finally, they retrieve the receipt and the card with no contact with, or work done by, anyone working for the gas station.

In this context, more needs to be said about the credit card as a highly efficient means for doing all sorts of shopping.[38] Indeed, the credit card, most generally, can be seen as having McDonaldized the process of obtaining credit. In the past, people had to go through lengthy and cumbersome application procedures to receive credit. Now, the credit card companies have streamlined the process, in some cases to the extent of mailing people a notice that they have been preapproved for a credit card. Thus, they now need do nothing, or virtually nothing, to receive a line of credit, often amounting to several thousand dollars. Now, that's efficiency, even from the point of view of the customer. Of course, the credit card company sees this as an efficient means of recruiting large numbers of potential debtors who will pay almost usurious interest rates in exchange for the right to run up a balance.

Shopping has become far more efficient with the widespread use of credit cards. People need not go to the bank to load up on cash or return to the bank if they run out of cash at the mall. They can even shop in other countries without needing to purchase foreign currency. While it still might be more efficient to pay cash, at least some clerks are surprised, even suspicious, when people make purchases, especially large ones, with cash. Credit cards are certainly a more efficient way of paying than writing personal checks, which often require several pieces of identification.

Entertainment

With the advent of videotapes and video-rental stores, many people no longer deem it efficient to drive to their local theater to see a movie. Movies can now be viewed, often more than one at a sitting, in people's own dens. Those who wish even greater efficiency can buy one of the new television sets that enables viewers to see a movie while also watching a favorite TV show on an inset on the screen.

The largest video rental franchise in the United States, Blockbuster, predictably "considers itself the McDonald's of the video business."[39] Blockbuster has almost 4,000 outlets, its revenues rose 69% in 1993, and its net income rose from $18 million in 1988 to $244 million in 1993.[40] However, Blockbuster may already be in danger of replacement by even more efficient alternatives such as the pay-per-view movies offered by many cable companies. Instead of trekking to the video store, people just turn to the proper channel and phone the cable company. New small dishes allow people access to a wider range of video offerings. Now in the experimental stage, video-on-demand systems may some day allow people to order the movies available in video stores from the comfort of their homes. Said one customer at a video store, "I'd definitely get video on demand. . . . I wouldn't have to come over here to pick this up. And I wouldn't have to bring it back tomorrow, which is going to be a pain in my butt."[41] Just as the video store replaced many movie theaters, video stores themselves may soon make way for even more efficient alternatives.

As briefly mentioned in chapter 2, travel to exotic foreign locales has also grown more streamlined. The best example of this is the package tour. Take, for example, a thirty-day tour of Europe. To make it efficient, tourists visit only the major locales in Europe. Buses hurtle through cities, allowing tourists to glimpse the maximum number of sites in the time allowed. At particularly interesting or important sights, the bus may slow down or even stop to permit some picture taking. At the most important locales, a brief stopover is planned; there, a visitor can hurry through the site, take a few pictures, buy a souvenir, then hop back on the bus to head to the next attraction. The package tour can be seen as a mechanism that permits the efficient transport of people from one locale to another.

New heights in people moving have been reached by modern amusement parks, particularly Disneyland and Walt Disney World.[42] At Disney World and Epcot Center, for example, a vast highway and road system filters many thousands of cars each day into the appropriate parking lots. Once the driver has been led to a parking spot (often with the help of information broadcast over the radio), jitneys come to whisk visitors to the gates of the park. Once in the park, visitors find themselves in a vast line of people, on what is, in effect, a huge conveyor belt that leads them from one ride or attraction to another. Once they actually reach an attraction, visitors find themselves on one conveyance or another—cars, boats, submarines, planes, rockets, or moving walkways—that moves them through and out of the attraction as rapidly as possible. The speed with which they move through each attraction enhances their experience and reduces the likelihood that they will question the "reality" of what they see. In fact, they are often not sure what they have witnessed, although it seems exciting. The entire system is set up to move large numbers of people through the entire park as efficiently as possible. Of course, Disney World has been victimized by its own success: even its highly efficient systems cannot handle the hordes that descend on the park at the height of the tourist season. Thus, visitors still must face long lines at many of the most popular attractions. However, the waits would be far longer were it not for the efficiency with which Disney World processes people.

People are not the only thing that Disney World must process efficiently. Another example of their efficiency is trash disposal.[43] The throngs that frequent such amusement parks eat a great deal (mostly fast/finger foods) and therefore generate an enormous amount of trash. If Disney World relied simply on trash receptacles emptied at the end of each day, the barrels would quickly overflow. To prevent this (and it must be prevented since cleanliness—some would say sterility—is a key component of the McDonaldized world in general and Disney World in particular), hordes of employees constantly sweep, collect, and empty trash. To take a specific example, bringing up the rear in the nightly Disney parade, a large group of cleaners almost instantly dispose of whatever trash and animal droppings have been left behind. Within a few minutes, they have eliminated virtually all signs that a parade has just passed by. Disney World also employs an elaborate system of underground tubes. Garbage receptacles are emptied into this system, which whisks the trash away at about sixty miles per hour to a central trash disposal plant far from the view of visitors. The trash magically disappears; Disney World is a "magic kingdom" in more ways than one. Thus, in various ways, the modern amusement park is a highly efficient place, especially in comparison to its ancestors, such as county fairs and Coney Island. Here is the way one observer describes another of the modern, highly rational amusement parks—Busch Gardens:

> Gone is the dusty midway, the cold seduction of a carnie's voice, the garish, gaudy excitement and all the harsh promise evoked by a thousand yellow lights winking in darkness. In its place is a vast, self-contained environment, as complex as a small city and endowed with the kind of *efficiency* beyond the reach of most cities of any size.[44] [Italics added.]

Sports

The new athletic stadiums built in the United States in recent years have also fostered the efficient movement of people. The new stadiums usually offer easy access to and from highways, as well as huge adjacent parking lots. Elaborate systems of ramps and escalators move people in and out of the stadiums. But people moving is not the only form of efficiency found in modern stadiums. In baseball, a rained-out game is highly inefficient, to say nothing of costly, because it must be played over again. To eliminate this, some stadiums have domes, while other stadiums without domes may have artificial turf, which drains far more readily than rain-soaked grass and may be more likely to allow games to resume after a storm.

Modern health clubs, including such chains as Holiday Spas, also strongly emphasize efficiency.[45] These clubs often offer, under one roof, virtually everything needed to lose weight and stay in shape, including a wide array of exercise machines, as well as a running track and a swimming pool. The exercise machines are highly specialized so that people can efficiently work specific areas of the body. Thus, using running machines and the StairMaster increases cardiovascular fitness, whereas using various weight-lifting machines increases strength and muscularity in targeted areas of the body. Another efficiency associated with many of these machines is that people can do other things while exercising. Thus, many clubs have television sets throughout the gym. The exerciser can also read, listen to music, or even listen to a book-on-tape (probably abridged) while working out. All of this is offered in the sterile environment associated with McDonaldization.[46]

Conclusion

The first dimension of McDonaldization, efficiency, involves the search for the optimum means to a given end. The fast-food restaurant has spearheaded the search for optimum efficiency and has been joined in that quest by other elements of our McDonaldizing society. The search for ever-greater efficiency can take many different forms, but in McDonaldizing systems, it has taken the form primarily of streamlining a variety of processes, simplifying goods and services, and using the customer to perform work that paid employees used to do.

4

Calculability
Big Macs and Little Chips

McDonaldization involves an emphasis on things that can be calculated, counted, quantified. In fact, quantity (especially a large quantity) tends to become a surrogate for quality.[1]

The emphasis on quantity relates both to processes (production, for example) and to end results (for example, goods). In terms of processes, the emphasis is on speed (usually high), whereas for end results the focus is on the number of products produced and served (usually large). This emphasis on quantity has a number of positive consequences, the most important being the ability to produce and obtain large amounts of things very rapidly. Customers in fast-food restaurants get a lot of food quickly, while the managers and owners get a great deal of work from their employees and the work is done speedily. However, the emphasis on quantity tends to affect adversely the quality of both the process and the result. For customers, this often means eating on the run (hardly a "quality" dining experience) and consuming food that is, at best, mediocre. For employees, there is little or no chance of obtaining any personal meaning from their work; therefore, the work as well as the products and service suffer.

All the basic dimensions of McDonaldization, including calculability, are intertwined. For instance, the emphasis on things that can be counted makes it easier to determine efficiency, that is, those steps that take the least time are usually the most efficient. Once quantified, products and processes become more predictable because they take the same amounts of materials or time from one place or time to another. Quantification is also linked to the creation of nonhuman technologies that perform tasks in the given amount of time or make products of a given weight or size. Finally, calculability is clearly linked to irrationality since, among other things, the emphasis on quantity tends to affect quality adversely.

The Fast-Food Industry: Of Whoppers
and Whalers

Conscious of quantification from the beginning, McDonald's has emphasized it in various ways. The three most important ways follow: emphasizing the quantity rather than the quality of products, giving the illusion of
quantity, and reducing the processes of production and service to numbers.

Emphasizing Quantity Rather than Quality of Products

McDonald's has emphasized bigness. For a long time, the most visible symbols of this emphasis were the large signs, usually beneath the even larger
golden arches touting the millions, and later billions, of hamburgers sold
by McDonald's. This was a rather heavy-handed way of letting everyone
know about McDonald's great success. (With the wide-scale recognition of
their success in recent years, there is less need for McDonald's to be so
obvious; hence the decline of such signs and the decrease in size of the
golden arches.[2]) The mounting number of hamburgers sold indicated to
potential customers not only the success of the chain, but also that the high
quality of the burgers presumably accounted for the immense sales. Hence,
the link was made, albeit implicitly, between large numbers of sales and
quality; quantity appeared to equal quality.

McDonald's carries this emphasis on quantity to its products' names,
especially the Big Mac. A large burger is considered desirable simply because the consumer receives a large serving. Furthermore, consumers are
led to believe that they are getting a *large* amount of food for a *small* price.
Calculating consumers come away with the feeling that they are not only
getting a good deal, but perhaps they are also getting the best of McDonald's.

Many other fast-food restaurants mirror this emphasis on quantity. The
most notable, Burger King, points to the quantity of meat in the "Whopper" and of fish in what used to be called the "Whaler" (now, not surprisingly, known as the "Big Fish"). Then there is Wendy's with its "Biggies,"
including Biggie fries. Not to be outdone, Jack in the Box has its "Colos-
sus," Pizza Hut its "BIGFOOT" pizza, Domino's touts its "Dominator,"
Little Caesar pushes its "Big! Big!," and Kentucky Fried Chicken offers a
"Mega" meal. Similarly, Seven-Eleven proffers its customers a hot dog called
the "Big Bite" and a large soft drink called the "Big Gulp," and now, the even
larger "Super Big Gulp."[3] In fact, in recent years the tendency has been for the

fast-food restaurants to push ever larger servings. For example, McDonald's now offers a "Super-Size" fries, 20% larger than a large order. Then there is the "Double Quarter Pounder" and the "Triple Cheeseburger."[4]

The franchised frozen yogurt businesses that have sprung up in recent years have also adopted this emphasis on quantity. Rather than simply filling a container to the brim as traditionally done in ice cream parlors, each container is weighed to be sure it includes the correct quantity of frozen yogurt.

All this emphasis on quantity suggests the fast-food restaurants' apparent lack of interest in communicating anything about quality.[5] Were they interested, they might give their products names such as "McDelicious," or "McPrime." But the fact is that typical McDonald's customers know they are not getting the highest quality food:

> No one, but no one, outside of a few top McDonald's executives, knows exactly what's in those hamburger patties, and, whatever they're made of, they're easy to overlook completely. I once opened up a bun . . . and looked at a McDonald's patty in its naked state. It looked like a Brillo pad and I've never forgotten it.
>
> Let's face it. Nobody thinks about what's between the bun at McDonald's. You buy, you eat, you toss the trash, and you're out of there like the Lone Ranger.[6]

Another observer has argued that people do not go to McDonald's for a delicious, pleasurable meal, but rather to "refuel."[7] McDonald's is a place to fill their stomachs with lots of calories and carbohydrates so that they can move on to the next rationally organized activity. Eating to refuel is far more efficient than eating to enjoy a culinary experience.

The propensity for fast-food restaurants to minimize quality in their search for many, rapidly made sales is well reflected in the sad history of Colonel Harland Sanders, the founder of Kentucky Fried Chicken. The quality of his cooking techniques and his secret seasoning (which his wife originally mixed, packed, and shipped herself) led to great success and a string of about 400 franchised outlets by 1960. Sanders had a great commitment to quality, especially to his gravy: "To Sanders himself the supreme stuff of his art was his gravy, the blend of herbs and spices that time and patience had taught him. It was his ambition to make a gravy so good that people would simply eat the gravy and throw away "the durned chicken."[8]

After Sanders sold his business in 1964, he became little more than the spokesman and symbol for Kentucky Fried Chicken. The new owners soon made clear their commitment to speed rather than quality: "The Colonel's gravy was fantastic, they agreed . . . but it was too complex, too time-consuming, too expensive. It had to be changed. It wasn't fast food." Ray Kroc, who befriended Colonel Sanders, recalls him saying, "That friggin' . . . outfit . . . They prostituted every goddamn thing I had. I had the greatest gravy in the world and those sons of bitches they dragged it out and extended it and watered it down that I'm so goddamn mad."[9]

At best, what customers expect from a fast-food restaurant is modest but strong-tasting food—hence, the salty/sweet french fries, highly seasoned sauces, saccharine shakes. Given such modest expectations of quality, customers do have greater expectations of quantity. They expect to get a lot of food *and* pay relatively little for it.

In response to the latter, Taco Bell recently announced five new menu items called "Big Fill." Included are five kinds of burritos that deliver up to a half pound of food for ninety-nine cents or less. A lot of Mexican food for little money, but of course there is no mention of the quality of that food.[10]

Giving the Illusion of Quantity

Getting a lot of food for little cost in a fast-food restaurant is often more illusion than reality. For example, the big, fluffy (and inexpensive) bun that surrounds the burger makes it seem bigger than it is. To further the illusion, the burger and various fixings are sized to stick out of the bun, as if the bun, as large as it is, cannot contain the "tremendous" portion within. Similarly, special scoops arrange fries in such a way that a portion looks enormous. The bags and boxes seem to bulge at the top, overflowing with french fries. The insides of the boxes for McDonald's large fries are striped to further the illusion. In fact, there are, given the price, relatively few fries in each package, a few pennies worth of potato. Indeed, there is a huge profit margin in the fries. Reiter reports that at Burger King, fries are sold at 400% of their cost! Drinks at Burger King involve a 600% markup.[11] (This is due, in part, to all the ice used to create the impression that people get more of a drink than they actually do.) Indeed, given the enormous rush of people into this business, and the huge growth in fast-food outlets, it is clear that there are great profits to be made. Thus, in fact, the consumers' calculus is wrong—they are *not* getting a lot for a little.

To be fair, fast-food restaurants probably give more food for less money than is the case in a traditional restaurant. However, fast-food restaurants make up for this by doing much more business than a traditional restaurant. They may earn less profit on each meal, but they sell many more meals.

Reducing Processes of Production and Service to Numbers

The emphasis on the number of sales made and the size of the products offered are not the only manifestations of calculability in fast-food restaurants. Another example is the great emphasis on the speed with which a meal can be served. In fact, Ray Kroc's first outlet was named *McDonald's Speedee Service Drive-In*. At one time, McDonald's sought to serve a hamburger, shake, and french fries in 50 seconds. The restaurant made a great breakthrough in 1959 when it served a record 36 hamburgers in 110 seconds. Today, Burger King seeks to serve a customer within three minutes of entering the restaurant.[12] The drive-through window drastically reduces the time required to process a customer through the fast-food restaurant. Speed is obviously a quantifiable factor of monumental importance in a *fast*-food restaurant.

Speed is even more important to the pizza-delivery business. Not only does the number sold depend on how quickly the pizzas can be delivered, but also, a hot, fresh pizza must be transported quickly to arrive so, even though special insulated containers keep the pizzas hot longer. However, this emphasis on rapid delivery has caused several scandals. Pressure to make fast deliveries has led young delivery people to become involved in serious and sometimes fatal automobile accidents.

Still another aspect of the emphasis on quantity lies in the precision with which every element in the production of fast food is measured. For example, great care is taken to be sure that each raw McDonald's hamburger weighs 1.6 ounces, no more, no less; there are ten hamburgers to a pound of meat. The precooked hamburger measures precisely 3.875 inches in diameter, the bun, exactly 3.5 inches. McDonald's invented the "fatilyzer" to ensure that its regular hamburger meat had no more than 19% fat.[13] This is important because greater fat content would lead to greater shrinkage during cooking and prevent the hamburger from appearing too large for the bun. Besides giving the illusion that there are a lot of fries in each package, the french-fry scoop helps make sure that each package has about the same number of fries. The new automatic drink dispensers ensure that each cup gets the correct amount of soft drink with nothing lost to spillage.

Arby's has reduced the cooking and serving of roast beef to a series of exact measures.[14] All roasts weigh ten pounds at the start. They are then roasted at 200 degrees Fahrenheit for 3.5 hours until the internal temperature is 135 degrees. They are then allowed to cook in their own heat for twenty minutes more until the internal temperature is 140 degrees. By following these steps and making these measurements, Arby's doesn't need a skilled chef; virtually anyone who can read and count can cook an Arby's roast beef. When the roasts are done, each weighs between nine pounds, four ounces, and nine pounds, seven ounces. Every roast beef sandwich has three ounces of meat. This allows Arby's to get forty-seven sandwiches (give or take one) from each roast.

Burger King has also quantified quality control. Hamburgers must be served within ten minutes of being cooked. French fries may stand under the heat lamp for no more than seven minutes. A manager is allowed to throw away 0.3 percent of all food.[15]

The performance of fast-food restaurants is also assessed quantitatively, not qualitatively. At McDonald's, for example, central management judges the performance of each restaurant "by `the numbers': by sales per crew person, profits, turnover, and QSC [Quality, Service, Cleanliness] ratings."[16]

Higher Education: Grades, Scores, Ratings, and Rankings

An increasing emphasis on quantifiable phenomena has developed in education. The focus seems to be on how many students (the "products") can be herded through the system and what grades they earn rather than the quality of what they have learned and of the educational experience. An entire high-school or college experience can be summed up in a single number, the grade-point average (GPA). Armed with their GPAs, students can take examinations with quantifiable results such as the PSAT, SAT, and GRE. Colleges, graduate schools, and professional schools can focus on three or four numbers in deciding whether or not to admit a student.

For their part, students may choose a university because of its rating. Is it one of the top ten universities in the country? Is its physics department in the top ten? Are its sports teams usually top ranked? Potential employers may decide whether or not to hire graduates on the basis of their scores, their class ranking, as well as the ranking of the university from which they graduated. To increase their job prospects, students may seek to amass a number of different degrees and credentials with the hope that prospective employers will believe that the longer the list of degrees, the higher the quality of the job candidate. Personal letters of reference, however important, are often replaced by standardized forms with quantifiable ratings (for example, "top 5 percent of the class," "ranks 5th in class of 25").

Most courses run for a standard number of weeks and hours per week. In the main, little attention is devoted to whether a given subject is best taught in a given number of weeks or hours per week. Even less attention is devoted to whether a student can actually learn the given material in the time period allotted.

The number of credentials a person possesses plays a role in situations other than obtaining a job. For example, people in various occupations increasingly use long lists of initials after their names to convince prospective clients of their competence. (My BA, MBA, and PhD are supposed to persuade the reader that I am competent to write this book, although a degree in "Hamburgerology" might be more relevant.) Said one insurance appraiser with ASA, FSVA, FAS, CRA, and CRE after his name, "the more [initials] you tend to put after your name, the more impressed they [potential clients] become."[17] However, the sheer number of credentials tells little about the competence of the person sporting them. Furthermore, this emphasis on quantity of credentials has led people to make creative use of letters after their names. For example, one camp director put "ABD" after his name to impress parents of prospective campers. While these letters may appear impressive to many, all academics know this informal, and largely negative, label—"All But Dissertation"—for people who have completed their graduate courses and exams, but who have not written their dissertations. Also noteworthy here is the development of organizations whose sole reason for existence is to supply meaningless credentials, often through the mail.

The emphasis on quantifiable factors is common even among college professors (the "workers" if students are "products"). For example, more and more colleges and universities have students use evaluation forms and systems. The students evaluate each course by answering questions that have, for example, a one-to-five range with one being low and five being high. At the end of the semester, the professor receives what is in effect a report card with an overall teaching rating. There is little or no room for students to offer qualitative evaluations of their teachers. While student ratings are desirable in a number of ways, they also have some unfortunate consequences. For example, they tend to favor professors who are performers, who have a sense of humor, or who do not demand too much from students. The serious professor who places great demands on students is not likely to do well in such ratings systems, even though he or she may offer higher quality teaching (for example, more profound ideas) than the performer does.

Quantitative factors are important not only in teaching, but also in research and publication. The "publish or perish" pressure on academicians in many colleges and universities tends to lead to great attention to the quantity of their publications. In hiring and promotion decisions, a resume with a long list of articles and books is generally preferred to one with a shorter list. Thus, an award-winning teacher was recently turned down for tenure at Rutgers University because, in the words of his department's tenure committee, his stack of publications was "not as thick as the usual packet for tenure."[18] This emphasis on quantity has unfortunate consequences such as causing a professor to publish less than high-quality works, rushing to publication before a work is fully developed, or publishing the same idea or finding several times with only minor variations.

The latter is one of the ways that professors, like those in charge of fast-food restaurants, create the illusion of quantity in their list of publications. Another is to include items such as self-published reports or books published by "vanity presses," which require payment from the author. Such books, often produced in very limited numbers, may reach few but the author's immediate family. Thus, what appears to be a lengthy list of publications may, on closer scrutiny, turn out to be very modest productivity.

Another quantitative factor in academia is the ranking of the place in which a work is published. In the hard sciences, articles in professional journals receive high marks; books are less valued. In the humanities, books are of much higher value and sometimes more prestigious than journal articles. Being published by some publishers (for example, university presses) yields more prestige than being published by others (for example, commercial presses).

There is an even more elaborate ratings system for professional journals. In sociology, for example, a formal ratings system assigns certain professional journals high ratings, others moderate ratings, and still others low ratings. Thus, a publication in the prestigious *American Sociological Review* would receive ten points, the maximum in this system, and one in the far less prestigious (and in order not to hurt anyone's feelings, fictional) *Antarctic Journal of Sociology* would receive only one point. With such a system, it is hypothetically possible to give all sociologists in the world point scores for their journal publications. By this system, the professor whose journal publications yield 340 points is supposed to be twice as "good" as one who earns only 170 points.

However, as is usually the case, such an emphasis on quantity adversely affects quality in many ways. For one thing, it is highly unlikely that the quality of a professor's life work can be reduced to a single number. In fact, it seems impossible to quantify the quality of an idea, theory, or research finding. Second, this ratings system deals with quality only indirectly. That is, the rating is based on the quality of the journal in which an article was published, not the quality of the article itself. No effort is made to evaluate the quality of the article or its contribution to the field. Furthermore, poor articles can appear in the highest-ranking journals, with excellent ones in low-ranking journals. Third, the academician who writes only a few, high-quality papers might not do well in this ratings system. In contrast, someone who produces a lot of mediocre work could well receive a far higher score. Thus, this kind of system tends to reward a lot of published work whether or not it is really any good. It can lead ambitious sociologists (and those in most other academic fields) to conclude that they cannot afford to spend years honing a single work because it will not pay off much in their point score. Any system that places so much emphasis on quantity of publications will produce a great deal of mediocre work.

The sciences have come up with another quantifiable measure in an effort to evaluate the quality of work: the number of times a person's work is cited in the work of other people. The assumption is that high-quality, important, and influential work is likely to be used and cited by other scholars. It supposedly follows, then, that the more times a scholar's work is cited by others, the higher the quality of that work. People can use the variety of citation indexes published each year to calculate the number of citations per year for every scholar. They might find that the work of one sociologist has been cited 140 times while that of another only 70 times. Again, people might conclude that the work of the first sociologist is twice as "good" as that of the second.

However, once again the problem of evaluating quality arises. Can the influence of a person's academic work be reduced to a single number? Perhaps a few central uses of one scholar's ideas will influence the field more than many trivial citations of another scholar's work. Furthermore, the mere fact that a work is cited tells people nothing about *how* the work was used by other scholars. A worthless piece of work attacked by many people and thereby cited in their work would lead to many citations for its creator. Conversely, scholars may ignore a truly important piece of work that is, for example, ahead of its time, leading to a minuscule number of citations for the author. As always, quantity does not necessarily translate easily into quality and may even indicate poor rather than high quality.

Not long ago, Donald Kennedy, then the president of Stanford University, announced a change in that university's policies for hiring, promoting, or granting tenure to faculty members. Disturbed by a report indicating "that nearly half of faculty members believe that their scholarly writings are

merely counted—and not evaluated—when personnel decisions are made,"
Kennedy said,

> First, I hope we can agree that the quantitative use of research output as
> a criterion for appointment or promotion is a bankrupt idea. . . . The
> overproduction of routine scholarship is one of the most egregious
> aspects of contemporary academic life: It tends to conceal really impor-
> tant work by sheer volume; it wastes time and valuable resources.[19]

To deal with this problem, Kennedy proposed to limit the number of publications used in making personnel decisions. He hoped that the proposed
limits would "reverse the appalling belief that counting and weighing are
the important means of evaluating faculty research."[20] It remains to be seen
whether Stanford, to say nothing of the rest of American academia, will be
able to limit the emphasis on quantity rather than quality.

Health Care: Patients As Dollar Signs

In profit-making medical organizations (for example, Humana), physicians,
along with all other employees, feel pressured to contribute to the
corporation's profitability. Efforts are also made to quantify various aspects
of medical practice. For example, limiting time with each patient and maximizing the number of patients seen in a day allows the corporation to reduce costs and increase profits. This emphasis on quantity can easily threaten
the quality of medical care. Profits can be increased by pushing doctors to
spend less time with patients, to see more patients, to abandon long-shot
diagnostic techniques and treatments, to turn down patients who probably
can't pay the bills, and to see only patients who have the kinds of diseases
likely to yield large profits.

Not only profit-making medical organizations, but all medical bureaucracies are pushing medicine in the direction of greater calculability. Even
nonprofit medical organizations (for example, nonprofit hospitals and health
maintenance organizations, or HMOs) are experiencing the external pressures, employing professional managers, and instituting sophisticated accounting systems. At least one physicians' union has engaged in a strike that
centered on quantified productivity issues such as required number of visits, number of patients seen, and an incentive system tying physician salaries to productivity.

Third-party payers, that is, health-insurance companies, and the federal government through its prospective payment and Diagnostic Related

Groups (DRG) programs are also pushing medicine in the direction of greater calculability. Outside agencies have grown increasingly concerned about spiraling medical costs and have sought to deal with the problem by limiting what they will pay for and how much they will pay for it. Thus, a third-party payer might refuse to pay for certain procedures or hospitalization for them, or perhaps pay only a given amount for each. Concentrating on quantities of money, time, and so on, can lead the medical profession away from an emphasis on quality of patient care. As one physician-union leader put it, however romantically, doctors are "the only ones who think of patients as individuals . . . not as dollar signs."[21]

The Workplace: A Penny the Size of a Cartwheel

With scientific management, Taylor intended to transform everything work-related into quantifiable dimensions. Instead of relying on the worker's "rule of thumb," scientific management sought to develop precise measurements of how much work was to be done by each and every motion of the worker. Everything that could be reduced to numbers was then analyzed using mathematical formulas.

Calculability was clearly an aim when Taylor sought to increase the amount of pig iron a worker could load in a day: "We found that this gang were loading on the average about 12-1/2 long tons per man per day. We were surprised to find, after studying the matter, that a first-class pig iron handler ought to handle between 47 and 48 long tons per day, instead of 12-1/2 tons."[22] To try to nearly quadruple the workload, Taylor studied the way the most productive workers, the "first-class men," operated. He divided their work into its basic elements and timed each step with a stop watch down to hundredths of a minute.

On the basis of this careful study, Taylor and his associates developed the one best way to carry pig iron. They then found a worker they could motivate to work this way—Schmidt, who was able and ambitious and to whom a penny looked "about the size of a cart-wheel," as one coworker said. Schmidt indicated that he wanted to be a "high-priced man." Taylor used a precise economic incentive: $1.85 per day, rather than the usual $1.15, if Schmidt agreed to work exactly the way Taylor told him to. After careful training and supervision, Schmidt successfully worked at the faster pace (and earned the higher pay); Taylor then selected and trained other workers to work the same way.

Schmidt and his successors were being asked to do about 3.6 times the normal amount of work for an approximately 60% increase in pay. Taylor defended this exploitation in various ways. For example, he argued that it would be unfair to workers in other areas who were working up to their capabilities to have pig handlers earn 3.6 times as much as they did. For another, Taylor argued that he and his associates had decided (without, of course, consulting the workers themselves) that a greater share of the profits would not be in the workers' interests. For Taylor, "the pig iron handler with his 60-percent increase in wages is not an object for pity but rather a subject for congratulations."[23]

Other Examples: The Computer Made Me Do It

The tendency to emphasize quantitative factors has strongly affected at least three areas—television, sports, and politics. Other areas worth mentioning in this context include cooking, newspapers, and computers.

Television

Television programs are heavily, if not almost exclusively, determined by quantitative rather than qualitative factors. The ratings, not the high quality, of a program determines its success and, therefore, the advertising revenue it is likely to generate. A vice president of programming for ABC made this emphasis on calculability quite clear: "Commercial television programming is designed to attract audiences to the advertisers' messages which surround the programming. . . . Inherent creative aesthetic values [quality] are important, but always secondary."[24] Thus, over the years the commercial networks have dropped many critically acclaimed programs for poor ratings.

Potential programs are tested on sample audiences in an effort to predict which shows will achieve high ratings. When pilots for new shows are broadcast, those that achieve or demonstrate potential for high ratings are selected for regular broadcast. Ratings services such as A. C. Nielsen determine the fate of television programs. In fact, it could be said that "Nielsen is television." Said one ABC executive, "The thing we've always had has been this set of numbers. . . . It's the foundation upon which program decisions are made."[25] For these ratings, sophisticated meters are placed in the homes of a sample of American television viewers. The current technology requires that the selected viewers push remote control buttons to indicate when television viewing begins and ends. Periodically the meter flashes, directing viewers to press the OK button if anyone is still watching. Soon an improved audience meter may be developed to measure viewing habits without requiring the viewers to do anything.

Ratings are derived from the number of Nielsen-selected homes that tune into a particular program. Of course, ratings reveal nothing about a program's quality. Indeed, high-quality programs often receive low ratings. A good example is the highly acclaimed *I'll Fly Away*, which has received consistently low ratings. This difference between ratings and quality has been one reason for the existence of the Public Broadcasting System (PBS). Because of its public funding, PBS is far more interested in the quality of a program than in its ratings. In fact, when *I'll Fly Away* was canceled by NBC, it was picked up by PBS.[26]

Historically, television stations in Europe have been far more likely to be run by the government than to be owned privately. As a result, they have been less responsive to the wishes of commercial sponsors for high ratings and far more interested in the quality of programs. Hence, people tend to see much more quality programming on European than American television. However, even these government-run stations do program a number of the most popular American shows. Further, the advent of various kinds of private European cable and satellite television networks will likely move the quality of European television toward that of American television.

Over the years, television rating systems have grown more sophisticated. Instead of relying solely on absolute numbers, some programs succeed or fail on the basis of their ratings within specific demographic groups. Advertisers who sell primarily to a particular demographic group will support a program with relatively low overall ratings as long as its ratings within the targeted group are high. Thus, for example, a program such as the highly acclaimed *thirtysomething*, with modest overall ratings, remained on the air because of high ratings among consumption-oriented "Yuppies."

Sports

The quality of various sports has been altered by, perhaps even sacrificed to, calculability. For instance, the nature of sporting events has been changed by the need for the enormous revenues derived from television contracts.[27] Because teams in many sports earn a large part of their revenue from television contracts, they will sacrifice the interests of paid spectators, even compromise the games themselves, to increase their television income.

A good example of this is the so-called "TV time-out." In the old days, commercials occurred during natural breaks in a game, for example, during a time-out called by one of the teams, at half-time, or between innings. But this meant that commercials appeared too intermittently and infrequently to bring in the increasingly large fees advertisers were willing to pay. This led to regular TV time-outs in sports such as football and basketball. The owners of sports franchises may be maximizing their incomes from advertising, but they may have sacrificed the quality of the sport. For example, the momentum of a team may be lost because of an inopportune TV time-out. Thus, these time-outs do alter the nature of some sports; they may even affect the outcome of a game. Also, for the fans who watch in person, these time-outs interrupt the flow of the game. The fans at home can at least watch the commercials; the spectators at the games have little to watch until the commercial ends and the game resumes. But the owners consider such negative effects on the quality of the game insignificant compared with the economic gain from increased advertising.

Clearly though, sports themselves place a premium on the quality of both individual and team performance: the power of basketball star Shaquille O'Neill and the teamwork of the New York Knickerbockers. At the same time, quantitative factors have always been enormously important in sports. In many cases quality is directly related to quantity—the better the performance, the higher the score and the greater the number of victories.

However, over the years there has been increasing emphasis on the quantifiable attributes of sports:

> Modern sports are characterized by the almost inevitable tendency to transform every athletic feat into one that can be quantified and measured. The accumulation of statistics on every conceivable aspect of the game is a hallmark of football, baseball, hockey, and of track and field too, where the accuracy of quantification has, thanks to an increasingly precise technology, reached a degree that makes the stopwatch seem positively primitive.[28]

Even a highly aesthetic sport such as gymnastics has been quantified:

> How can one rationalize and quantify a competition in gymnastics, in aesthetics? The answer now seems obvious. Set up an interval scale and a panel of judges and then take the arithmetic mean of the subjective evaluations. . . . Nadia Comeneci scored exactly 79.275 points in Montreal, neither more nor less. The ingenuity of *Homo Mensor* must not be underestimated.[29]

The growing emphasis on quantity can sometimes adversely affect the quality of play in a sport. For example, the basketball star motivated by a need to stand out individually and score as many points as possible may negatively affect teammates and the team's overall performance. The quality of play is even more compromised by owners' attempts to McDonaldize sports by seeking to maximize things such as points scored.

In basketball, McDonaldization has taken the form of the 24-second clock for professionals and the 35-second clock for college athletes. This means that the offensive team must attempt a shot within 24 or 35 seconds. Not long ago, basketball was a more leisurely game. A team brought the ball down the court and took as long as necessary to get a player into position to take a good shot. Basketball fans enjoyed the strategies and maneuvers players used. Toward the end of the game, a team holding a slim lead could attempt to "freeze" the ball, that is, not risk taking and missing a shot and thereby give their opponents a chance to take possession of the ball to narrow, or even take, the lead.

In the past few decades, the leadership of collegiate and professional basketball decided that fans raised in the McDonald's era wanted to see faster games and many more points scored. In other words, fans wanted from basketball what they got from their fast-food restaurant—great speed and large quantities. It was believed, apparently correctly, that faster and higher-scoring games would mean greater attendance and higher profits. Hence, the 24- and 35-second time clocks were established to provide a more fast-paced game with many more shots attempted and made. However, the "run and shoot" style of play generated by the time clocks may have adversely affected the quality of play by eliminating many maneuvers and strategies that made the game so interesting to "purists." But a "run and shoot" style of basketball fits in well with the McDonaldized "eat and move" world of dinners purchased at drive-through windows and consumed on the run.

Baseball owners decided long ago that fans preferred to see high-scoring games with lots of hits, home runs, and runs scored rather than pitchers' duels in which the final score might be 1–0. Thus, they took a number of steps to increase the number of runs scored. New, livelier baseballs can travel farther than old-fashioned ones. In some baseball parks, outfield fences have been brought closer to home plate to increase the number of home runs. Although growing in disrepute for, among other things, the injuries it causes, the artificial turf still used on many fields in place of natural grass makes routine ground balls roll faster and therefore more likely to skip by the infielders for base hits.

Found in the American League but not in the more traditional National League, the designated hitter is the most notable effort to increase hits and runs. Instead of the often weak-hitting pitcher taking his turn at bat, someone whose main (and sometimes only) skill is hitting replaces him. Designated hitters will get more hits, hit more home runs, and help produce more runs than pitchers who are allowed to bat.

Although use of the designated hitter in American League baseball has undoubtedly increased the number of runs scored, it has also affected, perhaps adversely, the quality of the game. For example, when pitchers bat in certain situations they often employ a sacrifice bunt, a very artful practice. But a designated hitter rarely sacrifices an at bat to advance a runner by bunting. Pinch hitters play less of a role with designated hitters replacing weak-hitting pitchers. Finally, because there is less need to pinch hit for them, starting pitchers can remain in games longer, which reduces the need for relief pitchers.[30] In these and other ways, baseball is a different game when a designated hitter is employed. In other words, the quality of the game has changed, some would say for the worse, because of the emphasis on quantity.

Politics

The political sector offers a number of interesting examples of the emphasis on calculability. For instance, political candidates and politicians, obsessed by their ratings in political polls, can adjust the nature of their positions or the actions they take because of what pollsters say will increase their rankings in the polls. How a specific political position affects ratings can become more important than the qualities of that position and whether the politician genuinely believes in those qualities.

Television has also affected politics in various ways, such as its effect on political speechmaking. On television, the visual images, not the words, tend to matter most. Thus, by the 1984 presidential campaign, only about fifteen seconds of a speech would likely find its way onto a national news program. Four years later, speaking time on such reports shrank to only nine seconds (called "sound bites").[31] The focus in candidates' speeches is on the limited, ten- or fifteen-second portion apt to be picked up by the national networks. This emphasis on length has clearly reduced the quality of public political speeches, and therefore the quality of public discourse on important political issues.

In addition to the decline in the length of televised reports of public speeches, televised speeches themselves have undergone a similar decline.

Prior to television, political speeches on radio at first usually lasted an hour; by the 1940s, the norm had dropped to thirty minutes. In the early years of television, speeches also lasted about half an hour, but because political campaign speeches became more tailored to television coverage and less to the immediate audience, speeches have grown shorter, less than 20 minutes on the average. By the 1970s the speech itself had been largely replaced by the sixty-second advertisement. Similarly, in today's televised presidential debates, candidates have a minute or two to offer their position on a given issue. By contrast, according to one observer, "In each of their seven senatorial debates of 1858, Lincoln and Douglas spoke for ninety minutes each on a single topic: the future of slavery in the territories."[32]

In foreign policy, one area that displays an absolute mania for numbers is nuclear deterrence.[33] Although this issue is less publicly visible now that the Cold War has ended, there are no signs that either the United States or Russia plan to give up their ability to deter the other from launching a nuclear attack. Both sides possess nuclear arsenals large enough to destroy each other many times over; nevertheless, their efforts to negotiate treaties reducing nuclear weapons often became bogged down in trying to assess accurately the size and power—"the relative throw weight"—of their respective nuclear arms. While accurate measures were undoubtedly important in trying to achieve parity, both sides tended to get lost in the minutia of the numbers and lose sight of the qualitative fact that both sides could eliminate most of their nuclear weapons and retain the ability to destroy the other side, even the world as a whole. Here we have one of the clearest manifestations of the irrationality of rationality.

Other Domains

The cookbook was an early example of great emphasis placed on calculability. In the original (1896) *The Boston Cooking School Cook Book*, Fannie Farmer emphasized precise measurement and in the process helped to rationalize home cooking:

> Before her death she had changed American kitchen terminology from "a pinch" and "a dash" and "a heaping spoonful"—all vague terms which she detested—to her own *precise*, standardized, scientific terms, presenting a model of cooking that was easy, reliable, and could be followed even by inexperienced cooks. To Fannie Farmer, "the mother of level measurement," we can attribute the popularity of such *precise* everyday kitchen terms as level teaspoon, 1/2 teaspoon,

measuring cup, oven thermometer, and "bake at 350 degrees for 40 minutes."[34]

Calculability plays an integral role in food production as well as in consumption of the finished products. For instance, the diet industry is obsessed with things that can be quantified.[35] Weight, weight loss (or gain), and time periods are measured precisely. Food intake is carefully measured and monitored. Packages of diet foods carefully detail the number of ounces of food, the number of calories, and many other things as well.

Not surprisingly, organizations such as Weight Watchers and Nutri/System carefully measure caloric intake per day, number of calories in each food product, and weight loss per week. What is striking is their increasing desire to provide foods that can be prepared rapidly. For example, Nutri/System boasts that most of its freeze-dried dinner entrees "can be ready in under five minutes. So you don't have to spend a lot of time in the kitchen." But in its endless search to reduce further the time devoted to food preparation, Nutri/System is now offering "an increasing number of microwavable entrees that can be on your plate, ready to eat, 90 seconds after you take them from your cupboard."[36]

Another interesting example of the emphasis on quantity over quality is the newspaper *USA TODAY*, noted for its "junk-food journalism," that is, the lack of substance in its stories.[37] Instead of detailed stories, *USA TODAY* offers many short, easily and quickly read stories. It is the kind of newspaper that can be read in about the time it takes a person to consume a meal at a fast-food restaurant.[38] Said one executive, "*USA TODAY* must sell news/info at a fast, hard pace." One observer underscored the newspaper's corresponding lack of concern for quality and, in the process, its relationship to the fast-food restaurant: "Like parents who take their children to a different fast-food joint every night and keep the refrigerator stocked with ice cream, *USA TODAY* gives its readers only what they want. No spinach, no bran, no liver."[39]

The package tour represents a clear emphasis on the quantity of sights visited rather than the quality of those visits. It is obviously impossible to get in a day or two any real sense of what Paris has to offer or in a brief visit do much more in the Louvre than rush to the Mona Lisa, glance at it, then rush back to the bus. A tourist can see *lots* of sights (often through a bus window) in *many* different countries, but the quality of the sight-seeing is very superficial. When tourists return from such a trip, they can crow about the large number of countries and sights visited, slides taken, and video-tapes filled. (They can even bore their friends for hours with interminable slide or video shows of their trip.) However, given the nature of such trips, devotees of packaged tours are hard-pressed to tell their friends very much about the countries they visited or the sights they saw.

The Computer

I cannot close this discussion of calculability in contemporary society without mentioning the impact of the computer.[40] The tendency to quantify virtually everything has obviously been expedited by its development and now widespread use. The first computer, constructed in 1946, weighed thirty tons, employed 19,000 vacuum tubes (that were constantly blowing out), filled an entire room, and had very limited capacity. Now, of course, there exist far more compact computers with infinitely greater capacity, to say nothing of the small computers in virtually every office and many homes. The massive expansion of the number and capacity of computers, as well as the ability to make them significantly smaller, was made possible by the invention of the silicon chip in the 1970s. The chip is a slice of a silicon crystal about half the size of a fingernail. It replaced the much larger transistor, which had in turn replaced the still larger vacuum tube. Because the silicon chip provides the necessary electronic circuitry in microscopic form, computers are being made ever smaller (laptops and notebook computers, for example), more powerful, cheaper, and, most important, able to do more and more calculations with increasing speed.

Many aspects of today's quantity-oriented society could not exist, or would need to be greatly modified, were it not for the computer. Examples include the following:

- The registration of masses of students at large state universities, the processing of their grades, and the constant recalculation of grade-point averages.

- Extensive medical testing in which a patient takes a battery of blood and urine tests, and the results are returned in the form of a series of numbers on a variety of factors as well as the normal ranges for each of them. This permits efficient diagnosis of medical problems and allows the patient to be a kind of do-it-yourself physician.

- The development and widespread use of the credit card ("plastic money"). The computer made possible the billions of transactions associated with the credit card. The growth of the credit card, in turn, made possible a massive increase in consumer spending and business sales.

- ◆ The ability of the television networks to give us almost instantaneous election results.
- ◆ Virtually continuous political polling and TV ratings.

Although society undoubtedly was already moving toward increased calculability, continuing advances in computer technology have greatly expedited and extended that movement.

Conclusion

Calculability, the second dimension of McDonaldization, involves an emphasis on quantification. In fact, in a McDonaldizing society, there tends to be an emphasis on quantity rather than quality. This emphasis shows up in various ways, but especially in the focus on the quantity rather than the quality of products, the widespread efforts to create the illusion of quantity, and the tendency to reduce production and service processes to numbers.

5

Predictability

It Never Rains on Those Little Houses on the Hillside

Rationalization involves the increasing effort to ensure predictability from one time or place to another. A rationalized society therefore emphasizes such things as discipline, order, systematization, formalization, routine, consistency, and methodical operation. In such a society, people prefer to know what to expect in most settings and at most times. They neither desire nor expect surprises. They want to know that when they order their Big Mac today it will be identical to the one they ate yesterday and the one they will eat tomorrow. People would be upset if the special sauce was used one day, but not the next, or tasted differently from one day to the next. They want to know that the McDonald's franchise they visit in Des Moines, Los Angeles, or Paris will appear and run much the same as their local McDonald's.

From the consumer's point of view, predictability thus makes for much peace of mind in day-to-day dealings. For workers, tasks are made easier and can be performed effortlessly and mindlessly. In fact, some workers prefer predictable, repetitive work.[1] If nothing else, it allows them to think of other things, even daydream, while they are doing their tasks. To managers and owners, predictability makes it easier to manage both workers and customers. It also makes many other things easier such as anticipating needs for supplies and materials, personnel requirements, income, and profits. However, predictability has a downside, especially the cost of turning everything—consumption, work, management—into a series of mind-numbing routines.

The Fast-Food Industry: "Howdy Pardner," "Happy Trails"

A good place to begin a discussion of predictability in the fast-food industry is with one of the other pioneers of rationalization—motel chains. Most notable are the Best Western motel chain, founded in 1946, and Holiday Inn, which started in 1952. Anticipating both, but less significant today, the Howard Johnson's chain arose in the 1920s and 1930s. By the late 1950s, there were about 500 standardized Howard Johnson's restaurants scattered around the United States, many with standardized motels attached to them. These three motel chains had opened in anticipation of the massive expansion of highways and highway travel.

Before the development of such franchises, motels were highly unpredictable and diverse places. Run by myriad local owners, every motel was different from every other. Because the owners and employees varied from one locale to another, guests could not always feel fully safe and sleep soundly. One motel might be quite comfortable, even luxurious, while another might well be a hovel. People could never be sure whether various amenities were going to be present—soap, shampoo, telephones, radio (and later television), air conditioning, and please don't forget the much-loved "Magic Fingers" massage system. Checking into a motel was an adventure: a traveler never knew what to expect.

The motel chains took pains to make their guests' experience predictable. They developed tight hiring practices to keep "unpredictable" people from managing or working in them. Travelers could predict that a motel equipped with the familiar orange and green Holiday Inn sign (now gone the way of McDonald's oversized golden arches) would have most, if not all, the amenities they could reasonably expect in a moderately priced motel. Faced with the choice between a local, no-name motel and a Holiday Inn, many travelers preferred the predictable even if it had liabilities (the absence of a personal touch, for example). The success of the early motel chains has led to many imitators, such as Ramada Inn, Rodeway Inn, as well as the more recent, more price conscious chains—Days Inn, Econo-Lodge, and Motel 6.

The budget motel chains were predictably barren. Guests found only the minimal requirements (eventually including a TV) for a motel stay. They expected the minimum, and that's what they got. They also expected, and received, bargain-basement prices for the rooms.

The fast-food industry quickly adopted and perfected practices pioneered by, among other precursors, the motel chains: replicated settings, predictable employee behavior, and predictable products. As Robin Leidner has put it, "The heart of McDonald's success is its uniformity and predictability . . . [its] relentless standardization." Later, she argues that "there is a McDonald's way to handle virtually every detail of the business, and that doing things differently means doing things wrong."[2] While McDonald's allows its franchisees and managers to innovate, "the object is to look for new innovative ways to create an experience that is exactly the same no matter what McDonald's you walk into, no matter where it is in the world."[3]

Replicating the Setting

Like the motel chains, McDonald's and many other franchises devised a large and garish sign that soon became familiar to customers. McDonald's logo evokes a sense of predictability: "Replicated color and symbol, mile after mile, city after city, act as a tacit promise of *predictability* and stability between McDonald's and its millions of customers, year after year, meal after meal."[4] (Italics added.) Each McDonald's presents a series of predictable elements—counter, menu posted above it, "kitchen" visible in the background, tables and uncomfortable seats, prominent trash bins, drive-through windows, and so on.

This predictable setting appears not only throughout the United States but also in many other parts of the world. Thus, homesick American tourists in far-off countries can take comfort in the knowledge that they will likely run into those familiar golden arches and the restaurant they have become so accustomed to.

Virtually all that some of the most recent participants in McDonaldization have in common is a sign and a physical structure. For example, hair-cutting franchises such as Hair-Plus cannot offer a uniform haircut because every head is slightly different and every barber or hairdresser operates in a slightly idiosyncratic fashion. To reassure the anxious customer longing for predictability, Hair-Plus and other hair-cutting franchises offer only a few signs, similar shop set-up, and perhaps a few familiar products.

Scripting Interaction with Customers

Much of what is said and done in fast-food restaurants by both employees and customers is ritualized,[5] routinized, even scripted.[6] These familiar and comfortable rituals and scripts help make fast-food restaurants attractive to legions of people. Because interaction between customer and counterperson is limited in length and scope, it can be largely routinized. Thus, McDonald's has a series of regulations that employees must follow in their dealings with customers. There are, for example, six steps to window service: greet the customer, take the order, assemble the order, present the order, receive payment, thank the customer and ask for repeat business.[7]

An example of scripted interaction, the Roy Rogers chain used to have its employees, dressed in cowboy and cowgirl uniforms, say, "Howdy pardner" to every customer about to order food. After paying for the food, people were sent on their way with "Happy trails."[8] The repetition of these familiar salutations visit after visit was a source of great satisfaction to regulars at Roy Rogers. Many people (including me) felt a deep personal loss when Roy Rogers ceased this practice. In a McDonaldized society, such pseudo interactions are increasingly the norm, so that people can look forward to them. Indeed, they might even look back on them longingly when all they have on their visits to fast-food restaurants are interactions with their favorite robot (see chapter 6).

Not only general scripts, but also a series of subscripts are followed in the case of unusual requests or behaviors. For example, there might be a subscript for customers who object to being subjected to the same scripted interaction as everyone else. In fact, the subscript might be written to appear as if it reflects the "real" feelings of the employee and is not scripted. For example, a subscript might direct employees to say they will bend the rules "just this once." Recalcitrant customers are satisfied because they feel as if they are getting individualized treatment and an authentic response, and managers are happy because their employees are following the subscripts.

Like all other aspects of rationalization, scripts can have positive functions. For example, scripts can be a source of power to employees, enabling them to control interaction with customers. Employees can fend off unwanted or extraordinary demands merely by refusing to deviate from the script. Employees can also use their routines and scripts to protect themselves from the insults and indignities that are frequently heaped upon them by the public. Employees can adopt the view that the public's hostility is aimed at the scripts and those who created them. Overall, rather than being hostile to scripts and routines, McDonald's workers often find them useful and even satisfying.[9]

However, employees and customers sometimes resist routines and scripts. As a result, the behavior of those who give and receive services "is never entirely predictable."[10] While this conclusion is undoubtedly on target, the fact is that *no* aspect of McDonaldization is, as yet, total. People do not yet live in an iron cage of McDonaldization. In fact, they are unlikely ever to live in a totally predictable, completely McDonaldized world. Nonetheless, it is clear that people live in an *increasingly* predictable, increasingly McDonaldized world.

Furthermore, the things McDonald's workers could do to exert some independence in their work are hardly overwhelming. First, they could go a

"bit" beyond the routine by providing extra services or exchanging pleas-
antries. Second, they could withhold smiles, act a bit impatient or irritated,
or refuse to encourage the customer to return. Third, they could focus on
offering speedy service to avoid demeaning behavior such as faking seem-
ing friendliness.[11] These all seem like very small deviations from an otherwise highly routinized workday.

For their part, customers do not follow scripts, but they do tend to behave predictably in fast-food restaurants. Three factors help to lead to predictable behavior among customers.[12] First, they receive cues (the presence
of lots of trash receptacles, for example) that indicate what is expected of
them. Second, a variety of structural constraints lead them to behave in
certain ways. For example, the drive-through window, as well as the written
instructions on the menu board at the entrance (and elsewhere), give customers few, if any, alternatives. Finally, there are taken-for-granted norms
customers have internalized and follow when they enter a fast-food restaurant. For example, when my children were young they admonished me after we finished our meal for not cleaning up the debris and carting it to the
trash can. My children were, in effect, serving as agents for McDonald's
teaching me the norms of behavior in such settings. I (and most others)
have long-since internalized these norms and I dutifully follow them these
days on the rare occasions that a lack of any other alternative leads me into
a fast-food restaurant.

As in the case of workers, customers also gain from scripts and routines:
"Routinization can provide service-recipients with more reliable, less expensive, or speedier service, can protect them from incompetence, can minimize the interactive demands on them, and can clarify what their rights
are." Such routines help guarantee equal treatment of all customers. Finally, routinization can help "establish a floor of civility and competence
for which many customers have reason to be grateful."[13]

Thus, rules and norms generally lead to predictable customer behavior
in the fast-food restaurant. However, there are exceptions. For example,
some customers may react negatively when employees mindlessly following scripts seem "unresponsive," or "robot-like."[14] Arguments may ensue,
and angry customers may even leave without being served. In a classic scene
from *Five Easy Pieces*, Jack Nicholson's character stops at a diner and en-
counters a traditional greasy-spoon waitress. The waitress angers the
Nicholson character, and displays an early manifestation of McDonaldization,
by following a script: he cannot get an order of toast even though he could
order a sandwich made *with* toast. Nicholson's character reacts even more

strongly and negatively to the unresponsive script than he does to the surly waitress.

The fake friendliness of scripted interaction reflects the insincere camaraderie that characterizes not only fast-food restaurants but also all other elements of McDonaldized ("have a nice day") society, a camaraderie that is used to lure customers and keep them coming back. For example, the TV screens have recently been saturated with scenes of Wendy's owner, Dave Thomas, extending a "personal invitation" to join him for a burger at his restaurant.[15]

After reviewing a range of routinized and scripted interactions from various settings, Leidner concludes,

> Collectively, these excerpts tell us that no detail is too trivial, no relationship too personal, no experience too individual, no manipulation too cynical for some organization or person, in a spirit of helpfulness or efficiency, to try to provide a standard, replicable routine for it.[16]

Predictable Employee Behavior

Interaction with customers does not exhaust the actions of employees in fast-food restaurants. Employers also seek to make other work as predictable as possible. For example, all employees are expected to cook hamburgers in the same, one-best way. In other words, "Frederick Taylor's principles can be applied to assembling hamburgers as easily as to other kinds of tasks."[17]

Furthermore, fast-food restaurants try in many ways to make the way workers look, speak, and feel more predictable.[18] For one, all employees must wear uniforms and follow dress codes for things such as makeup, hair length, and jewelry. Then, employees receive instructions not only about doing the work, but for thinking about the work, the customers, and even themselves as fast-food employees. For instance, training programs are designed to indoctrinate the worker into a "corporate culture"[19] such as the McDonald's attitude and way of doing things. The fast-food restaurant also uses surveillance techniques ("undercover" inspectors, for example) to keep tabs on employees. Finally, incentives (awards, for example) are used to reward employees who behave properly and disincentives, ultimately firing, to deal with those who do not.

Fast-food managers and their assistants also act predictably. To help ensure predictable managerial thinking and behavior, McDonald's has managers attend its central Hamburger University, which has branches throughout the United States and the world.[20] Even the "professors" at Hamburger University behave predictably since "they work from scripts prepared by the curriculum development department."[21] Potential managers trained by these teachers internalize the ethos and the techniques employed by McDonald's. As a result, in demeanor and behavior, McDonald's managers are hard to distinguish from one another. More important, because the managers train and oversee workers to help make them behave more predictably, managers use elaborate corporate guidelines that detail how virtually everything is to be done in all restaurants. McDonald's central headquarters periodically sends forth inspectors to be sure that these guidelines are being enforced. These inspectors also check to see that the food meets quality control guidelines.

Predictable Products

This brings up the predictability of the food purveyed in fast-food restaurants. A short menu of simple foods helps ensure predictability. Hamburgers, fried chicken, pizza, tacos, french fries, soft drinks, shakes, and the like are all relatively easy to prepare and serve in a uniform fashion. Predictability in such products is made possible by the use of uniform raw ingredients, identical technologies for food preparation and cooking, similarity in the way the food is served, and identical packaging. As a trainer at Hamburger University puts it, "McDonald's has standards for everything down to the width of the pickle slices."[22]

Packaging is an important component of predictability in the fast-food restaurant. In spite of the fast-food restaurants' best efforts, unpredictabilities can creep in because of the nature of the materials—the food might not be hot enough, the chicken might be gristly or tough, or there may be too few pieces of pepperoni on a particular slice of pizza. Whatever the (slight) unpredictabilities in the food, the packaging—containers for the burgers, bags for the small fries, cardboard boxes for the pizzas—can always be the same and imply that the food will be too.

Predictable food requires predictable ingredients. McDonald's has stringent guidelines on the nature (quality, size, shape, and so on) of the meat, chicken, fish, potatoes, and other ingredients purchased by each franchisee. I have already said, for example, that the precooked McDonald's hamburger must weigh 1.6 ounces, be 3.75 inches in diameter, and have no more than 19% fat, so that after it is cooked it just manages to jut out from the bun. The buns are made of the predictable white bread that many Americans prefer and some disparage. One wit said of Wonder Bread, "I thought they just blew up library paste with gas and sent it to the oven."[23] To give it this predictability, all the chewy and nutritious elements of wheat, such as bran and germ, have been milled out. Because buns otherwise might grow stale or moldy, preservatives are added to retard spoilage. Precut, uniform frozen french fries rather than fresh potatoes are used. In these and other ways, the serving of predictable foods is made possible by predictable ingredients.

The increasing use of frozen (or freeze-dried) foods in a McDonaldized society also deals with unpredictabilities related to the supply of raw materials. One of the reasons Ray Kroc eventually substituted frozen for fresh potatoes was that for several months a year it was difficult to obtain the desired variety of potato. Freezing potatoes made them readily available year-round. In addition, the potato peelings at each McDonald's outlet often created a stench anathema to Kroc and the sanitized (some would say, sterile) world he sought to create. Frozen, peeled, and precut french fries solved this problem as well.

Higher Education: Cookie-Cutter Texts

The educational arena in which people might expect to find the least amount of predictability, compared with grade schools and high schools, is the university. Nonetheless, there is a surprising amount even there.

Educational settings look much the same at every American university. In general, professors stand in the front of classrooms, before blackboards, and lecture to the seated students facing them. Ordinarily, the professor faces twenty-five to fifty students, but that number may reach 500, 1,000, or more. A number of smaller seminar rooms with conference tables allow professors and a much smaller number of students to interact more directly.

Most colleges and universities will offer similar courses, especially at lower levels of the curriculum. One reason for this is that teachers across the country usually choose from a limited number of textbooks, and these books tend to structure classes. There is also enormous pressure in the textbook industry for all lower-division texts to look like each other. A key factor in this is the desire on the part of publishers to emulate the best-selling texts. Predictable texts lead to predictable courses and, more generally, to a predictable educational experience.

Textbooks show conformity in many ways. They often have the same trim size, a similar page length, and glossaries, bibliographies, and indexes. Each chapter often follows the same format: chapter outline, introduction, boxes for tangential discussions, photos (most desirably in color), chapter glossary, and summary.

With the advent of the multiple-choice exam, testing has also become highly predictable. The student who takes such an exam knows that there will be a question followed by four or five possible answers. It is highly likely that at least two of the answers will be outrageous, which leaves the savvy student with only three to choose from. Grades will likely come from the computer, so there is little subjective grading by professors or graduate students. The exams and the grading are clearly far more predictable than essay exams, which are much more likely to be subject to the whim of the grader.

While these and many other elements of McDonaldization can be found in the university, it is certainly not nearly as McDonaldized as, say, the fast-food restaurant. For example, relatively little interaction in universities is scripted. There is a routinized quality to lectures, but there is a big difference between using one's own lecture over and over and employing a script created by others. Also, university employees, especially professors, have far more leeway to behave unpredictably than do the workers at a fast-food restaurant.

Health Care: Diagnosis by Computer

Historically, medicine has been anything but predictable. Physicians in private practice usually operated autonomously using their own methods. Even when they became affiliated with hospitals or group practices, they remained largely free of the organizational constraints that might have made their actions more predictable.

A variety of forces are pushing medicine in the direction of greater predictability, that is, various medical practices are becoming standardized. The growing influence of bureaucracies over physicians, especially over the increasing number employed by them, is leading to much more predictability in medical practice. Medical organizations, like all bureaucracies, are based on a series of rules, regulations, and formalized controls that in this case constrain physicians and lead them to practice medicine more predictably. That is, physicians' behaviors will not differ much; medical decisions made at one time or place will be similar to those made at other times or places. For-profit organizations are most likely to push medicine in this direction. To ensure profitability as well as predictable increases in profitability, they demand more and more predictability from the physicians they employ. The larger the organization, the greater the pressure toward predictability; the trend toward medical conglomerates clearly fosters this development. The advent of "McDoctors" also demonstrates the move toward greater predictability.

Pressures from third-party payers to control costs will also lead to greater predictability in medicine. Instead of the physician making independent judgments about such things as length of stay or tests required, federal policies and private third-party payers make these sorts of decisions.

There is also a tendency for less predictable, subjective judgments of the doctor to be replaced by more objective judgments rendered by advanced medical technologies. Thus, a physician need no longer determine from a series of diagnostic clues whether or not a coronary artery is clogged; he or she can order an arteriogram that will objectively demonstrate whether such a blockage exists. Says one observer,

> Medicine has now evolved to a point where diagnostic judgments based on 'subjective' evidence—the patient's sensations and the physician's own observations of the patient—are being supplanted by judgments based on "objective" evidence, provided by laboratory procedures and by mechanical and electronic devices.[24]

The Workplace: Even the Jokes Are Rehearsed

As work settings, bureaucracies are far more predictable than other kinds of organizations. In bureaucracies, people occupy "offices," or positions, each defined by a set of responsibilities and expected behaviors. Those who occupy an office are expected to live up to those expectations. Thus, coworkers or clients can expect the same performance from an office no matter who happens to occupy it. Although there is some leeway, occupants of given offices cannot refuse to perform their functions or do them very differently without being punished or fired.

There is also a clear hierarchy of offices in a bureaucracy so that people know whom to take orders from and whom they may give orders to. This means that bureaucrats do not usually operate in a setting in which anyone who wants to can give them orders.

Further, virtually everything in a bureaucracy exists in written form. Thus, those who read the organization's rules and regulations know what can be expected. With printed forms for virtually every conceivable circumstance, handling an issue often involves little more than filling out (in triplicate) a particular form. In fact, every issue of a given type is usually handled with the same form. Thus, bureaucracies engender predictability in at least three important ways: offices, hierarchies, and documentation.

Scientific management, as developed by Taylor, also placed great emphasis on predictability. Clearly, in delineating the one best way to do a job, Taylor sought an approach that each and every worker could use. Taylor dealt with the issue of predictability largely under the heading of "standardization." Taylor believed that most managers allowed workers to choose their own tools and methods of doing a job. While this may have given the work some individuality, Taylor thought it led to low productivity and poor quality. Instead, he sought the complete standardization of tools and work processes. In fact, he felt that poor standards were better than no standards at all because they caused at least some improvement in productivity and quality. Of course, Taylor favored the clear and detailed standards that made sure all workers did a given type of job in exactly the same way and would therefore consistently produce high-quality work. Standardized tools and procedures would also permit such consistent production.

So, too, the assembly line enhanced the likelihood of predictable work and products. The alternative to the assembly line, the use of highly skilled craftspeople, presented several problems. The steps each craftsperson took were somewhat unpredictable, varying from person to person and over time. Similarly, small but significant differences in the finished products cropped up. This, in turn, led to unpredictabilities in the functioning and quality of the products. For instance, one car would run far better or be much less prone to breakdowns than another.

The assembly line eliminated much of this unpredictability. Highly specialized workers did one or a few things in the same way. If they did not perform as expected, quality control inspectors would catch errors down the line. As a result, the finished product was far more predictable than that produced by a small number of skilled craftspeople. For example, all automobiles from an assembly line were virtually identical, with much more similar performance and quality.

Another factor in workplace predictability is the use of scripts. Robin Leidner has detailed how Combined Insurance has made life-insurance sales predictable. While she found some flexibility and adaptability, she concludes that "the most striking thing about Combined Insurance's training for its life insurance agents was the amazing degree of standardization for which the company was striving. The agents were told, in almost hilarious detail, what to say and do." In fact, a large portion of the agents' sales pitch was "supposed to be memorized and recited precisely as possible." One of the trainers told of a foreign salesman whose English was poor: "He learned the script phonetically and didn't even know what the words meant. . . . He sold twenty applications on his first day and is now a top executive."[25] The insurance agents were even taught the company's standard joke, as well as "the Combined shuffle," the standardized movements, body carriage and intonation.

While McDonald's uses only external constraints on its workers, Combined Insurance attempts to go further—to transform them as people, to lead them to embrace a new identity. Combined workers are supposed to transform their selves, while, in contrast, McDonald's employees are expected to suppress their selves. This difference is traceable to differences in the nature of the work in the two settings. Since McDonald's workers perform their tasks within the work setting, they can be controlled by external constraints. In contrast, Combined Insurance salespeople work door-to-door, with most of their work done inside customers' homes. Because external constraints do not work, Combined tries to change the agents into the kind of people the company wants. In spite of the efforts to control their personalities, however, the insurance agents retain some discretion as well as a sense of autonomy. Thus, though control over Combined workers goes deeper, McDonald's workers are still more controlled because virtually all decision making is removed from their jobs.

Other Settings: That Disney Look

Entertainment

In his classic thriller, *Psycho*, Alfred Hitchcock beautifully exploited the concerns about old-fashioned, unpredictable motels (discussed earlier). The motel in the movie was creepy, but not as creepy as its owner, Norman Bates. Although it offered few amenities, the Bates Motel room did come equipped with a peephole (something most travelers could do without) so that Norman could spy on his victims. Of course, the Bates Motel offered the ultimate in unpredictability—a homicidal maniac and a horrible death to unsuspecting guests. Although few motels were likely to house crazed killers, all sorts of unpredictabilities confronted the traveler at that time.

Psycho brings to mind the fact that the movie industry, too, values predictability. *Psycho* was followed by several sequels, as were other horror films, such as *Halloween* and *Nightmare on Elm Street*. Outside the horror genre, many other movies have been succeeded by one or more sequels: *Star Wars*, *Raiders of the Lost Ark*, *The Godfather*, and *Back to the Future*. Predictable products, particularly sequels to successful movies—at the expense of movies based on new concepts, ideas, and characters—abound.

The studios like sequels because the same characters, actors, and basic plot lines can be used again and again. Furthermore, there seems to be a greater likelihood that sequels will succeed at the box office than completely original movies; profits are therefore more predictable. Presumably, viewers like sequels because they enjoy the comfort of encountering favorite characters played by familiar actors who find themselves in accustomed settings. In a series of *Vacation* movies, Chevy Chase plays the same character. The only thing that varies is the vacation setting in which he practices his very familiar antics. Moviegoers seem more willing to shell out money for a familiar and therefore "safe" movie than for a completely new one. Like a McDonald's meal, many sequels are not very good, but at least the consumers know what they are getting.

Movies themselves seem to require increasingly predictable sequences and highly predictable endings. Dustin Hoffman contends that today's movie audiences would not accept the many flashbacks, fantasies, and dream sequences of his classic movie from 1969, *Midnight Cowboy*. Hoffman believes that this may be "emblematic of the whole culture":

> My friend [director Barry Levinson] says we live in a McDonald's culture . . . because you aren't going to stop [at a restaurant] until you get what you already know. . . .
>
> . . . and in our culture now people want to know what they're getting when they go to the movies.[26]

The movie rating system allows people to predict the amount of violence, nudity, and potentially objectionable language they will see and hear. On the one hand, a "G" rating means that the movie contains no nudity and objectionable language, and only mild forms of violence; on the other hand, an "NC–17" rating means that all three will appear in the movie. The ratings are quantified by age: "PG" means that children under thirteen may attend, "PG–13" indicates that a movie may be inappropriate for children under thirteen, "R" means that children under seventeen need parental consent (supposedly), and "NC–17" is supposed to ban all children under seventeen from the movie.

Modern amusement parks, especially compared with their honky-tonk ancestors, are in many ways highly predictable places. The Disney organization quite clearly knew that to succeed it had to overcome the unpredictabilities of old amusement parks. For example, Disneyland and Walt Disney World take great pains to be sure that the visitor is not subject to any disorder. You have already seen how the garbage is whisked away so that people do not have to be disturbed by the sight of trash. Vendors do not sell peanuts, gum, and cotton candy because they would make a mess underfoot. The average American family who visits the Disney parks will not likely have their day disturbed by the sight of public drunkenness. Disney offers a world of predictable, almost surreal, orderliness.

In fact, the Disney amusement parks demonstrate all the subdimensions of predictability. The layouts of the parks, and many of the attractions, are very similar. Much of the success of the parks is based on the familiarity of the various Disney characters. All the parks are littered with the predictable Disney products available for sale to eager visitors each time they come. Disney employees often follow scripts in their interaction with the public.

One of the most important problems facing older amusement parks was the unpredictable appearance and behavior of their employees. To overcome this problem, Disney has developed detailed guidelines about what Disney employees should look like (the "Disney look") and how they should act. Thus, there is a long list of "do's" and "don'ts" for different kinds of employees. For example, female "cast members" (a Disney euphemism for its park employees) not in costume must not wear jeans, clinging fabrics, athletic shoes, socks of any kind, hoop earrings, bracelets, or more than two necklaces. Female hosts may not use eyeliner or frost their hair, but they *must* use a deodorant or antiperspirant. Mustaches and beards are unacceptable for male hosts. The list goes on and on, but the point is that the visitor meets Disney employees who look predictably alike.[27]

Disney is not alone among amusement parks in the effort to make behavior at such parks predictable. At Busch Gardens, Virginia, "a certain amount of energy is devoted to making sure that smiles are kept in place. There are rules about short hair (for the boys) and no eating, drinking, smoking, or straw chewing on duty (for everyone). 'We're just supposed to be perfect, see,' one employee . . . said cheerfully."[28]

Not only do the employees at Busch Gardens all look alike, but they are also supposed to act alike:

> Controlled environments hinge on the maintenance of the right kind of attitude among the lower echelons.
>
> "It is kind of a rah-rah thing. We emphasize cleanliness, being helpful, being polite."

Consequently, there is a lot of talk at Busch Gardens about All American images and keeping people up and motivated. At the giant, *somewhat* German restaurant, the Festhaus, there are contests to determine who has the most enthusiasm and best attitude. One of the prizes is free trips to King's Dominion, Busch Garden's arch rival up the road.[29] [Italics added.]

Thus, visitors to Busch Gardens and parks like it can expect to see and deal with highly predictable employees throughout their visit.

In addition, few unanticipated things happen on any of the rides or in any of the attractions in such parks. Of the Jungle Cruise ride at Disney World, a company publication says, "The *Jungle Cruise* is a favorite of armchair explorers, because it compresses weeks of safari travel into ten minutes [efficiency!] of fun, *without mosquitoes, monsoons, or misadventures.*"[30] (Italics added.)

Sports

Promoters have taken various steps to make sporting events, as products, more predictable. Domes and artificial turf make rainouts unlikely. Artificial turf also allows the baseball to bounce more truly, making for fewer unpredictable hops caused by clumps of grass or clods of earth. The more symmetrical baseball stadiums make the balls that hit the walls carom more predictably. They also enable greater consistency from one park to another in the distance and height a baseball must be hit to be a home run.

The classic nonrationalized and unpredictable baseball stadium is Boston's Fenway Park, with its grass playing field and asymmetrical dimensions. Its famous "Green Monster," a close but high wall in left field, makes home runs of relatively short high flies (routine outs in other stadiums), and well-hit but low line drives hit the wall for base hits. At Wrigley Field in Chicago, balls sometimes get lost in the ivy that covers the fences. Stadiums such as these are the exception in major league baseball.

Interestingly, a reaction seems to have set in against symmetrical baseball parks. Some of the newest baseball parks such as Oriole Park at Camden Yards are quite asymmetrical. In fact, such parks seek to exploit nostalgia by bringing back many things associated with the older ballparks. For example, Oriole Park retained and rebuilt an old warehouse, which serves as an old-fashioned backdrop for the stadium.

In tennis (as a product), a relatively recent development, the tie breaker, has made tennis matches more predictable. Prior to tie breakers, to win a set, a player needed to win six games with a two-game margin over his or her opponent. But if the opponent was never more than one game behind, the set could go on and on. Some memorable, interminable tennis matches produced scores on the order of 12–10. With limitations imposed by television and other mass media, the tennis establishment decided to institute the tie breaker in many tournaments. If a set is deadlocked at six games each, a twelve-point tie breaker is played. The first player to get seven points with a two-point margin wins. A tie breaker might go beyond twelve points (if the players are tied at six points each), but it rarely goes on as long as close matches occasionally used to.

An interesting example of predictability in a previously highly unpredictable area is the rationalization of racehorse training. Trainer Wayne Lukas has set up a string of stables around the United States labeled "McStables." In the past, training stables have been independent operations specific to a given track. Thus, training has greatly varied from one race track to another, and from one stable to another. However,

> Lukas has thrived by establishing and supervising far-flung divisions of his stable. "I think the absolute key to doing this is quality control," he said. "You cannot ever see a deviation of quality from one division to the other. The barns are the same. The feeding program is the same . . .
>
> "This is what makes it easy to ship horses around the country. Most horses, when they ship, have to adjust. There's never an adjustment necessary in our divisions. *It's the McDonald's principle.* We'll give you a franchise, and that franchise is going to be the same wherever you go."[31] [Italics added.]

Malls

The attraction of the shopping mall can also be credited, at least in part, to its ability to make the shopping center more predictable. For example, "One kid who works here told me why he likes the mall. . . . It's because no matter what the weather is outside, it's always the same in here. He likes that. He doesn't want to know it's raining—it would depress him."[32] Those who wander through malls are also relatively free from the unpredictabilities of crime that might beset them in city streets. The lack of bad weather and the relative absence of crime point to another predictable aspect of shopping malls—they are always upbeat. As physical settings, the malls, like fast-food restaurants, are virtually the same from one place or time to another.

Avoiding crime is a key factor in the rise of so-called "family fun" or "pay-to-play" centers (it costs about six dollars per visit per child, although, in a cute gimmick, parents are "free"). The leader here, the Discovery Zone, runs over 300 play centers nationwide. They offer ropes, padded "mountains," tubes, tunnels, giant blocks, trapezes, and so on. These centers have proven popular in urban areas because they provide a safe haven in the crime-ridden cities.[33] Children are also seen as less likely to injure themselves in fun centers than in community playgrounds because of the nature of the equipment and the presence of staff supervisors. And there are safety checks to be sure that children do not leave with anyone but their parents. However, though fun centers are undoubtedly safer and less unpredictable, they have also been described as "antiseptic, climate-controlled, plastic world[s]."[34]

Home Cooking

The predictability of foods in a McDonaldized society has led to a disturbing fact:

> Regional and ethnic distinctions are disappearing from American cooking. Food in one neighborhood, city, or state looks and tastes pretty much like food anywhere else. Americans are sitting down to meals largely composed of such items as instant macaroni and cheese, soft white bread, oleomargarine, frozen doughnuts, and Jell-O. Today it is possible to travel from coast to coast, at any time of year, without feeling any need to change your eating habits. . . . Sophisticated processing and storage techniques, fast transport, and a creative variety of formulated convenience-food products have made it possible to ignore regional and seasonal differences in food production.[35]

One watershed in the evolution of predictable meals prepared at home was the frozen TV dinner. Within the nicely uniform packaging, an aluminum tray with a consistent set of four or five compartments holds a complete meal, perhaps a few slices of turkey and a dollop of stuffing in one section, a predetermined number of peas in another, a mound of mashed potatoes or other starch, and a dessert, such as peach cobbler. Diners may feel a rush of emotion when they peel away the aluminum foil and there before their eyes is that beloved familiar meal. Diners know that it isn't going to be a gourmet meal, but it will be just like the TV dinner they had last time and presumably will be just like their next TV dinner.

Of course, the TV dinner has now been joined and, in some cases, superseded by even more rational meals eaten at home. The microwavable dinner, just as predictable as the TV dinner, can be stored more easily and "cooked" more quickly. Add to this list of advances the freeze-dried foods that blossom into a predictable dish with merely the addition of boiling water.

Vacations

The package tour is as oriented to predictability as it is to efficiency. That is, a person who signs up for a package tour wants a trip that offers no surprises. To accommodate (or create) this demand, tour operators have turned travel into a highly predictable product. What this often means is an effort to allow minimal contact with the people, culture, and institutions of visited countries. This creates a paradox: People go to considerable expense and effort to go to foreign countries where they have as little contact as possible with native culture.[36] A tour group from the United States will likely be made up of like-minded Americans, with the majority of one's time spent with those (highly predictable) people. Agencies use American carriers wherever possible or else local transports that offer the amenities expected by the American tourist (perhaps even air conditioning, stereo, bathroom). Tour guides are usually Americans or people who have spent time in America—at the very least, natives fluent in English who know all about the needs and interests of Americans. Restaurants visited on the tour are either American (perhaps an American fast-food chain) or cater to the American palate. Hotels are also likely to be either American chains, such as the Sheraton and Hilton, or European hotels that have structured themselves to suit American tastes.[37] Each day offers a firm, often tight schedule, with little time for spontaneous activities. Tourists can take comfort from knowing exactly what they are going to do on a daily, even hourly, basis.

The package tour is also designed to shelter travelers from other unpredictabilities of travel. People take such tours because they believe they are much less likely to be accosted by beggars or pickpockets, to be humiliated because of their lack of facility with foreign languages, or to fall ill from polluted water or bad food. Of course, this process also eliminates the unanticipated events that can make foreign travel so interesting—meeting a fascinating native, discovering a charming little shop or restaurant, or happening upon an unexpected sight.

While the package tour represents the McDonaldization of travel, a similar thing has happened to camping. At one time people went camping to escape the predictable routines of their daily lives. City dwellers fled their homes in search of life in nature with little more than a tent and a sleeping bag. Little or nothing lay between the camper and the natural environment. This led to some unpredictable events, but that was the whole point. Campers might see a deer wander close to their campsite, perhaps even venture into it. Of course, they might also encounter the unexpected thunderstorm, tick bite, or snake, but these were accepted as an integral part of escaping one's routine activities. Here is the way one person describes the ups and downs of this kind of camping:

> Of course it began to pour. We had neglected to pack the main tent pole, which is like forgetting the mast on a sailboat. There is no tent without the tent pole. At first we failed to grasp this, so we kept trying to get the tent to stand. The whole structure kept collapsing like some big green bear that had been shot. Just when we were exasperated and began to dream of Holiday Inns, a deer appeared not two feet from our son.
>
> "Look!" our child said, enraptured. "Look, my first deer!"[38]

Some people still camp this way; however, many others have sought to eliminate unpredictability from camping. Said the owner of one campground, "All they wanted [in the past] was a space in the woods and an outhouse. . . . But nowadays people aren't exactly roughing it."[39] Instead of simple tents, modern campers might venture forth in a recreational vehicle (RV) such as a Winnebago, or take a trailer with an elaborate pop-up tent, to protect them from the unexpected. Of course, "camping" in an RV also tends to reduce the likelihood of catching sight of wandering wildlife. Furthermore, the motorized camper carries within it all the elements that one has at home—refrigerator, stove, television, VCR, and stereo.

Camping technology has made for not only great predictability, but also changes in the modern campgrounds. Relatively few people now pitch their tents in the unpredictable wilderness; most find their way into rationalized campgrounds, even "country-club campgrounds," spearheaded by such franchises as Kampgrounds of America (KOA).[40] Said one camper relaxing in his air-conditioned thirty-two-foot trailer, "We've got everything right here. . . . It doesn't matter how hard it rains or how the wind blows."[41] Modern campgrounds are likely to be divided into sections—one for tents, another for RVs, each section broken into neat rows of usually tiny campsites. Hook-ups allow those with RVs to operate the various technologies encased within them. After campers have parked and hooked up their RVs or popped up their tents, they can gaze out and enjoy the sights—other tents, RVs, children on bikes—in other words, many of the sights they tried to leave be-hind in the cities or suburbs. Campsite owners might also provide campers who are "roughing it" with such amenities as a well-stocked delicatessen, bathrooms and showers, heated swimming pools, a game room loaded with video games, a laundromat, a TV room, a movie theater, and even enter-tainment such as bands or comedians.

Housing

Modern suburban housing demonstrates predictability in a McDonaldized society. As the famous folk song puts it,

> Little boxes on the hillside,
> Little boxes made of ticky-tacky,
> Little boxes, little boxes, little boxes
> Little boxes all the same.[42]

In the post–World War II housing boom, an effort was made to make houses as products, and home building more predictable. This effort led to the birth of suburban communities made up of houses with interiors and exteriors little different from each other. Indeed, people could wander into someone else's house and not realize for a moment that they were not in their own home. Though some diversity exists in the more expensive developments, many suburbanites live in houses nearly identical to their neighbors'.

Furthermore, the communities themselves look very much alike. To replace mature trees bulldozed to allow for the more efficient building of houses, rows of saplings held up by posts and wire were planted. Similarly, hills were often bulldozed to flatten the terrain. Streets were laid out in straight, symmetrical patterns. With such predictable landmarks, suburban-ites may well enter the wrong suburban community or get lost in their own community.

Several of Steven Spielberg's movies take place in these rationalized and highly predictable suburbs. Spielberg's strategy is to lure viewers into this highly predictable world and then hit them with a highly unpredictable event. For example, in *E.T.* an extraterrestrial wanders into a suburban de-velopment of tract houses and is discovered by a child there who, up to that point, has lived a highly predictable suburban existence. The unpredictable E.T. eventually disrupts not only the lives of the child and his family, but also the entire community. Similarly, *Poltergeist* takes place in a suburban household, with evil spirits disrupting its predictable tranquility. (The spirits first manifest themselves through another key element of a McDonaldized society—the television set.) The great success of Spielberg's movies may be traceable to people's longing for some unpredictability, even if it is frightening and menacing, in their increasingly predictable lives.

Conclusion

Predictability is the third dimension of McDonaldization. It involves the emphasis on things such as discipline, systematization, and routine so that things are the same from one time or place to another. Predictability is achieved in various ways, including the replication of settings, the use of scripts to control what employees say, the routinization of employee behavior, and the offering of uniform products.

6

Control

Human and Nonhuman Robots

This chapter presents the fourth dimension of McDonaldization—increased control and the replacement of human with nonhuman technology. In fact, the replacement of human with nonhuman technology is very often motivated by a desire for greater control. The great source of uncertainty, unpredictability and inefficiency in any rationalizing system is people—either those who work within it or those served by it. Hence, the efforts to increase control are usually aimed at people.

McDonaldization involves the search for the means to exert increasing control over both employees and customers. Over the years, a variety of technologies designed to control people have been developed and deployed.[1] Furthermore, and more extremely, nonhuman technologies have steadily replaced the people who work in rationalized settings because, among other things, robots and computers are far easier to control than humans. Technology is treated very broadly here to include not only machines and tools, but also materials, skills, knowledge, rules, regulations, procedures, and techniques. Thus, technologies include not only the obvious, such as robots, computers, and the assembly line, but also the less obvious, such as bureaucratic rules and manuals prescribing accepted procedures and techniques.

The basic idea, historically, is for organizations to gain control over people gradually and progressively through the development and deployment of increasingly effective technologies. Once people are controlled, it is possible to begin reducing their behavior to a series of machinelike actions. And once people behave like machines, they can be replaced with actual machines such as robots. The replacement of humans by machines is the ultimate stage in control over people—people can cause no more uncertainty and unpredictability because they are no longer involved, at least directly, in the process.

Before the age of sophisticated nonhuman technologies, people were largely controlled by other people. In the workplace, owners and supervisors controlled subordinates directly, face-to-face. But such direct, personal control is difficult, costly, and likely to engender personal hostility among those being controlled. Subordinates will likely strike out at an immediate supervisor or an owner who exercises excessively tight control over their activities. However, control through a technology is easier, less costly in the long run, and less likely to engender hostility toward supervisors and owners. Thus, over time, control by people has shifted toward control by technologies.[2]

It is clearly not the case that the *only* goal of nonhuman technologies is control. These technologies are created and implemented for many reasons such as increased productivity, greater quality, and lower cost. However, this chapter is mainly concerned with the ways nonhuman technologies have increased control over people as employees and clients in a McDonaldizing society.

The Fast-Food Industry: Eat, and Get Out!

One of the main sources of uncertainty in a traditional restaurant is the chef or cook. The cook's mood can lead to great variation in meals. A cook who chooses not to show up for work could spell disaster for a restaurant. Another major source of uncertainty in the traditional restaurant is the customer, who may request special foods or linger over a meal. Fast-food restaurants, however, have found ways to control both employees and customers.

Controlling the Product and the Process

Fast-food restaurants have coped with problems of uncertainty by doing away with a cook, at least in the conventional sense. Grilling a hamburger is so simple that anyone can do it with a bit of training. Furthermore, even when more skill is required (as in the case of Arby's roast beef), the fast-food restaurant develops a routine involving a few simple procedures that almost anyone can follow. Cooking fast food is like a game of connect-the-dots or painting-by-numbers. Following prescribed steps eliminates most of the uncertainties of cooking. Like the military, fast-food restaurants have generally recruited teenagers because they surrender their autonomy to machines, rules, and procedures more easily than adults do.[3]

Much of the food prepared at McDonald's arrives at the restaurant pre-formed, precut, presliced, and "pre-prepared," often by nonhuman technologies. This serves to limit drastically what employees need to do—there is usually no need for them to form the burgers, cut the potatoes, slice the rolls, or prepare the apple pie. All they need to do is, where necessary, cook or often merely heat the food and pass it on to the customer. The more that is done by nonhuman technology before the food arrives at the restaurant, the less workers need to do and the less room they have to exercise their own judgment and skill. At Taco Bell, workers used to spend hours cooking meat and shredding vegetables. Now, bags of frozen ready-cooked beef arrive—all the workers do is drop the bags in boiling water. They have used preshredded lettuce for some time, and now preshredded cheese and prediced tomatoes have appeared. As a result, there is less and less for human workers to do at Taco Bell.[4]

McDonald's has developed a variety of machines to control its employees. If a worker must decide when a cup is full and the soft drink dispenser needs to be shut off, there is always the risk that the worker may be distracted and allow the cup to overflow. Thus, a sensor has been developed that automatically shuts off the soft-drink dispenser when the cup is full. When an employee controls the french-fry machine, misjudgment may lead to undercooked, overcooked, or even burned fries. Ray Kroc fretted over this problem: "It was amazing that we got them as uniform as we did, because each kid working the fry vats would have his own interpretation of the proper color and so forth."[5] Kroc's dissatisfaction with the vagaries of human judgment led to its elimination and the development of french-fry machines that ring or buzz when the fries are done, or that shut themselves off and automatically lift the french-fry baskets out of the hot oil.

When a worker at the cash register has to look at an item being purchased and then to the price list, the wrong (even lower) amount could be rung up. Computerized cash registers forestall that possibility. All the employee need do is press the image on the register that matches the item purchased; the machine then produces the correct price. In all these ways, work traditionally done by people has been taken away from them and built into machines.

It could be argued that the objective in a fast-food restaurant is to reduce its employees to functioning at the level of human robots. There have even been experiments with mechanical robots that serve food. For example, one university has built a robot that serves hamburgers at the campus restaurant.

The robot looks like a flat oven with conveyor belts running through and an arm attached at the end. A red light indicates when a worker should slide in a patty and bun, which bob along in the heat for 1 minute 52 seconds. When they reach the other side of the machine, photo-optic sensors indicate when they can be assembled.

The computer functioning as the robot's brain determines when the buns and patty are where they should be. If the bun is delayed, it slows the patty belt. If the patty is delayed, it slows bun production. It also keeps track of the number of buns and patties in the oven and determines how fast they need to be fed in to keep up speed.[6]

Robots offer a number of advantages—lower cost, increased efficiency, fewer workers, no absenteeism, and a solution to the decreasing supply of teenagers needed to work at fast-food restaurants. The professor who came up with the idea for the robot that serves hamburgers said, "Kitchens have not been looked at as factories, which they are. . . . Fast-food restaurants were the first to do that. We're just at the beginning."[7] However, this robot still costs a great deal, can make only hamburgers, is relatively slow, and breaks down a lot.

Taco Bell is developing "a computer-driven machine the size of a coffee table that . . . can make and seal in a plastic bag a perfect hot taco."[8] Pepsico (which owns Kentucky Fried Chicken, Pizza Hut, and Taco Bell) has a prototype for an automated drink dispenser that produces a soft drink in fifteen seconds: "Orders are punched in at the cash register by a clerk. A computer sends the order to the dispenser to drop a cup, fill it with ice and appropriate soda, and place a lid on top. The cup is then moved by conveyor to the customer."[9] When the technology is refined and affordable, fast-food restaurants will widely employ such robots.

In fact, McDonald's already has a limited program in operation called ARCH, or Automated Robotic Crew Helper. There is a french-fry robot that fills the fry basket, cooks the fries, empties the basket when its sensors tell it the fries are done, and even shakes the fries while they are being cooked. In the case of drinks, an employee pushes a button on the cash register to place an order. The robot then puts the proper amount of ice in the cup, moves the cup under the correct spigot, and allows the cup to fill. It then places the cup on a conveyor, which moves it to the employee, who passes it on to the customer.[10]

While most of these technological changes are aimed at controlling lower-level employees, managers are not immune from such efforts. Another aspect of McDonald's ARCH program is a computerized system that, among other things, tells managers how many hamburgers or orders of french fries they will require at a given time (the lunch hour, for example). As a result, the computerized system takes away the need to make such judgments and decisions from managers.[11]

Controlling Customers

Fast-food restaurants have, of course, greatly refined their methods for controlling the customer. Whether they go into the restaurant or use the drive-through window, customers enter a kind of conveyor system that moves them through the restaurant in the manner desired by the management. This is clearest in the case of the drive-through window (the energy for this conveyor comes from one's own automobile), but it is also true for those who enter the restaurant. Consumers know that they are supposed to line up, move to the counter, order their food, pay, carry the food to an available table, eat, gather up their debris, deposit it in the trash receptacle, and return to their cars. People are moved along in this system not by a conveyor belt, but by the unwritten, but universally known, norms for eating in a fast-food restaurant.

One of the ways that fast-food restaurants have tried to tighten control over their customers is by influencing them to leave quickly. This is motivated by the restaurant's need for tables to be vacated rapidly in order to allow other diners to have a place to eat their food. Perhaps today's fast-food restaurant owners fear what befell the famous chain of cafeterias, the Automat, which was partly undermined by people who occupied tables for hours on end. The Automat became a kind of social center, leaving less and less room for people looking for tables to eat their meals. The death blow was struck when street people began to monopolize the Automat's tables.

To keep people moving through fast-food restaurants, owners may employ security personnel to prevent diners from lingering at their tables or loitering. In the cities, this keeps street people on the move, while in the suburbs it prevents potentially rowdy teenagers from monopolizing tables or parking lots. Seven-Eleven has sought to deal with loitering teenagers outside its stores by playing saccharine tunes such as *Some Enchanted Evening*. Said a Seven-Eleven spokesperson, "They won't hang around and tap their feet to Mantovani."[12]

Some fast-food restaurants have even put up signs limiting a customer's stay in the restaurant, say to twenty minutes.[13] More generally, fast-food restaurants have structured themselves so that people do not need or want to linger over meals. Easily consumed finger foods make the meal itself a quick one. Some fast-food restaurants have even developed chairs that make customers uncomfortable after about twenty minutes.[14]

Education: Learning to Be Docile

Universities have developed a variety of nonhuman technologies to exert control over the process of education. For instance, professors must follow certain rules and regulations. Class periods are set by the university and determine when classes must end. Students leave at the assigned time no matter where the professor happens to be in the lecture. So, too, because the university requires grading, the professor must test students. In some universities, final grades must be submitted within forty-eight hours of the final exam, which may force professors to employ computer-graded multiple-choice exams. Required evaluations by students may force professors to teach in a way that will lead to high ratings. The publishing demands of the tenure and promotion system may force professors to devote far less time to their teaching than they, and their students, would like.

Of course, students are even more controlled than professors by the university system. For example, besides the constraints already mentioned, universities often give students little leeway in the courses they may take. The courses themselves, often highly structured, force the students to perform in specific ways.

Control over the university's "customers"—that is, the students—actually begins long before they enter the university. Grade schools in particular have developed many technologies to control students. Many schools strive, right from the start, to have students conform to their rules. Kindergarten has been described as educational "boot camp."[15] Those who conform to the rules are thought of as good students, while those who don't are labeled bad students. Thus, as a general rule, the students who end up in college are the ones who have successfully submitted to the control mechanisms. Students are taught not only to obey authority, but also to embrace the rationalized procedures of rote learning and objective testing. More important, spontaneity and creativity tend not to be rewarded, and may even be discouraged, leading to what one expert calls "education for docility."[16]

The clock and the lesson plan also exert control over students, especially in grade school and high school. Because of the "tyranny of the clock," a class must last until, and end at, the sound of the bell, even though learning does not often conform to the clock. Thus, even if students are just about to comprehend something, the lesson must end and the class must move on to something else. Because of the "tyranny of the lesson plan," a class must focus on what the plan requires for the day, no matter what the class (and perhaps the teacher) may find interesting. There is the example of a teacher "who sees a cluster of excited children examining a turtle with enormous fascination and intensity. Now children, put away the turtle, the teacher insists. We're going to have our science lesson. The lesson is on crabs."[17] Overall, the emphasis tends to be on producing submissive, malleable students; creative, independent students are often, from the educational system's point of view, "messy, expensive, and time-consuming."[18]

An even more extreme version of this emphasis appears in the child-care equivalent of the fast-food restaurant, Kinder-Care. Kinder-Care tends to hire short-term employees with little or no training in child care. What these employees do in the "classroom" is largely determined by an instruction book with a ready-made curriculum. Staff members open the manual to find activities spelled out in detail for each day. Clearly, a skilled, experienced, and creative teacher is not the kind of person "McChild" care centers seek to hire. Rather, relatively untrained employees are more easily controlled by the nonhuman technology of the omnipresent "instruction book."

Another example of this is the franchised Sylvan Learning Center, labeled the "McDonald's of Education."[19] Sylvan learning centers are after-school centers for remedial education. The corporation "trains staff and tailors a McDonald's type uniformity, down to the U-shaped tables at which instructors work with their charges."[20] Through its training methods, rules, and technologies, for-profit systems like the Sylvan Learning Center exert great control over their "teachers."

Health Care: Who's Deciding Our Fate?

As all rational systems have, medicine has moved away from human toward nonhuman technologies. The two most important examples of this are the growing importance of bureaucratic rules and controls and the growth of modern medical machinery. Instead of physicians making independent subjective evaluations of patients, that process is increasingly constrained by bureaucratic rules. For example, the prospective payment and DRG (Diagnostic Related Groups) systems—not physicians and their medical judgment—tend to determine how long a patient must be hospitalized. Similarly, the doctor operating alone out of a black bag with a few simple tools has virtually become a thing of the past. Instead, doctors serve as dispatchers, sending patients on to the appropriate machines and specialists. Even computer programs that diagnose illnesses have begun to appear.[21] Although it is unlikely that they will ever replace the physician, computers may one day be the initial, if not the prime, diagnostic agents. There is also a trend toward various types of do-it-yourself medical testing (for pregnancy, diabetes, high blood pressure, cholesterol and so on). These relatively new technologies take control completely away from the physician and serve as yet another example of the tendency in a McDonaldizing society to put the client to work.

These and other developments in modern medicine demonstrate increasing external control over the medical profession by third-party payers, employing organizations, for-profit hospitals, HMOs, the federal government, and "McDoctors"-like organizations. Even in its heyday the medical profession was not free of external control, but now the nature of the control is changing and its degree and extent is increasing greatly. Instead of the mostly autonomous decision making of the doctor in private practice, many organizations control, in some cases even determine, the decision-making process with their rules and regulations. In bureaucracies, employees are controlled by their superiors. So are physicians, whose superiors are more and more likely to be professional managers and not other doctors. The result is that the much more constraining control "from the top" is replacing peer control in the medical profession. Bureaucracies are also characterized by formalized and codified technical standards. What the physician does in such organizations is likely to be controlled by such codes. Also, the existence of hugely expensive medical technologies often mandates that they be used by the medical profession. As the machines themselves grow more sophisticated, physicians come to understand them less and are therefore less able to control them. Instead, control shifts to the technologies as well as to the experts who create and handle them.

For the patient also, control is shifting from the primary care physician to these various structures and technologies. Minimally this involves a qualitative shift in the nature of control over patients; maximally it means a vast increase in the control of patients by large, impersonal systems. For example, in many medical insurance programs, patients can no longer decide on their own to see a specialist. Rather, the primary physician must decide whether a specialist is necessary, with great pressure on the primary physician to perform many functions previously handled by specialists. Because of the effort to keep costs down, fewer patients visit specialists; as a result, the patient, like the physician, loses a great deal of autonomy.

The Workplace: Do As I Say, Not As I Do

Bureaucracies can be seen as large-scale nonhuman technologies with innumerable rules, regulations, guidelines, positions, lines of command, and hierarchies designed to dictate what people do within the system and how they do it. The consummate bureaucrat thinks little about what is to be done: he or she simply follows the rules, deals with incoming work, and passes it on to the next step in the hierarchy. Forms further limit human choice and error: employees need do little more than fill out the required form and pass it on, up, or across the bureaucratic hierarchy.

Scientific management clearly strove to limit or replace human with nonhuman technology. For instance, the "one best way" required workers to follow a series of steps in a mindless fashion. More generally, Taylor believed that the most important part of the work world was not the workers, or even the managers, but rather the organization that would plan, oversee, and control their work.

While Taylor wanted all employees to be controlled by the organization, he accorded managers much more leeway than manual workers. It was the task of management to study the knowledge and skills of workers and to record, tabulate, and, ultimately, reduce that knowledge and skill to laws, rules, and even mathematical formulas. To put this slightly differently, managers were to take a body of *human skills*, abilities, and knowledge and transform them into a set of *nonhuman rules*, regulations, and formulas. Once human skills were codified, the organization no longer needed skilled workers. Management would hire, train, and employ unskilled workers in accord with a set of strict guidelines.

In effect, Taylor separated "head" from "hand" work. In the past, the skilled worker had performed both. Taylor and his followers studied what was in the heads of those skilled workers, then translated that knowledge into simple, mindless routines that virtually anyone could learn and follow. Workers were thus left with little more than repetitive "hand" work. This principle remains at the base of the movement throughout our McDonaldizing society to replace human with nonhuman technology.

Behind Taylor's scientific management, and all other efforts to replace human with nonhuman technology, lies the goal of employing human beings with minimal intelligence and ability. In fact, Taylor sought to hire people who resembled animals:

> Now one of the very first requirements for a man who is fit to handle pig iron as a regular occupation is that he shall be so stupid and so phlegmatic that he more nearly resembles in his mental make-up the ox than any other type. The man who is mentally alert and intelligent is for this very reason entirely unsuited to what would, for him, be the grinding monotony of work of this character. Therefore the workman who is best suited to handling pig iron is unable to understand the real science of doing this class of work. He is so stupid that the word "percentage" has no meaning to him, and he must consequently be trained by a man more intelligent than himself into the habit of working in accordance with the laws of this science before he can be successful.[22]

Taylor's attitude is one precursor to the contemporary effort to reduce human activities to robot-like actions so that the humans can actually be replaced by robots. Because Taylor did not have robots at his disposal, all he could do was hire humans, then dictate to them in great detail what they were to do on the job.

It is no coincidence that Henry Ford had a similar view of the kinds of people who were to work on his assembly lines:

> Repetitive labour—the doing of one thing over and over again and always in the same way—is a terrifying prospect to a certain kind of mind. It is terrifying to me. I could not possibly do the same thing day in and day out, but to other minds, perhaps I might say to the majority of minds, repetitive operations hold no terrors. In fact, to some types of mind thought is absolutely appalling. To them the ideal job is one where creative instinct need not be expressed. The jobs where it is necessary to put in mind as well as muscle have very few takers—we always need men who like a job because it is difficult. The average worker, I am sorry to say, wants a job in which he does not have to think. Those who have what might be called the creative type of mind and who thoroughly abhor monotony are apt to imagine that all other minds are similarly restless and therefore to extend quite unwanted sympathy to the labouring man who day in and day out performs almost exactly the same operation.[23]

The kind of person sought out by Taylor was the same kind of person Ford thought would work well on the assembly line. In their view, such people would more likely submit to external technological control over their work and perhaps even crave such control. This perspective also lies behind the effort in fast-food restaurants, and many other businesses in a McDonaldizing society, to hire teenagers and have them operate as automatons. Control of such employees also allows managers rigid control of the work process.

Not surprisingly, a perspective similar to that held by Taylor and Ford can be attributed to other entrepreneurs, notably Ray Kroc and W. Clement Stone (the founder of Combined Insurance): "The obvious irony is that the organizations built by W. Clement Stone and Ray Kroc, both highly creative and innovative entrepreneurs, depend on the willingness of employees to follow detailed routines precisely."[24]

Other Settings: Phoneheads Need to Push the Potty Button

You can find the replacement of human with nonhuman technology—and the consequent increase in control—in many realms of daily life, some of which might surprise you. Two other broad areas where technology has been used to increase control are (1) food production, cooking, and vending and (2) marketing and sales.

Food Production, Cooking, and Vending

Technologies designed to reduce the uncertainties caused by people are found throughout the manufacture of food. For example, the mass manufacturing of bread is not controlled by skilled bakers who lavish love and attention on a few loaves of bread at a time. Such skilled bakers cannot produce enough bread to supply the needs of our society. Furthermore, the bread they do produce can suffer from the uncertainties involved in having humans do the work. That is, the bread may, for example, be either too brown or doughy. To increase productivity and eliminate these unpredictabilities, mass producers of bread have developed an automated system in which, as in all automated systems, humans play a minimal role rigidly controlled by the technology:

> The most advanced bakeries now resemble oil refineries. Flour, water, a score of additives, and huge amounts of yeast, sugar and water are

mixed into a broth that ferments for an hour. More flour is then added, and the dough is extruded into pans, allowed to rise for an hour, then moved through a tunnel oven. The loaves emerge after 18 minutes, to be cooled, sliced, and wrapped.[25]

In one food industry after another, technologies in which humans play little more than a planning and maintenance role have replaced production processes dominated by skilled craftspeople. The warehousing and shipping of food has been similarly automated.

Some rather startling technological developments have occurred in the ways in which people raise animals for food. Here, unpredictabilities stem not only from human workers but also from the animals. Thus, rational techniques have been developed to cope with both types of uncertainty.

For instance, "aquaculture," a $5-billion-a-year business, is growing dramatically because of the spiraling desire for seafood in an increasingly cholesterol-conscious population.[26] Instead of a lone angler inefficiently casting a line with unpredictable results, or even huge boats catching tons of fish at a time in huge nets, the much more predictable and efficient "farming" of seafood has increased. For example, more than 50% of the fresh salmon found in restaurants is raised in huge sea cages off the coast of Norway.

Sea farms provide a series of rational benefits. Most generally, aquaculture allows humans to exert far greater *control* over the unpredictabilities that beset fish in their natural habitat, thus producing a more predictable supply. Various drugs and chemicals also increase predictability in the amount and quality of seafood. Aquaculture also permits a more predictable and efficient harvest because the creatures are confined to a limited space. In addition, geneticists can manipulate them to produce seafood more efficiently. For example, it takes a halibut about ten years to reach market size, but a new dwarf variety can reach the required size in only three years. Sea farms also allow for greater calculability—the greatest number of fish for the least expenditure of time, money, and energy.

Similarly, relatively small, family-run farms for raising other animals are being rapidly replaced by "factory farms."[27] The first animal to find its way into the factory farm was the chicken. Here is the way one observer describes a chicken "factory":

> A broiler producer today gets a load of 10,000, 50,000, or even more day-old chicks from the hatcheries, and puts them straight into a long, windowless shed. . . . Inside the shed, every aspect of the birds' environment is controlled to make them grow faster on less feed. Food and water are fed automatically from hoppers suspended from

the roof. The lighting is adjusted. . . . For instance, there may be bright light twenty-four hours a day for the first week or two, to encourage the chicks to gain [weight] quickly. . . .

Toward the end of the eight- or nine-week life of the chicken, there may be as little as half a square foot of space per chicken—or less than the area of a sheet of quarto paper for a three-and-one-half-pound bird.[28]

Among its other advantages, such chicken farms allow one person to raise over 50,000 chickens.

Raising chickens this way involves a series of predictable steps that ensure control over all aspects of the business, from the farmers' procedures to the chickens themselves. For instance, the chickens' size and weight is more predictable than that of free-ranging chickens. It is also more efficient to "harvest" chickens confined in this way than it is to catch chickens that roam over large areas.

However, confining chickens in such crowded quarters creates unpredictabilities such as violence and even cannibalism. Farmers deal with these irrational "vices" in a variety of ways, such as dimming the light as chickens approach full size and "debeaking" chickens so they cannot harm each other.

Hens have another use—producing eggs. In modern factory farming, hens are viewed as little more than "converting machines" that transform raw material (feed) into a finished product (eggs). Peter Singer describes the technology employed to rationalize egg production:

> The cages are stacked in tiers, with food and water troughs running along the rows, filled automatically from a central supply. They have sloping wire floors. The slope . . . makes it more difficult for the birds to stand comfortably, but it causes the eggs to roll to the front of the cage where they can easily be collected . . . in the more modern plants, carried by conveyor belt to a packing plant. . . . The excrement drops through [the wire floor] and can be allowed to pile up for many months until it is all removed in a single operation.[29]

This obviously imposes great control over the production of eggs by hens and is a very efficient way to produce eggs; it also leads to a more predictable supply and more uniform quality.

Other animals—pigs, lambs, steer, and calves especially—are raised in similar settings. To prevent their muscles from developing, which toughens the veal, calves are immediately confined to tiny stalls where they cannot exercise and, as they grow in size, may not even be able to turn around. Being kept in stalls also prevents the calves from eating grass that would cause their meat to lose its pale color. The stalls are kept free of straw, which, if eaten by the calves, would also darken the meat. "They are fed a totally liquid diet, based on nonfat milk powder with added vitamins, minerals, and growth-promoting drugs," says Peter Singer in his book, *Animal Liberation*.[30] To make sure the calves take in the maximum amount of food, they are given no water, which forces them to keep drinking their liquid food. By rigidly controlling the size of the stall and the diet, veal producers can maximize two quantifiable objectives—the production of the largest amount of meat in the shortest possible time and the creation of the tenderest, whitest, and therefore most desirable veal.

Thus, the production of chicken, eggs, and meat has witnessed a transition from more human small farms and ranches to nonhuman technologies. These technologies obviously lead to greater control over the process by which animals produce meat, thereby increasing the efficiency, calculability, and predictability of meat production. In addition, they exert control over farm workers. For example, left to their own devices, ranchers might feed young steer too little or the wrong food or permit them too much exercise. In fact, in the rigidly controlled factory ranch, human ranch hands (and their unpredictabilities) are virtually eliminated.

Nonhuman technologies have also affected how people cook food. Technologies such as ovens with a temperature probe "decide" when food is done for the cook. Many ovens, coffee makers, and other appliances can now turn themselves on and off. The instructions on all kinds of packaged foods dictate precisely how to prepare and cook the food. Premixed products, such as Mrs. Dash eliminate the need for the cook to come up with creative combinations of seasonings. Nissin Foods' new Super Boil soup is "the soup that cooks itself!" There is a special compartment in the bottom of the can of soup. A turn of a key starts a chemical reaction that eventually boils the soup.[31] Even the cookbook, now old-fashioned, was designed to take creativity away from the cook, who would normally flavor to taste, offering in its place the recipes' rigid guidelines. All of the above exert control over the cook ("customer"), the process of cooking, and the food (product).

Just as in the production and cooking of food, nonhuman technologies have come to control the sale of food. Take, for example, some recent developments at the site in which most food is sold these days—the supermarket. In the past, prices were marked: the supermarket checker had to read prices marked on food products and enter them into the cash register. As with all human activities, the process was slow, with a chance of human error. To counter these problems, many supermarkets have installed optical scanners. A mechanical scanner "reads" a code preprinted on each item. Each code number calls up a price already entered into the computer that controls the modern cash register. This nonhuman technology has thus reduced the number and sophistication of the tasks performed by the checker. Only the less skilled tasks, such as scanning the food and bagging it, remain. In other words, the work performed by the supermarket checker has been "deskilled"—that is, a decline has occurred in the amount of skill required for the job.

The next step at supermarket checkout stands is to have the customer do the scanning, thereby eliminating the need for a checkout clerk. The developer of one of these systems predicted that "within five years, self-service grocery technology could be as pervasive as the automatic cash machines used by bank customers."[32] In fact, a suburban Maryland Safeway has instituted such a technology. To make things easier, this Safeway provides its customers with a brochure entitled, "Checkout for Yourself Just How Easy It Is." (Of course, you might ask, Easy for whom?) Here are the three "easy" steps for customers to perform:

1. Pass the item's barcode over the scanner. Wait for beep. Place item on conveyor belt.

2. When you are finished scanning all items, touch END ORDER button on screen.

3. Pick up receipt at the end of the lane. Proceed to the pay station.

Like the scanner itself, such militaristic orders exert great control over the customer.[33]

Self-checkout is also linked to many other aspects of McDonaldization, such as greater efficiency. One customer, apparently a strong believer in McDonaldization, said of the system, "It's quick, easy and efficient. . . . You get in and out in a hurry."[34] The new systems that allow customers to pay with credit cards may even eliminate the need for cashiers. Thus, self-check-out also involves passing more and more work on to the customer. Indeed, after scanning, the customers must bag their own groceries.

Supermarket scanners also give the supermarket other kinds of control over customers. Before the scanner, prices were marked on all products, and customers could examine their purchases and see how much each item cost; they could also check the price on each item to be sure that they were not being overcharged at the cash register. With scanners, prices no longer appear on goods. In an increasing number of states, it is almost impossible for the consumer to keep tabs on the checkers.

Supermarkets also control shoppers with food placement. For example, supermarkets take pains to put foods children find attractive in places where youngsters can readily grab them (for example, low on the shelves). Also, what a market chooses to feature through sale prices and strategic placement in the store profoundly affects what is purchased. Manufacturers and wholesalers battle one another for coveted display positions, such as at the front of the market. Foods placed in these positions will likely sell far more than they would if they were relegated to their usual positions.

Marketing and Sales

The shopping mall exerts great control over shops and shopkeepers. Before allowing shops to open, mall developers often must approve their design, logo, colors, and even names. Once open, mall managers proliferate rules and regulations and enforce them on shopkeepers. Security people inspect shops and take note of those that violate the rules (for example, opening or closing a few minutes early or late). Persistent violators may be expelled from the mall. Efforts are also made to exclude controversial groups.

Malls also exert control over customers, especially children and young adults, who are programmed by the mass media to be avid consumers. Malls operate in a way that encourages people to make them an integral part of their lives. For instance, parents often visit the mall because it provides them with a safe and controlled environment, safer than the streets. With mall-going a deeply ingrained habit, some people are reduced to what Kowinski calls "zombies" shopping the malls hour after hour, weekend after weekend.[35]

Telemarketing is an increasingly popular sales device. Many people receive calls several times a day from telemarketers trying to sell them something. Those who work in these telemarketing "factories" usually have scripts they must follow unerringly. The scripts are designed to handle most foreseeable contingencies. Supervisors often listen in on solicitations to make sure employees follow the correct procedures. With requirements for the number of calls made and sales completed in a given time, if employees fail to meet the quotas, they may be fired summarily.

Similar control is exerted over the "phoneheads" who work for many companies, including those who make reservations for United Airlines. Every minute spent on the job must be logged, with each moment away from the phone justified. Employees even have to punch a "potty button" on the phone to let management know of their intentions. Supervisors sit in an elevated "tower" in the middle of the reservations floor, "observing like guards the movements of every operator in the room." They also monitor phone calls to make sure that employees say and do what they are supposed to. This control is part of a larger process of:

> omnipresent supervision increasingly taking hold in so many work-
> places—not just airline reservations centers but customer service
> departments and data-processing businesses where computers make
> possible an exacting level of employee scrutiny.[36]

The people who deal with the representatives of these businesses usu-ally deal with automatons. Said one employee of United Airlines, "My body became an extension of the computer terminal that I typed the reservations into. I came to feel emptied of self."[37] Following the usual progression, instead of having people solicit us over the phone, some companies now use computer calls.[38] Computer voices are far more predictable and control-lable than even the most rigidly controlled human operator. Indeed, in our increasingly McDonaldized society, I have had some of my most "interest-ing" conversations with such computer voices.

Beyond these calls, some computers can respond to the human voice via voice recognition systems. A person receiving a collect call might be asked by the computer voice whether she will accept the charges. The computer voice requests, "Please say yes or no." While efficient and cost-saving, such a system is anonymous and dehumanizing:

> The person senses that he cannot use free-flowing speech. He's being
> constrained. The computer is controlling him. It can be simply
> frustrating. . . . People adapt to it, but only by filing it away subcon-
> sciously as another annoyance of living in our technological world.[39]

In addition, people are daily bombarded by a mountain of computer-ized letters, or "junk mail."[40] Great pains are sometimes taken to make a letter seem personal, even though in most cases it is fairly obvious that a computer has generated the letter from a database of names. These letters are full of the kind of false fraternization described earlier in the case of the Roy Rogers' workers. For example, the letters often adopt a friendly, per-sonal tone designed to lead people to believe that the leader of some busi-ness has fretted over the fact that they haven't shopped in his or her department store or used his or her credit card in the past few months. For example, a friend of mine recently received a letter from a franchise, The

Lube Center, a few days after he had his car lubricated (note the use of the first name and the "deep" personal concern):

> Dear Ken:
>
> We want to THANK YOU for choosing The Lube Center for all of your car's fluid needs. . . .
>
> We strongly recommend that you change your oil on a regular basis. . . . We will send you a little reminder card. . . . This *will help remind* you when your car is next due to be serviced. . . .
>
> We spend the time and energy to make sure that our employees are trained properly to give you the service that you *deserve*. . . .
>
> > Sandy Grindstaff/Randall S. Simpson
> > The Lube Center Management
> > [Italics added.]

Also, several years ago, I received the following letter from a congressman from Long Island even though I live in Maryland. Though I had never met Congressman Downey and knew nothing about him, this didn't prevent him from writing me a "personal" letter:

> Dear George:
>
> It is hard to believe, but I am running for my NINTH term in Congress! . . .
>
> When I think back over the 8,660 votes I've cast. . . . I realize how many battles *we've shared*.
>
> Please let me know that I can count on *you*.
>
> > Sincerely,
> > *Tom* Downey (Italics added.)

A *Washington Post* correspondent offers the following critique of false friendliness in junk mail:

> By dropping in peoples' names and little tidbits gleaned from databases hither and yon in their direct mail pitches, these marketing organizations are trying to create the illusion of intimacy. In reality, these technologies conspire to *corrupt and degrade intimacy*. They cheat, substituting the insertable fact for the genuine insight. These pitches end up with their own synthetic substitutes for the real thing."[41]

However false it may be, such junk mail is designed to exert control over customers by getting them to take desired courses of action.

Marketing, of course, is not restricted to goods. Even religion and politics are being marketed today and are therefore subjected to McDonaldization.

For example, religion is marketing itself through television.[42] The Roman Catholic Church has gotten into the act with its Vatican Television Center. More generally, instead of worshipping with a human preacher, millions of worshippers now "interact" with a televised image. Television permits preachers to reach far more people than they could in a conventional church; thereby they can exert, or so they hope, greater control over what people believe and do. TV preachers use the full panoply of techniques developed by media experts to control their viewers. Thus, some TV preachers use a format much like that of the talk shows hosted by Jay Leno or David Letterman. Jokes, orchestras, singers, and guests all entertain the viewer to better communicate the preacher's message and, not insignificantly, to extract enormous contributions. Here is the way one observer describes Vatican television: "The big advantage to the Vatican of having its own television operation . . . is that they can put their own spin on anything they produce. If you give them the cameras and give them access, they are in control."[43]

A similar point can be made about politics, also dramatically affected by nonhuman technologies. Again, the most obvious example is the use of television to market politicians and manipulate voters. Indeed, most people never see a politician except on TV, most likely in a firmly controlled format designed to communicate the exact message and image desired by the politicians and their media advisers. President Ronald Reagan raised political marketing to an art form in the 1980s. On many occasions, visits were set up and TV images arranged so that the viewers and potential voters received precisely the visual message intended by Reagan's media advisers. Most of Reagan's TV appearances were carefully managed to be sure that the right message was communicated. Conversely, press conferences were held to a minimum because the questions and many of the answers could not be determined in advance.

Clearly, the future will bring with it an increasing number of nonhuman technologies with greater ability to control people. For example, such military hardware as "smart bombs" adjust their trajectories without human intervention. In the future, smart bombs may be developed that scan an array of targets and "decide" which one to hit. Perhaps the next great step will be the expansion of artificial intelligence, which gives machines the apparent ability to think and make decisions as humans do.[44] Artificial intelligence promises many benefits in a wide range of areas (medicine, for example). However, it also constitutes an enormous step in taking skills away from people. In effect, more and more of people's ability to think will be taken from them and built into nonhuman technology.

Conclusion

The fourth dimension of McDonaldization is the replacement of human with nonhuman technology. There are many objectives involved in the development of nonhuman technologies, but the most important from the point of view of this book is increased control over the uncertainties created by employees. In controlling employees, nonhuman technologies also lead to greater control over work-related processes as well as the finished product. The ultimate in control is reached when employees are replaced by nonhuman technologies such as robots. Nonhuman technologies are also employed to control the uncertainties created by customers. The objective is to make them more pliant participants in McDonaldized processes.

7

The Irrationality of Rationality

Traffic Jams on Those "Happy Trails"

M cDonaldization has swept across much of the social landscape because it offers increased efficiency, predictability, calculability, and control through the substitution of nonhuman for human technology. It also offers many more specific advantages in numerous settings. Despite these advantages, I have shown some of the drawbacks of McDonaldization in the preceding chapters. This chapter presents the great costs of McDon- aldization more systematically. Rational systems inevitably spawn a series of irrationalities that limit, eventually compromise, and perhaps even undermine their rationality.

At the most general level, the irrationality of rationality is simply a label for many of the negative aspects and effects of McDonaldization. More specifically, this irrationality can be seen as the opposite of rationality and its several dimensions. That is, McDonaldization can be viewed as leading to inefficiency, unpredictability, incalculability, and loss of control.[1] Most specifically, irrationality means that rational systems are *unreasonable systems* that deny the humanity, the human reason, of the people who work within them or are served by them. In other words, rational systems are dehumanizing. Please note that though the terms *rationality* and *reason* are often used interchangeably, in this book they are viewed as antithetical phenomena.

However, before I discuss the main irrationality of rationality—dehumanization—I will present some of the lesser irrationalities, beginning with inefficiency.

Inefficiency: Long Lines at the Checkout

Rational systems, contrary to their promise, often end up being quite inefficient. For instance, in fast-food restaurants, long lines of people often form at the counters, or parades of cars snake by the drive-through windows. What is purported to be an efficient way to obtain a meal often turns out to be quite inefficient.

To combat this inefficiency, McDonald's is now considering a private television network in its stores. The network would beam entertainment, news, and advertisements to a daily audience estimated to be fifteen million people. A similar effort, Checkout Channel for people waiting in supermarket checkout lines, is also under development. On the one hand, this represents another forward step in rationalization because now people will be able to do two things at once—wait in line *and* watch television. On the other hand, and of central interest here, this represents a tacit admission that people are waiting in line for their fast food—that fast food isn't so fast, that these efficient systems aren't so efficient. Thus, an executive of the firm developing the new television network says, "One of the biggest customer concerns is the problem of queuing. . . . Anything a retailer can do to lessen the perceived wait is going to be a benefit."[2]

The fast-food restaurant is far from the only aspect of a McDonaldized society that exhibits inefficiency. Interestingly, even the vaunted Japanese industry has its inefficiencies. Take the "just-in-time" system discussed in chapter 3. Because this system often requires that parts be delivered several times a day, the streets and highways are cluttered with trucks. Thus, people are often late for work or for business appointments, resulting in lost productivity. The situation has grown even worse now because Japanese convenience stores, supermarkets, and department stores have also begun to use a just-in-time system, bringing even greater numbers of delivery trucks onto the streets. But the irrationalities go beyond traffic jams and missed appointments. All these trucks waste fuel, very expensive in Japan, and contribute greatly to air pollution.[3]

Here is the way columnist Richard Cohen describes another example of inefficiency in the McDonaldized world:

> Oh Lord, with each advance of the computer age, I was told I would benefit. But with each "benefit," I wind up doing more work. This is the ATM [automated teller machine] rule of life. . . . I was told—nay promised—that I could avoid lines at the bank and make deposits or withdrawals any time of the day. Now, there are lines at the ATMs, the bank seems to take a percentage of whatever I withdraw or deposit, and, of course, I'm doing what tellers (remember them?) used to do. Probably, with the new phone, I'll have to climb telephone poles in the suburbs during ice storms.[4]

Cohen underscores at least three different irrationalities—rational systems are not less expensive, they force people to do unpaid work, and, most important here, they are often inefficient. It might be more efficient to deal with a human teller, either in the bank or drive-through window, than to wait in line at an ATM. For many, it would be far more efficient to prepare a meal at home than to pack the family in the car, drive to McDonald's, load up on food, and then drive home again. This may not be true of some meals cooked at home from scratch, but it is certainly true of TV dinners, microwave meals, or full-course meals brought in from the supermarket. Yet many people persist in the belief, fueled by propaganda from the fast-food restaurants, that it is more efficient to eat there than to eat at home.

Though these and other elements of a rational society may be inefficient for the customer, they are quite efficient for purveyors of goods and services. Banks gain efficiency when people line up at an ATM (unless it breaks down or runs out of money) rather than call on employees for help. McDonald's benefits in a similar way when people use the drive-through window, taking all their wrappings and mess with them.

Supermarkets find it efficient to pack themselves full of foods of all types. A Giant supermarket in Virginia has about 45,000 different products strung out along twenty-three aisles. In addition, the store includes a "florist shop, a wine store, a Fanny May candy store, a deli, a soup-and-salad bar, and machines that dispense cold soda and hot coffee, just in case a shopper's strength starts to wane."[5] However, is it efficient for consumers in search of a loaf of bread and a quart of milk to wend their way through this labyrinth? Of course not, which partly accounts for the popularity of chains such as Seven-Eleven.

Although the forces of McDonaldization trumpet their greater efficiency, they never tell us whom the system is more efficient for. Most of the gains in efficiency go to those who push rationalization. People need to ask: Efficient for whom? Is it efficient for consumers to push their own food over the supermarket scanner and then bag it themselves? Is it efficient for people to pump their own gasoline? Is it efficient for them to push numerous combinations of telephone numbers before they speak to a human voice? Most often, people will find that such systems are not efficient for them.

Similarly, rational systems impose a double standard on employees. Those at the top of an organization impose rationalization on those who work at or near the bottom of the system—the assembly-line worker, the counterperson at McDonald's. The owners, franchisees, top managers, want to control subordinates through the imposition of rational systems. However, they want their own positions to be as free of rational constraints—as nonrational—as possible. They need to be free to be creative, but not their underlings. Subordinates are to follow blindly the rules, regulations, and other structures of the rational system. Thus, the goal is to impose efficiency on subordinates while those in charge remain as creative (and often as inefficient) as possible.

Besides being inefficient, many McDonaldized institutions suffer from low productivity. This means that, as a rule, workers in such settings produce relatively few goods or services per hour of work. In the main, these settings are labor-intensive, that is, the organization needs large numbers of workers to accomplish its goals. The best example is the fast-food restaurant with its hordes of teenagers working relatively unproductively. The fast-food restaurant can tolerate this low level of productivity because it pays most of its employees the minimum wage. Of course, elements of the McDonaldizing society, such as banks that rely on ATMs, do not suffer from this problem. Further, it seems likely that this problem will be solved as more and more rational institutions use increasingly sophisticated technologies either to replace unproductive workers or to render them more productive.

In general, McDonaldized institutions have also not developed notable new products. Please recall Ray Kroc's failures in this realm, notably the Hulaburger. As a general rule, such systems excel at selling familiar products and services in shiny new settings or packages. For instance, the fast-food restaurant wraps that prosaic hamburger in bright packages and sells it in a carnival-like atmosphere. This point extends to many other manifestations of McDonaldization. For example, Jiffy Lube and its imitators sell people nothing more than the same old oil change and lube job, but with well-known logos and bright colors.

High Cost: Better off at Home

McDonaldization does not ordinarily save people money. For example, a small soda costs a franchise owner eleven cents, but it is sold for eighty-five cents.[6] A fast-food meal for a family of four might easily cost over twenty dollars, which would go further spent on ingredients for a home-cooked meal.

As Cohen demonstrated in the case of ATMs, people must pay extra to deal with the inhumanity and inefficiency of a rationalized society. The great success and profitability of McDonaldized systems, the rush to extend them to ever new sectors of society, and the fact that so many people want to get into such businesses indicate that these systems generate huge profits.

Bob Garfield noted the expense of McDonaldized activities in an article entitled, "How I Spent (and Spent and Spent) My Disney Vacation." Garfield took his family of four to Walt Disney World and found that it might be more aptly named "Expense World." The five-day vacation cost $1,700; admission to Disney World alone cost $551.30. He calculates that in the five days, they had less than seven hours of "fun, fun, fun. That amounts to $261 c.p.f.h. (cost per fun hour)." Because most of his time in the Magic Kingdom was spent riding buses, "queuing up and shlepping from place to place, the 17 attractions we saw thrilled us for a grand total of 44 minutes."[7] Thus, what is thought to be an inexpensive family vacation turns out be quite costly.

The Illusion of Fun: Ha, Ha, the Stock Market Just Crashed

If it really isn't efficient, and it really isn't cheap, then what does McDonaldization, more specifically, the fast-food restaurant, offer people? Why has it been such a worldwide success? For one thing, it offers the *illusion* of efficiency and frugality. As long as people *believe* it, the actual situation matters little. Perhaps more important, what fast-food restaurants really seem to offer, as Stan Luxenberg has pointed out, is fun (or Garfield's "fun, fun, fun"). As another observer notes, "Restaurants have become a form of entertainment." Today's diner often looks for theater more than food. This is true even of those who frequent upscale restaurants: "I would rather eat mediocre food in a fabulous room than sit somewhere dull and boring and eat fabulous food. . . . I'm looking for decor, scale, *theatrics*, a lot going on."[8] Fast-food restaurants and others are really amusement parks for food, with their bright colors and garish signs and symbols. McDonald's even uses a ubiquitous clown, Ronald McDonald, and an array of cartoon characters to remind people that fun awaits them on their next visit.

Some outlets even offer playgrounds and children's rides. Further, as part of its continuing attempt to diversify, McDonald's actually went into the playground business. Its wholly owned subsidiary, Leaps & Bounds, Inc., eventually opened forty-nine playgrounds before it was sold to Discovery Zone in September, 1994. Begun in 1989, Discovery Zone now has 330 playgrounds nationwide. In exchange for Leaps & Bounds, McDonald's received a 10% stake in Blockbuster, the majority owner of Discovery Zone.[9] The playground equipment at Leaps & Bounds was derived from the sort of equipment found in the playgrounds at many McDonald's restaurants. A McDonald's spokesperson said that the idea grew out of the advertising theme of "food, folks and fun . . . We just turned it around and put the fun first."[10] There are more than a few cynics who would say that McDonald's *always* put fun before food.

In another recent development, McDonald's in Japan (there were over 1000 McDonald's restaurants in Japan at the end of 1993[11]) is joining forces with Toys "Я" Us. A number of Toys "Я" Us outlets to be built will include McDonald's restaurants. In aligning itself more closely with playgrounds and toys, McDonald's is making it increasingly clear that it is in the business of providing "fun."[12]

Furthermore, fast-food restaurants serve the kinds of finger foods bought at the stands in an amusement park. In what may be termed the "cotton candy principle," people will buy, and even pay comparatively high prices for, a few pennies worth of food as long as it has a strong, pleasant, and familiar flavor. Indeed, as Luxenberg shows, what fast-food restaurants often sell is "salty candy."[13] One of the secrets of the McDonald's french fry is that it is coated with *both* salt and sugar.[14] People taste the salt and the sugar, but rarely if ever the potato slice, little more than an excuse for the rest.

McDonald's offers a kind of "public theater."[15] Instead of a private, folded menu, McDonald's offers a marquee that, like the movie options at the local cineplex, presents the diner's alternatives. In this, and many other ways, dining becomes a public rather than a private and personal experience, at times even a public spectacle.

Supermarkets have also increasingly become entertainment centers, selling more and more "fun foods" such as Count Chocula and Teenage Mutant Ninja Turtles cereals, Snausages in a Blanket (dog food), and Funny Feet fruit snacks. As one observer said,

> When The Shopper was young, Americans used to sing, "There's no business like show business," but they don't sing it much anymore, probably because just about every business is like show business now. Supermarkets are certainly no exception. These days, supermarkets are like theme parks.[16]

The owner of large supermarkets in Connecticut invested a half million dollars in cartoon characters for his stores and has people dressed as Daisy Duck wandering through them. Said the owner, "This is a people business. Customers are happy here. People come here to shop together with friends because it's fun."[17]

All this is part of the United States' obsession with amusement. Neil Postman, in his aptly titled book, *Amusing Ourselves to Death*, argues that Las Vegas has become the symbol of this obsession because it "is a city entirely devoted to the idea of entertainment, and as such proclaims the spirit of a culture in which all public discourse increasingly takes the form of entertainment."[18] If Las Vegas, with its McDonaldized gambling, symbolizes the obsession with entertainment, then McDonald's symbolizes the emphasis on entertainment in the fast-food industry.

Entertainment is also central to the shopping mall. Malls are designed to be fantasy worlds, theatrical settings for what Kowinski calls "the Retail Drama."[19] Both consumers and mall employees play important roles in this drama. After all, many Americans' favorite form of entertainment is shopping. The mall is loaded with props, with a backdrop of ever-present Muzak to soothe the savage shopper. Some of the props remain all year, while others (for example, Christmas decorations) are brought in for special occasions and promotions. Then there are the restaurants, bars, movie theaters, and exercise centers to add to the fun. On weekends, clowns, balloons, magicians, bands, and the like further entertain those on their way from one shop to another. Faced by the threat of shop-at-home alternatives, one marketing expert said, "You've got to make your centers more fun."[20] Thus, people can expect shopping centers to become an even more integral part of show business.

That future has arrived with the coming of the Mall of America in Bloomington, Minnesota.[21] At the center of the Mall of America is a huge amusement park, Knott's Camp Snoopy, including a full-size roller coaster, an arcade, and shooting galleries. A system of acrylic tubes allows visitors to walk *through* an aquarium. Golf Mountain provides an eighteen-hole miniature-golf course on several levels. The mall also houses the largest Lego structure ever built. There is a huge sports bar, a Hooters, and a Planet Hollywood. And, of course, there is a movie theater—with fourteen screens! Said one critic, "Mall of America is not a mall, it's a circus."[22]

Journalism has also become more geared to entertainment. For example, *Business Week*, a rationalized magazine, is designed to be not only more efficient to read than the *Wall Street Journal*, but also more enjoyable. An ad for *Business Week* claims, "We don't just inform you but we entertain you." Two critics say of this advertisement, "Is *Business Week* really serious? Are we to expect the following: Ha Ha Ha, Ha! The stock market just crashed! What a laugh! . . . Your company is going down the tubes. What fun!"[23] Similarly, television news is often described as "infotainment" because it combines news and show business.

The Illusion of Reality: Even the "Singers" Aren't Real

Many aspects of a McDonaldized society involve deceptive settings and events (Daniel Boorstin's "pseudo events"[24]), including the package tour, the modern campground, the international villages at amusement parks such as Busch Gardens, the computer phone call, and false fraternization at Roy Rogers and Nutri/System. All of this may be viewed as part of Ian Mitroff and Warren Bennis's "unreality industry."[25] By this, they mean the fact that whole industries attempt to produce and market unreality. McDonald's, for example, creates the illusion that people are having fun, that they are getting lots of french fries, and that they are getting a bargain when they purchase their meal. In a famous example of such unreality, Milli Vanilli's two "singers" did not actually sing on their record album.[26] From the wide range of unrealities, here are a few examples from the supermarket where fewer and fewer things are what they appear to be:

- Sizzlean (fake "bacon") is made out of beef and turkey, and kosher bacon has no pork.
- Molly McButter and Butter Buds have no butter.
- The turkey flavor in the frozen turkey TV dinner may well be artificial since the natural flavor was removed during processing.
- The lemon smell in the laundry detergent usually does not come from lemons.

Such unreality, along with various pseudo events, has become integral to McDonaldized society.

Dehumanization: Getting Hosed at "Trough and Brew"

The main reason to think of McDonaldization as irrational, and ultimately unreasonable, is that it tends to become a dehumanizing system that may become antihuman or even destructive of human beings.

Health and Environmental Hazards

There are a number of ways progressive rationalization has threatened the health, and perhaps the lives, of people. One example is the danger posed by the content of most fast food: a lot of fat, cholesterol, salt, and sugar. Such meals are the last things many Americans need, suffering as many of them do from obesity, high cholesterol levels, high blood pressure, and perhaps diabetes. Fast-food restaurants also help create eating habits in children that contribute to the development of these, and other, health problems later in life. With their appeal to children, fast-food restaurants are creating not only life-long devotees of fast food, but also people who may well grow addicted to diets high in salt, sugar, and fat.[27]

Attacks against the fast-food industry's harmful effects on health have mounted over the years. As a result, many of the franchises have been forced to respond in various ways. Salads have been one response, although the dressings for them are often loaded with salt and fat. Some fast-food restaurants have ceased cooking french fries in beef tallow and instead use less-cholesterol-laden vegetable oil. Though these restaurants have had to adapt to increasing health concerns, the typical McDonald's meal of a Big Mac, large fries, and shake has more than 1,000 calories, loaded with salt, sugar, and fat.

McDonaldization poses even more immediate health threats. Regina Schrambling links various diseases, especially salmonella, to the rationalization of food production:

> Salmonella proliferated in the poultry industry only after beef became a four-letter word and Americans decided they wanted a chicken in every pot every night. But birds aren't like cars: you can't just speed up the factory line to meet demand. Something has got to give—and in this case it's been safety. Birds that are rushed to fryer size, then killed, gutted, and plucked at high speed in vast quantities are not going to be the cleanest food in the supermarket.[28]

Schrambling also links salmonella to the more rational production of eggs, fruit, and vegetables. More generally, she traces a wide range of illnesses to various rationalized production systems.[29]

McDonaldized systems pose a health hazard not only to humans, but also to pets. Chains of supermarket-like pet stores such as Petstuff and Petsmart have been employing automatic hair dryers to groom dogs. Unfortunately, some dogs have been locked in cages and under the dryers for too long. Several have died or been injured in the process. Said the founder of a watchdog group, Grooming Accidents, Supervision and Prevention (GASP): "The whole notion of leaving a dog unsupervised with an electrical heater blowing makes no sense. They are treating animals like cars in an assembly line."[30]

One Marxist critic, Tim Luke, has recently attacked the invasion of Russia by McDonald's as well as other aspects of a McDonaldized society. He labels what is being created a "McGulag Archipelago." The "Gulag Archipelago" refers to the elaborate system of prison camps in the former Soviet Union. Thus, Luke implies that McDonaldization is a new kind of system to imprison Russian citizens, in other words, a new kind of "iron cage." Luke also attacks McDonald's for a variety of other reasons, such as being "nutritionally questionable," "waste-intensive," and "environmentally-destructive."[31]

The fast-food industry has run afoul not only of nutritionists, but also of environmentalists. It produces an enormous amount of trash, some of which is nonbiodegradable. The litter from fast-food meals has created a public eyesore across the countryside. It takes hundreds, if not thousands, of square miles of forest to provide the paper needed each year by McDonald's alone.[32] Whole forests are being devoured by the fast-food industry, even though some paper containers have been replaced by styrofoam and other products. In fact, the current trend may be back to paper products because even greater criticism has been leveled at the fast-food industry for its widespread use of styrofoam. Virtually indestructible, styrofoam piles up in landfills, creating mountains of waste that simply remain there for years, if not forever.

Dehumanization of Customers and Employees

As shown, the fast-food restaurant offers its employees a dehumanizing work setting. Said Burger King workers, "A moron could learn this job, it's so easy" and "Any trained monkey could do this job."[33] Workers can use only a small portion of their skills and abilities. This is irrational from the organization's viewpoint, because it could obtain much more from its employees for the money (however negligible) it pays them. This is one of the secrets of the success of Japanese industry. The Japanese have developed a number of mechanisms, such as quality circles, to elicit a wide variety of contributions from their employees.

The minimal skill demands of the fast-food restaurant are also irrational from the employee's perspective. Besides not using all their skills, employees are not allowed to think and be creative on the job. This leads to a high level of resentment, job dissatisfaction, alienation, absenteeism, and turnover among those who work in fast-food restaurants.[34] In fact, the fast-food industry has the highest turnover rate—approximately 300% a year—

of any industry in the United States. That means that the average fast-food worker lasts only about four months; the entire work force of the fast-food industry turns over approximately three times a year.

Although the simple and repetitive nature of the jobs makes it relatively easy to replace workers who leave, such a high turnover rate is still undesirable from the organization's perspective. It would clearly be better to keep employees longer. The costs involved in turnover, such as hiring and training, greatly increase with extraordinarily high turnover rates.

The fast-food restaurant also dehumanizes the customer. By eating on a sort of assembly line, the diner is reduced to an automaton made to rush through a meal with little gratification derived from the dining experience or from the food itself. The best that can usually be said is that it is efficient and it is over quickly.

Some customers might even feel as if they are being fed like livestock in a highly rationalized manner. This point was made on TV a number of years ago in a *Saturday Night Live* skit, "Trough and Brew," a parody of a small fast-food chain called "Burger and Brew." In the skit, some young executives learn that a new fast-food restaurant called Trough and Brew has opened, and they decide to try it for lunch. When they enter the restaurant, bibs are tied around their necks. Then, they discover what resembles a pig trough filled with chili and periodically refilled by a waitress scooping new supplies from a bucket. The customers bend over, stick their heads into the trough, and lap up the chili as they move along the trough making high-level business decisions. Every so often they come up for air and lap some beer from the communal "brew basin." After they have finished their "meal," they pay their bills "by the head." Since their faces are smeared with chili, they are literally "hosed off" before they leave the restaurant. The young executives are last seen being herded out of the restaurant, which is being closed for a half-hour so that it can be "hosed down." *Saturday Night Live* was clearly ridiculing the fact that fast-food restaurants tend to treat their customers like lower animals.

Customers are also dehumanized by scripted interactions, and other efforts to make interactions uniform. "Uniformity is incompatible when human interactions are involved. Human interactions that are mass-produced may strike consumers as dehumanizing if the routinization is obvious or manipulative if it is not."[35] Dehumanization occurs when prefabricated interactions take the place of authentic human relationships.

Garfield's critique of Walt Disney World provides another example of dehumanized customers:

I actually believed there was real fun and real imagination in store only to be confronted with an extruded, injection-molded, civil engineered brand of fantasy, which is to say: no fantasy at all.

From the network of chutes and corrals channeling people into attractions, to the chillingly programmed Stepford Wives demeanor of the employees, to the compulsively litter-free grounds, to the generalized North Korean model Socialist Society sense of totalitarian order, to the utterly passive nature of the entertainment itself, Disney turns out to be the very antithesis of fantasy, a remarkable technospectacle. . . .

Far from liberating the imagination, Disney succeeds mainly in confining it. Like the conveyor "cars" and "boats" that pull you along steel tracks through "Snow White" and "World of Motion" and the "Speedway" rides, Disney is a plodding, precise, computer controlled mechanism pulling an estimated 30 million visitors along the same calculated, unvarying, meticulously engineered entertainment experience. It occupies its customers without engaging them. It appeals to everybody while challenging nobody. . .

Imagine, for example, a fake submergence in a fake submarine for a fake voyage past fake coral and fake seafood, knowing full well that there are two magnificent aquariums within a 70-minute drive of your house.[36]

Thus, instead of being a creative and imaginative human experience, Disney World turns out to be an uncreative, unimaginative, and ultimately inhuman experience.

Negative Effect on Human Relationships

Another dehumanizing aspect of fast-food restaurants is that they minimize contact among human beings. For example, the nature of the fast-food restaurant makes the relationships between employees and customers fleeting at best. Because the average employee works part-time and stays only a few months, even the regular customer can rarely develop a personal relationship with him or her. All but gone are the days when one got to know well a waitress at a diner or the short order cook at a local greasy spoon. Few are the places where an employee knows who you are and knows what you are likely to order.

Contact between workers and customers is very short. It takes little time at the counter to order, receive the food, and pay for it. Both employees and customers are likely to feel rushed and to want to move on, customers to their dinner and employees to the next order.[37] There is virtually no time for customer and counterperson to interact in such a context. This is even truer of the drive-through window, where thanks to the speedy service and the physical barriers, the server is even more distant.

These highly impersonal and anonymous relationships are heightened by the training of employees to interact in a staged, scripted, and limited manner with customers. Thus, the customers may feel that they are dealing with automatons rather than with fellow human beings. For their part, the customers are supposed to be, and often are, in a hurry, so they also have little to say to the McDonald's employee. Indeed, it could be argued that one of the reasons the fast-food restaurants succeed is that they are in tune with our fast-paced and impersonal society (see chapter 8). People in the modern world want to get on with their business without unnecessary personal relationships. The fast-food restaurant gives them precisely what they want.

Not only the relationships between employee and customer, but other potential relationships are limited greatly. Because employees remain on the job for only a few months, satisfying personal relationships among employees are unlikely to develop. Again it is useful to contrast this with the Japanese case, where more permanent employment helps foster long-term relationships on the job. Furthermore, Japanese workers are likely to get together with one another after work hours and on weekends. The temporary and part-time character of jobs in fast-food restaurants largely eliminates the possibility of such personal relationships among employees.

Relationships among customers are largely curtailed as well. Although some McDonald's ads would have people believe otherwise, gone for the most part are the days when people met in the diner or cafeteria for coffee or a meal and lingered to socialize. Fast-food restaurants clearly do not encourage such socializing. If nothing else, the chairs by design make people uncomfortable, so that they move on quickly. The drive-through windows completely eliminate the possibility of interaction with other customers.

Because fast-food restaurants greatly restrict or even eliminate genuine fraternization, what people have left is either no human relationships or "false fraternization." Rule Number 17 for Burger King workers is "Smile at all times."[38] The Roy Rogers employees who used to say, "Happy trails" to me when I paid for my food really had no interest in what happened "on the trail." (In fact, come to think of it, they were really saying, in a polite way, "Get lost!") This phenomenon has been generalized to the many workers who say "Have a nice day" as customers depart. In fact, of course, they usually have no real interest in, or concern for, how the rest of a customer's day goes. Again, in a polite and ritualized way, they are really saying, "Get lost," or move on so someone else can be served.

At Nutri/System, counselors receive a list of things to do to keep dieters coming back. The counselors are urged to "greet client by name with enthusiasm." Knowing the client's name creates a false sense of friendliness, as does the "enthusiastic" greeting. Counselors are also urged to "converse with client in a *sensitive* manner." The counselors are provided with a small, glossy card entitled, "Personalized Approach at a Glance." The card rationalizes the personal greeting with pseudo-personalized responses to problematic situations. For example, if clients indicate that they feel they are receiving little support for the diet, the script urges the counselor to say, "I'm so glad to see you. I was thinking about you. How is the program going for you?" Is the counselor *really* glad to see the client? *Really* thinking about the client? *Really* concerned about how things are working out for the client? The answers to such questions are clear in a McDonaldized society.

Fast-food restaurants also tend to have negative effects on other human relationships. There is, for example, the effect on the family, especially the so-called "family meal." The fast-food restaurant is not conducive to a long, leisurely, conversation-filled dinnertime. Furthermore, as the children grow into their teens, the fast-food restaurant can lead to separate meals as the teens go at one time with their friends, and the parents go at another time. Of course, the drive-through window only serves to reduce further the possibility of a family meal. The family that gobbles its food while driving on to its next stop can hardly enjoy "quality time." Here is the way one journalist describes what is happening to the family meal:

> Do families who eat their suppers at the Colonel's, swinging on plastic seats, or however the restaurant is arranged, say grace before picking up a crispy brown chicken leg? Does dad ask junior what he did today as he remembers he forgot the piccalilli and trots through the crowds over to the counter to get some? Does mom find the atmosphere conducive to asking little Mildred about the problems she was having with third conjugation French verbs, or would it matter since otherwise the family might have been at home chomping down precooked frozen food, warmed in the microwave oven and watching "Hollywood Squares"?[39]

There is much talk these days about the disintegration of the family, and the fast-food restaurant may well be a crucial contributor to that disintegration.

In fact, as implied above, dinners at home may now not be much different from meals at the fast-food restaurant. Families tended to stop having lunch together by the 1940s and breakfast together by the 1950s. Today, the family dinner is following the same route. Even at home, the meal will probably not be what it once was. Following the fast-food model, people have ever more options to "graze," "refuel," nibble on this, or snack on that, rather than sit down at a formal meal. Also, because it may seem inefficient to do nothing but just eat, families are likely to watch television while they are eating. Furthermore, the din, to say nothing of the lure, of dinnertime TV programs such as *Wheel of Fortune* is likely to make it difficult for family members to interact with one another.

A key technology in the destruction of the family meal is the microwave oven and the vast array of microwavable foods it helped generate.[40] More than 70% of American households have a microwave oven. A *Wall Street Journal* poll indicated that Americans consider the microwave their favorite household product. In fact, the microwave in a McDonaldizing society is seen as an advance over the fast-food restaurant. Said one consumer researcher, "It has made even fast-food restaurants not seem fast because at home you don't have to wait in line." As a general rule, consumers demand meals that take no more than ten minutes to microwave, whereas in the past people were more often willing to spend a half hour or even an hour cooking dinner. This emphasis on speed has, of course, brought with it lower quality, but people do not seem to mind this loss: "We're just not as critical of food as we used to be."[41]

The speed of microwave cooking, as well as the wide variety of microwavable foods, make it possible for family members to eat at different times and places. Even children can "zap" their own meals with products such as "Kid's Kitchen," "Kid Cuisine," and "My Own Meals." As a result, "Those qualities of the family meal, the ones that imparted feelings of security and well-being, might be lost forever when food is 'zapped' or 'nuked' instead of cooked."[42]

The advances in microwave cooking continue. On some foods, plastic strips turn blue when the food is done. The industry has even promised strips that communicate cooking information directly to the microwave oven. "With cooking reduced to pushing a button, the kitchen may wind up as a sort of filling station. Family members will pull in, push a few buttons, fill up and leave. To clean up, all we need do is throw away plastic plates."[43] What is lost, of course, is the family meal; people need to decide whether they can afford the loss:

> The communal meal is our primary ritual for encouraging the family to gather together every day. If it is lost to us, we shall have to invent

new ways to be a family. It is worth considering whether the shared joy that food can provide is worth giving up.[44]

Homogenization

Another dehumanizing effect of the fast-food restaurant is that it has increased homogenization in the United States and, increasingly, throughout the world. This decline in diversity is manifest in the extension of the fast-food model to all sorts of ethnic foods. People are hard-pressed to find an authentically different meal in an ethnic fast-food chain. The food has been rationalized and compromised so that it is acceptable to the tastes of virtually all diners. Paradoxically, while fast-food restaurants have permitted far more people to experience ethnic food, the food that they eat has lost many of its distinguishing characteristics. The settings are also all modeled after McDonald's in one way or another.

The expansion of these franchises across the United States means that people find little difference between regions and between cities. Tourists find more familiarity and less diversity as they travel around the nation, and this is increasingly true on a global scale. Exotic settings are increasingly likely sites for American fast-food chains. The McDonald's and Kentucky Fried Chicken in Beijing are but two examples of this. Furthermore, in many nations, restaurant owners are applying the McDonald's model to native cuisine. In Paris, tourists may be shocked by the number of American fast-food restaurants there, but even more shocked by the incredible spread of indigenous forms such as the fast-food croissanterie. One would have thought that the French considered the croissant a sacred object and would have found it obscene to rationalize its manufacture and sale, but that is just what has happened. While the fast-food system has demeaned the quality of the croissant, the spread of such outlets throughout Paris indicates that many Parisians are willing to sacrifice quality for speed and efficiency. (And, you may ask, if the Parisian croissant can be tamed and transformed into a fast-food success, what food is safe?) In any case, the spread of American and indigenous fast food throughout much of the world causes less and less diversity from one setting to another. The human craving for new and diverse experiences is being limited, if not progressively destroyed, by the spread of fast-food restaurants. The craving for diversity is being supplanted by the desire for uniformity and predictability.

Just as the fast-food restaurants are leveling food differences, mail-order catalogues are eliminating seasonal differences. When Ellen Goodman received her Christmas catalogue just as fall was beginning, she critiqued this particular aspect of rationalization: "The creation of one national mail-order market has produced catalogues without the slightest respect for any season or region. Their holidays are now harvested, transported and chemically ripened on the way to your home. . . . I refuse to fast forward through the fall."[45] There is another irrationality here. Those who buy things through catalogues find that their deliveries are often late or they never arrive at all. Said the President of the Better Business Bureau of Metropolitan New York, "With mail order, the biggest problem is delivery and delay in delivery."[46]

Health Care: You're Just a Number

As has been made clear throughout this book, medicine is becoming progressively rationalized, that is, dominated by structures and institutions characterized by efficiency, predictability, calculability, and control through the substitution of nonhuman for human technology. Like all others, however, these rational systems bring with them a series of irrational consequences. That is not to say that prerationalized medicine is some sort of ideal to which people ought to return. For one thing, it is difficult, if not impossible, to turn back the process of rationalization. For another, medical practice in the past was rife with its own problems. Finally, although I focus on irrationalities here, rational medical systems also clearly have reasonable consequences. For example, advances in technology have improved medical practice and introduced lifesaving techniques. Control by third-party payers and the government may bring about greater control over spiraling medical costs and may benefit all those requiring medical care.

For the physician, the process of rationalization carries with it a series of irrationalities. At or near the top of the list is the shift in control away from the physician toward rationalized structures and institutions. The private practitioner of the past had a large degree of control over his or her work, with the major constraints being peer control as well as the needs and demands of patients. In rationalized medicine, external control increases and shifts to social structures and institutions. Not only is the physician more likely to be controlled by these structures and institutions, but also by managers and bureaucrats who are not themselves physicians. The ability of physicians to control their own work lives is declining. External control as a problem for physicians may manifest itself in increased levels of job dissatisfaction and alienation (perhaps even a turn toward unionization).

Rationalization often brings with it the removal of mystery or excitement from the work lives of physicians. Instead of relying on personal medical judgment in a given case, physicians increasingly tend to base their decision on rules, regulations, decisions of superiors, or technological imperatives. This, too, will likely increase job dissatisfaction and alienation among physicians.

The process of rationalization is likely to bring with it some degree of deprofessionalization of physicians. Professions are occupations that have the power to win and keep professional status. The erosion of physicians' power therefore, by definition, leads to a decline in their professional status. Such a loss is highly irrational from the physician's point of view.

From the patient's viewpoint, the rationalization of medicine causes a number of irrationalities. The drive for efficiency can make them feel like products on a medical assembly line. The effort to increase predictability will likely lead patients to lose personal relationships with physicians and other health professionals because rules and regulations lead physicians to treat all patients in essentially the same way. This is also true in hospitals, where instead of seeing the same nurse regularly, a patient may see many different nurses. The result, of course, is that such nurses never come to know their patients as individuals.

As a result of the emphasis on calculability, the patient is more likely to feel like a number in the system rather than a person. Minimizing time and maximizing profits may lead to a decline in the quality of health care provided to patients. Like physicians, patients are apt to be increasingly controlled by large-scale structures and institutions, which will probably appear to them as distant, uncaring, and impenetrable. Finally, patients are increasingly likely to interact with technicians and impersonal technologies. In fact, because more and more technologies may be purchased at the drug store, patients can test themselves and thereby cut out human contact with both physicians and technicians. Thus, the rationalization of medicine has increased the dehumanization and depersonalization of medical practice.

The ultimate irrationality of this rationalization would be the unanticipated consequences of a decline in the quality of medical practice and a deterioration in the health of patients. Increasingly rational medical systems, with their focus on lowering costs and increasing profits, may reduce the quality of health care, especially for the poorest members of society. At least some people may become sicker, and perhaps even die, because of the rationalization of medicine. Health in general may even decline. These possibilities can only be assessed in the future as the health-care system continues to rationalize. Since the health-care system will continue to rationalize, health professionals and their patients may need to learn how to control rational structures and institutions to ameliorate their irrational consequences.

Higher Education: It's Like Processing Meat

The modern university has, in various ways, become a highly irrational place. Many students and faculty members are put off by its huge, factorylike atmosphere. They may feel like automatons processed by the bureaucracy and computers, or even cattle run through a meat-processing plant. In other words, education in such settings can be a dehumanizing experience. The masses of students; large, impersonal dorms; and huge lecture classes make getting to know other students difficult. The large lectures, constrained tightly by the clock, make it virtually impossible to know professors personally. At best, students might get to know a graduate assistant teaching a discussion section. Grades may be derived from a series of machine-graded multiple-choice exams and posted impersonally, often by social-security number rather than name. In sum, students may feel like little more than objects into which knowledge is poured as they move along an information-providing and degree-granting educational assembly line.

Of course, technological advances are leading to even greater irrationalities in education. The minimal contact between teacher and student is being further limited by such advances as educational television, closed-circuit television,[47] computerized instruction, and teaching machines. We may soon see the ultimate step in the dehumanization of education—the elimination of a human teacher and of human interaction between teacher and student.

The Workplace: You Become a Mechanical Nut

Bureaucracies are often critiqued as dehumanizing settings in which to work. Often people employed in bureaucracies must deal with or respond to nameless, faceless bureaucrats. This is an even greater problem for the clients who have trouble reaching, let alone developing personal contacts with, these bureaucrats. A number of recent advances in telephone technology have added to this problem. Telephones in large bureaucracies are now often answered by prerecorded voices that tell the caller how important his or her call is to them (another form of fake fraternization that people rarely fall for), and return over and over again (often interrupting the beloved strains of Muzak) to tell the caller to keep hanging on. Then there are the fully computerized systems in which the caller must push a number of buttons in response to instructions from a computer's voice. When he or she ultimately reaches the right office, the caller may hear yet another prerecorded message. Because no humans exist on the other end of the phone line, dealing with such voices is obviously even more dehumanizing than dealing with the anonymous bureaucrat.

In spite of being set up to operate efficiently, bureaucracies are often notoriously inefficient. Trying to get anything out of a bureaucracy, especially something the least bit out of the ordinary, can require endless contacts with the relevant bureaucrats. Even normal business with a bureaucracy can mire clients in "red tape" from which it seems they may never extricate themselves.

The modern, computerized airplane (such as the Boeing 757 and 767) as a work setting for pilots represents an interesting case of the irrationality of rationality. Instead of flying "by the seat of their pants," or using old-fashioned autopilots for simple maneuvers, modern pilots can "push a few buttons and lean back while the plane flies to its destination and lands on a predetermined runway." Said one FAA official, "We're taking more and more of these functions out of human control and giving them to machines." These airplanes are in many ways safer and more reliable than older, less technologically advanced models. However, pilots, dependent on these technologies, may lose the ability to handle emergency situations creatively. Said one airline manager, "If we have human operators subordinated to technology, then we're going to lose that creativity. I don't have computers that will do that [be creative]; I just don't."[48] Thus, in an emergency situation, these airplanes pose the threat of ultimate dehumanization: the deaths of their passengers.

Undoubtedly, the automobile assembly line is the classic example of a rational system that has produced a seemingly never-ending string of irrationalities. For example, the mass production of automobiles has led to a voracious need for gasoline that, in turn, has made the United States (and many other countries) dependent on oil-producing nations and willing to go to war to protect its oil supplies and keep oil prices low. To take another irrationality, the automobile assembly line has experienced extraordinary success in churning out millions of cars a year. But all those cars, created year after year, have wreaked havoc on the environment, polluted by their emissions. An ever-expanding number of highways and roads has torn up and scarred the countryside. Then there are the thousands of people killed and the far greater number injured each year in traffic accidents.

Another example of the irrationality of the rationality in the automobile industry relates to calculability. Take the famous case of the Ford Pinto.[49] Because of competition from small foreign cars, Ford rushed the Pinto into and through production, even though preproduction tests had indicated its fuel system would rupture easily in a rear-end collision. Because the expensive assembly-line machinery for the Pinto was already in place, Ford decided to go ahead with the production of the car without any changes. Ford based its decision on a quantitative comparison. The company estimated that the defects would lead to 180 deaths and about the same number of injuries. Placing a value, or rather a cost, on them of $200,000 per person, Ford decided that the total cost from these deaths and injuries would be less than the $11 per car it would cost to repair the defect. Although this may have made sense from the point of view of profits, it was an unreasonable decision in that human lives were sacrificed and people maimed in the name of lower costs and higher profits. This is only one of the most extreme of a number of such decisions made daily in the automobile industry as well as in many other components of a society undergoing McDonaldization.

Although putting people at mortal risk in the name of rationality is the ultimate dehumanization, the automobile assembly line is best known for the way it dehumanizes life on a day-to-day basis for those who work on it. As you have read in chapter 2, Henry Ford felt that while he could not do the kind of repetitive work required on the assembly line, most people, with their limited mental abilities and aspirations, could adjust to it quite well. Ford said, "I have not been able to discover that repetitive labour injures a man in any way. . . . The most thorough research has not brought out a single case of a man's mind being twisted or deadened by the work."[50] However, people now know that the dehumanizing character of assembly-line work has profound negative effects on those who work on the line.

Objective evidence on the destructiveness of the assembly line is found in the high rates of absenteeism, tardiness, and turnover among employees. More generally, most people seem to find assembly-line work highly alienating. Here is the way one worker describes it:

> I stand in one spot, about a two- or three-feet area, all night. The only time a person stops is when the line stops. We do about thirty-two jobs per car, per unit, forty-eight units an hour, eight hours a day. Thirty-two times forty-eight times eight. Figure it out, that's how many times I push that button.[51]

Another worker offers a similar view: "What's there to say? A car comes, I weld it; a car comes, I weld it; a car comes, I weld it. One hundred and one times an hour." Others do more than describe the work, they get quite sarcastic about it: "There's a lot of variety in the paint shop. . . . You clip on the color hose, bleed out the color and squirt. Clip, bleed, squirt; clip, bleed, squirt, yawn; clip, bleed, squirt, scratch your nose."[52] Another assembly-line worker sums up the dehumanization he feels: "Sometimes I felt just like a robot. You push a button and you go this way. You become a mechanical nut."[53]

These workers' observations are supported by many scientific studies that show high degrees of alienation among assembly-line workers. This alienation is traceable to the rationality of the line and the fact that it produces the unreasonable consequence of dehumanizing work. Alienation affects not only those who work on the automobile assembly line, but also people in the wide range of settings built, at least in part, on the principles of the assembly line.[54] In our rapidly McDonaldizing society, the assembly line has implications for many of us and for many different settings.

Conclusion

Contrary to McDonald's propaganda and the widespread belief in it, fast-food restaurants and their rational clones are not reasonable, or even truly rational, systems. They spawn problems for the health of their customers and the well-being of the environment; they are dehumanizing and, therefore, unreasonable; and they often lead to the opposite of what they are supposed to create, for example, inefficiency rather than increased efficiency. None of this denies the advantages of McDonaldization, but these examples clearly indicate the counterbalancing and perhaps even overwhelming problems associated with this process. These problems, these irrationalities, need to be understood because most people have been exposed to little more than an unrelenting set of superlatives created by McDonaldized systems to describe themselves.

8

The Iron Cage of McDonaldization?

McDonaldization is clearly with us for the foreseeable future. While such a future will bring people many benefits, the profound irrationalities associated with McDonaldization raise serious questions about such a future, particularly about the "iron cage of McDonaldization," as Max Weber might have phrased it. By "iron cage," I mean that as McDonaldization comes to dominate ever more sectors of society, it will become ever less possible to "escape" from it.

The phrase "iron cage" implies a negative view of the nature of that which imprisons people, that is, McDonaldization. Furthermore, the interlocking rational systems of a McDonaldized society can fall into the hands of a small number of leaders who through them can exercise enormous control over society as a whole.

Perhaps the ultimate irrationality of McDonaldization is the possibility that people could come to lose control over the system—that it could someday come to control them. Already, these rational systems control many aspects of people's lives. Furthermore, though it at least appears that people still control them, these rational systems can spin beyond the control of even those who occupy the highest positions within those systems. Thus, the most extreme sense of the "iron cage of McDonaldization" is this: it can become an inhuman system that controls everyone, leaders included. With no people to appeal to, oppose, or overthrow in their efforts to escape, people may become even more hopelessly imprisoned.

The fear of such control has animated science fiction writers to write such classics as *1984*, *Brave New World*, and *Fahrenheit 451*. These novels describe a feared and fearsome future world; however, McDonaldization exists now, has existed for awhile, and continues to extend its reach throughout society.

The Forces Driving McDonaldization: It Pays, We Value It, It Fits

You may ask: Why must people face such a future? Why can't they back away from the further institutionalization of McDonaldization? To answer these questions, I will discuss three factors that drive McDonaldization: (1) material interests, especially economic goals and aspirations; (2) the culture of the United States, which values McDonaldization as an end in itself; and (3) McDonaldization's attunement to certain changes taking place within society. Here is a brief look at each of these factors.

Higher Profits and Lower Costs

Max Weber would argue that ultimately it is material, or more specifically, economic interests that drive rationalization in capitalist societies. Profit-making enterprises pursue McDonaldization because it leads to lower costs and higher profits. Clearly, greater efficiency and increased use of nonhuman technology are often implemented to increase profitability. Greater predictability provides, at the minimum, a climate that is needed for an organization to be profitable and for its profits to increase steadily from year to year. An emphasis on calculability, on things that can be quantified, helps lead to decisions that can produce and increase profits and makes possible measurements of profitability. In short, people and organizations profit greatly from McDonaldization and, as a result, they aggressively seek to extend its reach.

Though not oriented to profits, nonprofit organizations also press McDonaldization for material reasons. Specifically, it leads to lower costs, which permit nonprofit agencies to remain in operation and perhaps even expand. Greater efficiency and the increased use of nonhuman technology tend to lower costs directly. Further, the more predictable the environment, the more directly cost-reduction can be addressed. Calculability allows the nonprofit organization to determine whether it is in fact lowering costs. Officials in nonprofit organizations are also directly interested in increasing revenues and in lowering costs so they can raise salaries. Thus, the elements of McDonaldization permit nonprofit organizations to enhance income and lower costs.

Interestingly, the dramatic changes currently taking place in Russia and Eastern Europe can be explained in terms of McDonaldization. Because communism constituted a barrier to rationalization, such societies failed to

McDonaldize. As such, communist societies tended to be characterized by inefficiency, incalculability, unpredictability, and to be relatively slow to introduce advanced technologies (except in the military). These societies therefore suffered the economic (and social) problems that forced them to abandon their economic system and move toward a more marketlike economy. In other words, Russia and Eastern Europe are now rushing headlong toward greater rationalization, driven by a desire to improve their economic situation.

McDonaldization for Its Own Sake

Although it is clear that economic factors lie at the root of McDonaldization, it has become such a desirable process that many people and enterprises pursue it as an end in itself. That is, many people, either as individuals or as the representatives of institutions, have come to value efficiency, calculability, predictability, and control, and seek them out whether or not economic gains will result. For example, eating in a fast-food restaurant, or having a microwave dinner at home, may be efficient, but it is more costly than if people prepared the meal "from scratch." Because they value efficiency, people are willing to pay the extra cost.

At a more macroscopic level, while it may make economic sense for yet another entrepreneur to open still another McDonaldized institution, does it make economic sense at the societal level to have so many of them concentrated in given locales? After all, except for its square shape, the Wendy's burger is about the same as the McDonald's burger. Thus, McDonaldization does not always make economic sense yet continues to be pursued. This means that McDonaldization cannot be explained solely in terms of material interests. It has become valued in and of itself, with people willing to accept it even when it does not make sound economic sense.

The reasons for the value placed on rationalization are not difficult to find. Since its proliferation in the late 1950s, McDonald's (to say nothing of the myriad other agents of rationalization) has invested enormous amounts of money and effort in convincing people of its value and importance. Indeed, it now proclaims itself as a part of the rich tradition of the United States rather than, as many people believe, a threat to it. Many Americans have eaten at McDonald's in their younger years; gone out with teenage buddies for a burger; taken their children there at various times as they grew up; or gone there to have a cup of coffee with their parents. McDonald's has exploited the emotional baggage wrapped up in it to create a large number of highly devoted customers. Even though McDonald's built its position on rational principles, its customers' loyalty is as much emotional as it is rational. Thus, McDonaldization is likely to proceed apace for two reasons: it offers the advantages of rationality and people are committed to it. This commitment leads people to ignore and overlook McDonald's disadvantages; this, in turn, helps open the world to even further advances in McDonaldization.

McDonaldization and the Changing Society

A third explanation of the rush toward McDonaldization is that it meshes well with other changes occurring in American society and around the world. For example, the number of women working outside the home has increased greatly. In the old-fashioned family, in which the husband earned the money and the wife stayed home to cook and tend to the house and children, an elaborate meal prepared from scratch and eaten in a leisurely manner was possible. But in the modern family, in which both spouses are likely to work (or in which there is only one spouse), there is less likely to be anyone with time to shop, prepare the ingredients, cook the food, and clean up afterward. There may not even be time (or money), at least during the work week, for meals at traditional restaurants. Thus, the speed and efficiency of a fast-food meal fits in well with the demands of the modern, dual-career or single-parent family. Many other McDonaldized institutions offer similar advantages to the single-parent and dual-career families.

The fast-food model also thrives in a society that emphasizes mobility, especially by automobile. Clearly, the automobile occupies an increasingly central place in the United States and much of the rest of the world. Automobiles are common, especially among teenagers and young adults, the most likely devotees of the fast-food restaurant. And people need automobiles to frequent most fast-food restaurants, except those found in the hearts of large cities.

More generally, the fast-food restaurant suits a society in which people prefer to be on the move. Going out for a McDonaldized dinner, or any other rationalized activity, is in tune with the demands of such a society; even better is the use of the drive-through window so that people do not even have to stop to eat. Further serving McDonaldization is the increasing number of people who travel about, either on business or for vacations. People on the move seem to like the idea that even though they are in a different part of the country, they can still go to a familiar fast-food restaurant to eat the same foods they enjoy at home.

The increasing affluence of at least a portion of the population, accompanied by more discretionary funds, is another factor in the success of fast-food restaurants. As shown, those restaurants are not nearly as economical as they would have people believe. People who have extra funds can support a fast-food "habit." At the same time, the fast-food restaurant offers poor people the possibility of a meal out, out of the question at many traditional restaurants.

The increasing influence of the mass media also contributes to the success of fast-food restaurants. Without saturation advertising and the ubiquitous influence of television and other mass media, fast-food restaurants would not have succeeded as well as they have. Similarly, the extensive advertising employed by such McDonaldized systems as H & R Block, Jenny Craig, and Pearle Vision Centers has helped make them resounding successes.

Of course, technological change has probably played the greatest role in the success of McDonaldized systems. Initially, technologies such as bureaucracies, scientific management, the assembly line, and the major product of that production system, the automobile, all contributed to the birth of the fast-food society. Over the years, innumerable technological developments have both spurred, and been spurred by, McDonaldization: the "fatilyzer," automatic drink dispensers, supermarket scanners, foods that cook themselves, the microwave oven, aquaculture, factory farming, credit and debit cards, the StairMaster, videotapes, domed stadiums, the 24-second clock, RV's, cash machines, voice mail, and HMO's. In recent years, the computer has also come to play a central role in the growth of McDonaldization.[1] Many technological marvels of the future will either arise from the expanding needs of a McDonaldizing society or help create new areas to be McDonaldized.

In this light, mention should be made of the burgeoning importance of cyberspace, of the Internet, and of those who spend a good portion of their day "surfing the net." For example, one on-line service, Compuserve, grew from 1.1 million members in 1992 to 2.7 million in 1994.[2] This new technology, made possible by the computer, can be related to McDonaldization in various ways. It is certainly an efficient way to communicate with large numbers of people. Counting the number of messages received can be quite pleasing, although that number tells people nothing about the "quality" of those messages. The messages are generally quite predictable, although it is certainly the case that the most unpredictable of messages may appear on one's screen,[3] and it is still true that there is little or no control over the Internet. Perhaps most important, most of the messages in the "virtual community" of cyberspace are impersonal; communication via the "net" is thus dehumanizing. It is worth noting that McDonald's has taken the lead in using cyberspace to advertise its wares—yet another way the Internet spreads McDonaldization.

McDonaldization and Some Alternative Perspectives: Fast Food in the Era of the "Posts"

Because I present McDonaldization as a central process in the *modern* world, this book constitutes an analysis and critique of *modernity*. However, a number of contemporary perspectives, especially postindustrialism, post-Fordism, and postmodernism contend that we have already moved beyond the modern world and into a new, starkly different society. These views imply that this book is retrograde because it deals with a "modern" phenomenon (McDonaldization) that will soon disappear with the emergence of a new societal form. This book contends, however, that McDonaldization and its "modern" (as well as industrial and Fordist) characteristics not only are here for the foreseeable future, but also are influencing society at an accelerating rate. Thus, though important post-industrial, post-Fordist, and postmodernist trends are also occurring, some thinkers associated with these perspectives have been too quick to declare an end to modernity, at least in its McDonaldized form. This book constitutes a critique, in whole or in part, of extreme versions of these alternative viewpoints. Here is a brief look at each of these perspectives and the ways McDonaldization relates to them.

Postindustrialism: McDonaldization or Sneakerization?

Of those who argue that people have moved beyond industrial society to a new, postindustrial society, the most important is Daniel Bell.[4] Among other things, Bell argues that society has moved from goods-production to service provision. That is, fifty or seventy-five years ago the economy of the United States centered on the production of goods such as steel or automobiles. Today, however, the economy is dominated by the provision of services such as health care and fast food. Bell also points to the rise of new technologies and the growth in knowledge and information-processing. He observes as well that professionals, scientists, and technicians have increased in number and importance.

However, in spite of this growth, low-status service occupations show no sign of disappearing, and, in fact, they have expanded and are central to a McDonaldized society. Above all, however, McDonaldization, as we have seen, is built on many of the ideas and systems of industrial society, especially bureaucratization, the assembly line, and scientific management. The growth of McDonaldization at least in part contradicts Bell's idea that we have moved into a postindustrial society. Society is certainly postindustrial in many ways, but the spread of McDonaldization indicates that some aspects of industrial society will remain for some time to come.

Recently, in their book, *Post-Industrial Lives*, Jerald Hage and Charles Powers have argued in favor of the postindustrial thesis.[5] Among other things, they contend that a new postindustrial organization has arisen and that it coexists with the classic industrial organization, as well as other organizational forms. The postindustrial organization has a number of characteristics, including a leveling of hierarchical distinctions, a blurring of boundaries between organizations, a more integrated and less specialized organizational structure, an increase in behavior that is not bound by rules, and hiring policies that emphasize the creativity of potential employees.

There is no question that such organizations are on the ascent, but McDonaldized organizations are also increasing. Thus, the evidence supports *both* the postindustrial and McDonaldization theses: modern society contains contradictory organizational developments. In most cases the characteristics of McDonaldized organizations are diametrically opposed to those of postindustrial organizations. Thus, McDonaldized organizations continue to be hierarchical, behavior of employees and even managers is tightly bound by rules, and the last thing in the mind of those hiring for most jobs is creativity. Hage and Powers see jobs involving "tasks that are most clearly defined, technically simple, and most often repeated" being eliminated by automation.[6] While many such jobs have been eliminated in heavy industry, they are not only alive and well, but growing, in McDonaldized organizations. Postindustrial organizations are also characterized by customized work and products, while standardized work (everyone follows the same procedures, scripts) and uniform products are the norm in McDonaldized settings.

Relatedly, a process called the "sneakerization" of society has arisen.[7] Not quite customization, this process involves the diversification of product lines. Where there was once a single sneaker for all purposes, there are now specialized sneakers for all sorts of purposes—running, walking, aerobics, basketball, bicycling, and so on. Similar developments are everywhere—there are over 100 types of Walkman, 3,000 kinds of Seiko watches, and 800 models of Phillips color televisions. These examples reflect the replacement of the mass production market by the agile marketplace.

Does sneakerization and the agile market represent a critique of, and alternative to, McDonaldization? While it is easier to McDonaldize a single type of sneaker, nothing prevents the McDonaldization of the production and sale of a wide range of sneakers. Indeed, manufacturers such as Nike and Adidas and retail chains such as The Athlete's Foot and Foot Locker have done just that. The production and sale of a wide product line represents no barrier to McDonaldization. Indeed, that is precisely where the future of McDonaldization lies.

Hage and Powers envision a broader change in society as a whole in which the emphasis has come to be on creative minds, complex selves, and communication among people who have these characteristics. Though some aspects of modern society are congruent with that image, McDonaldization demands uncreative minds, simple selves, and minimal communication dominated by scripts and routines.

In sum, the postindustrial thesis is not wrong, but more limited than many of its adherents believe. Postindustrialization coexists with McDonaldization. The latter not only shows no sign of disappearing, but is in fact dramatically increasing in importance. This stands in contrast to the position taken by Hage and Powers who argue that not rationalization, but *"complexification will be the prevailing pattern of social change in post-industrial society."*[8] My view is that both complexification *and* rationalization will prevail but in different sectors of the economy and the larger society.

Fordism and Post-Fordism: Or, Is It McDonaldism?

A similar issue concerns a number of Marxist thinkers, who claim that industry has undergone a transition from Fordism to post-Fordism. Fordism, of course, refers to the ideas, principles, and systems spawned by Henry Ford.

Fordism has a number of characteristics. First, it involves the mass production of homogeneous products. To take a classic example, Model-T Fords were identical down to their black color. Even today's automobiles are largely homogeneous, at least by type of automobile being produced. In fact, in the United States in 1995 Ford came out with a so-called "world car" (e.g., the Contour), an automobile that could be sold in all world markets. Second, Fordism involves inflexible technologies, such as the assembly line. In spite of experiments with altering assembly lines, especially those undertaken by Volvo in Sweden, today's lines look much like they did in Ford's day. Third, Fordism involves the adoption of standardized work routines, or Taylorism.

Thus, the person who puts hubcaps on cars does the same task over and over, more or less the same way each time.

Fourth, increases in productivity come from "economies of scale as well as the deskilling, intensification, and homogenization of labor."[9] *Economy of scale* means simply that larger factories producing larger numbers of products can manufacture each individual product more cheaply than small factories producing goods in small numbers. *Deskilling* means that productivity increases if many workers do jobs requiring little or no skill (for example, putting hubcaps on cars) rather than, as had been the case in the past, a few workers with great skill doing all the work. *Intensification* means the more demanding and faster the production process, the greater the productivity. *Homogenization of labor* means that each worker does the same kind of highly specialized work (hubcaps, for example). This makes workers interchangeable.

Finally, Fordism involves the growth of a market for mass-produced items, which causes the homogenization of consumption patterns. In the automobile industry, Fordism led to a national market for automobiles in which similarly situated people bought similar, if not identical, automobiles.

Although Fordism grew throughout the twentieth century, especially in the United States, it reached its peak and began to decline in the 1970s, especially after the oil crisis of 1973 and the subsequent decline of the American automobile industry and the rise of its Japanese counterpart. Some argue that this indicates not only the decline of Fordism but also the rise of post-Fordism, which has a number of distinguishing characteristics.

First, interest in mass products declines, while interest in more customized and specialized products, especially those high in style and quality, grows. Rather than drab and uniform products, people want flashier goods that are easily distinguishable.[10] Today's post-Ford consumers are also more interested in quality and willing to pay extra for it.

Second, the more specialized products demanded in post-Fordist society require shorter production runs resulting in smaller and more productive systems. Thus, society will witness a move away from huge factories producing uniform products to smaller plants turning out a wide range of products.

Third, in the post-Fordist world, new technologies make flexible production profitable. For example, computerized equipment that can be reprogrammed to produce different products is replacing the old, single-function technology. This new production process is to be controlled through more flexible systems, for example, a more flexible form of management.

Fourth, post-Fordist systems require more from workers than their predecessors. For example, workers need more diverse skills and better training to handle the new, more demanding, and more sophisticated technologies.

These new technologies also mean that workers must be able to handle more responsibility and operate with greater autonomy. Thus, post-Fordism requires a new kind of worker.

Finally, as post-Fordist workers become more differentiated, they come to want more differentiated commodities, life-styles, and cultural outlets. In other words, greater differentiation in the workplace leads to greater differentiation in the society as a whole. This in turn leads to more diverse demands and still greater differentiation in the workplace.

Though these elements of post-Fordism have emerged in the modern world, it is equally clear that elements of Fordism persist and show no signs of disappearing: there has been no clear historical break with Fordism. In fact, "McDonaldism," a phenomenon that clearly has many things in common with Fordism, is growing at an astounding pace in contemporary society. Among the things McDonaldism shares with Fordism are homogeneous products, rigid technologies, standardized work routines, deskilling, homogenization of labor (and customer), the mass worker, and homogenization of consumption. Here is a look at each of these elements of McDonaldization from the vantage point of Fordism.

First, homogeneous products dominate a McDonaldized world. The Big Mac, the Egg McMuffin, and Chicken McNuggets are identical from one time and place to another. Second, technologies such as Burger King's conveyor system, as well as the french-fry and soft-drink machines throughout the fast-food industry, are as rigid as many of the technologies in Henry Ford's assembly-line system. Further, the work routines in the fast-food restaurant are highly standardized. Even what the workers say to customers is routinized. The jobs in a fast-food restaurant are deskilled; they take little or no ability. The workers are homogeneous and the actions of the customers homogenized by the demands of the fast-food restaurant (for example, don't dare ask for a rare burger). The workers at fast-food restaurants are interchangeable. Finally, what is consumed and how it is consumed is homogenized by McDonaldization.

Thus, in these and other ways Fordism is alive and well in the modern world, although it has been transformed into McDonaldism. Furthermore, classic Fordism, for example in the form of the assembly line, remains a significant presence in the American economy.

As you have seen, some argue that post-Fordism rather than Fordism is attuned to the production and sale of quality products. This is inconsistent with one of the fundamental tenets of McDonaldization—the emphasis on quantity and the corresponding lack of interest in quality. While this is generally the case, is it impossible to McDonaldize quality products? In some cases it is (for example, haute cuisine or outstanding cakes from skilled bakers), but in others, quality and McDonaldization are not inimical.

Take the boom in Starbucks coffee shops.[11] Starbucks clearly sells, at high prices, high quality coffee. A local Seattle business in 1987, by the end of 1994 Starbucks had grown to 470 company-owned stores (there are no franchises) with net sales of $285 million compared with $176 million the preceding fiscal year. The company plans to have 1,500 such stores in the United States by the turn of the century, with expansion into international markets underway. Starbucks has been able to McDonaldize the coffee business without sacrificing quality. I think their secret is that they deal with a very simple product (coffee) to which they do little (brew it) or nothing (sell bags of the beans). Simple products and processes can be McDonaldized without sacrificing quality, but more complex processes and products cannot. Even burgers and fries, to say nothing of Big Macs, are far more complex than coffee.

Regarding service, which is of similar complexity in McDonald's and Starbucks, the latter has self-consciously sought to counter the problems found in McDonaldized systems, as Starbuck's founder states:

> Service is a lost art in America. I think people want to do a good job, but if they are treated poorly they get beaten down. . . . It's not viewed as a professional job in America to work behind a counter. We don't believe that. We want to provide our people with dignity and self-esteem, and we can't do that with lip service. So we offer tangible benefits. The attrition rate in retail fast food is between 200 and 400 percent a year. At Starbucks, it's 60 percent.[12]

Since service is more complex than brewing coffee, it remains to be seen whether Starbucks can offer high quality service on a widespread and continuing basis.

Postmodernism: Are We Adrift in Hyperspace?

Finally, there is the more general perspective known as "postmodernism."[13] Although there are many varieties of postmodernism,[14] the most extreme view is that we have entered, or are entering, a new postmodern society that represents a break with modern society; postmodernity follows and supplants modernity. Among many other differences, modernity is generally thought of as highly rational and rigid, while postmodernity is seen as less rational, more irrational, and more flexible.

A number of writers, most notably Jean-Francois Lyotard, have explicitly viewed McDonald's as a postmodern phenomenon. Arthur Kroker, Marilouise Kroker, and David Cook have discussed McDonald's under the heading of "postmodern hamburgers."[15] In an essay entitled "Writing McDonald's, Eating the Past: McDonald's as a Postmodern Space," Allen Shelton extensively analyzes the relationship between McDonald's and postmodernism, concluding, "I portray McDonald's as an emblem of postmodernism, a moral symbol that acts as a signpost for the times."[16]

To the degree that postmodernity is seen as a successor to modernity, postmodernism stands in opposition to the McDonaldization thesis: the idea that there is an increase in irrationality contradicts the view that there is an increase in rationality. Given the extreme postmodern thesis, McDonald's cannot be the symbol of both modernity and postmodernity. However, less radical postmodern orientations allow us to see phenomena like McDonald's as having *both* modern and postmodern characteristics.[17]

Thus, while Shelton associates McDonald's with postmodernism, he also links it to various phenomena that I would identify with modernism (as well as industrialism and Fordism). For example, Shelton makes the excellent point that McDonald's succeeded in automating the customer. That is, when customers enter the fast-food restaurant or wend their way along the drive-through, they enter a kind of automated system through which they are impelled and from which they are ultimately ejected when they are "refueled." In his view, McDonald's thus looks more like a factory than a restaurant. However, it is not a "sweat shop for its customers, but a high tech factory."[18] Therefore, from this postmodernist perspective, McDonald's is as much a modern as a postmodern phenomenon.

David Harvey also offers a moderate postmodernist argument. While Harvey sees great changes and argues that these changes lie at the base of postmodern thinking, he believes that there are many continuities between modernity and postmodernity. His major conclusion is that while "there has certainly been a sea change in the surface appearance of capitalism since 1973 . . . the underlying logic of capitalist accumulation and its crisis tendencies remain the same."[19]

Central to Harvey's approach is the idea of time-space compression. He believes that modernism served to compress both time and space and that that process has accelerated in the postmodern era, leading to "an intense phase of time-space compression that has a disorienting and disruptive impact." But this is not essentially different from earlier epochs in capitalism: "We have, in short, witnessed another fierce round in that process of annihilation of space through time that has always lain at the center of capitalism's dynamic."[20]

As an example of space compression within the McDonaldized world, foods once available only in foreign countries or large cities are now quickly and widely available throughout the United States because of the spread of fast-food chains dispensing Italian, Mexican, or Cajun food. Similarly, as an example of time compression, foods that formerly took hours to prepare can now take seconds in a microwave oven or be purchased in minutes at a fast-food restaurant. To take a different kind of example, in the 1991 war with Iraq, television (especially CNN) transported viewers instantaneously from one place to another—from air raids in Baghdad to SCUD attacks on Tel Aviv to military briefings in Riyadh. Viewers learned about many military developments as they occurred at the same time the generals and the president of the United States did. Thus, to Harvey, postmodernity is not discontinuous with modernity; they both reflect the same underlying dynamic.

The best-known argument that there is no discontinuity between modernity and postmodernity is made by Fredric Jameson in the essay (later, book), "Postmodernism, or The Cultural Logic of Late Capitalism."[21] This title clearly indicates Jameson's Marxist position that capitalism (certainly a "modern" phenomenon), now in its "late" phase, continues to dominate today's world. However, it has now spawned a new cultural logic—postmodernism. In other words, though the cultural logic may have changed, the underlying economic structure remains continuous with earlier forms of capitalism, that is, it is still "modern." Furthermore, capitalism continues to be up to its same old tricks of spawning a cultural system to help it maintain itself.

The late phase of capitalism involves "a prodigious expansion of capital into hitherto uncommodified areas."[22] Jameson sees this expansion as not only consistent with Marxist theory, but as creating an even purer form of capitalism. For Jameson, the key to modern capitalism is its multinational character and the fact that multinational corporations have greatly increased the range of products transformed into commodities. Even aesthetic elements that people usually associate with culture have been turned into commodities to be bought and sold in the capitalist marketplace. As a result, extremely diverse elements make up the new postmodern culture.

Jameson offers a clear image of a postmodern society composed of five basic elements. Here I will present these elements and relate them to the McDonaldization of society.

First, as seen, Jameson associates postmodernity with late capitalism. There is no question that McDonaldization can be associated with earlier forms of capitalism. For example, McDonaldization is motivated by material interests, intimately associated with capitalism. But McDonaldization also exemplifies the multinationalism of late capitalism. Many McDonaldized businesses are international, with their major growth now taking place in the world marketplace.

Second, postmodern society is characterized by superficiality. Its cultural products do not delve deeply into underlying meanings. A good example is Andy Warhol's famous painting of Campbell's soup cans, which appear to be nothing more than perfect representations of those cans. To use a key term associated with postmodern theory, the painting is a *simulacrum* in which people cannot distinguish between the original and the copy. A simulacrum is also a copy of a copy; Warhol reputedly painted his soup cans not from the cans themselves, but from a photograph of them. Jameson describes a simulacrum as "the identical copy for which no original ever existed."[23] By definition, a simulacrum is superficial.

Clearly, a McDonaldized world is characterized by such superficiality. People pass through McDonaldized systems without being touched by them; for example, customers maintain a fleeting and superficial relation with McDonald's, its employees, and its products. McDonald's products also provide wonderful examples of simulacra. Each Chicken McNugget is a copy of a copy; no original Chicken McNugget ever existed. The original, the chicken, is hardly recognizable in the McNugget.

Third, Jameson characterizes postmodernity by a waning of emotion or affect. He contrasts another of Warhol's paintings, a near-photographic representation of Marilyn Monroe, to a classic modernist piece—Edvard Munch's, *The Scream*. This surreal painting represents a person in the depth of despair, or in sociological terms, anomie or alienation. Warhol's painting of Marilyn Monroe expresses no genuine emotion. This reflects the postmodernist assertion that it was the modern world that caused the alienation depicted by Munch. In the postmodern world, however, fragmentation has tended to replace alienation. Since the world, and the people in it, have become fragmented, the affect that remains is "free-floating and impersonal."[24]

There is also a peculiar kind of euphoria associated with these postmodern feelings, or what Jameson prefers to call "intensities." As an example, he presents a photorealist cityscape "where even automobile wrecks gleam with some new hallucinatory splendour."[25] Euphoria based on automobile disasters in the midst of urban squalor is, indeed, a peculiar kind of emotion.[26]

Clearly, the McDonaldized world is one in which the sincere expression of emotion and affect have been all but eliminated. At McDonald's, little or no emotional bond can develop among customers, employees, managers, and owners. The company strives to eliminate genuine emotion so things can operate as smoothly, as rationally, as possible. A McDonaldized world is also fragmented as people go to McDonald's today, Denny's tomorrow, and Pizza Hut the day after. Though alienation in the McDonaldized world, especially among employees, reflects the modern world, McDonaldization also offers the free-floating affect described by Jameson. People may feel angry about, and hostile toward, the McDonaldized world, but this feeling will take a free-floating form since it is difficult to know where to direct it; after all, so many different things seem to be undergoing McDonaldization. In spite of the lack of affect in a McDonaldized society, people often feel a kind of intensity, a euphoria when they enter one of its domains. The bright lights, colors, garish signs, children's playgrounds, and so on give visitors the impression that they have entered an amusement park and are in for an exciting time.

Fourth, Jameson cites a loss of historicity in the postmodern world. Not being able to know the past has led to the "random cannibalization of all styles of the past" and the creation of what postmodernists call *pastiches*. That is, since historians can never find the truth about the past, or even put together a coherent story about it, they must be satisfied with creating pastiches, or hodgepodges of ideas, sometimes contradictory and confused, about the past. Further, there is no clear sense of historical development, of time passing, in the postmodern world. Past and present are inextricably intertwined. For example, historical novels such as E.L. Doctorow's *Ragtime* present the "disappearance of the historical referent. This historical novel can no longer set out to represent historical past; it can only 'represent' our ideas and stereotypes about that past."[27] Another example is the movie *Body Heat*, which while clearly about the present, creates an atmosphere reminiscent of the 1930s. To do this,

> the object world of the present-day—artifacts and appliances, even automobiles, whose styling would serve to date the image—is elaborately edited out. Everything in the film, therefore, conspires to blur its official contemporaneity and to make it possible for you to receive the narrative as though it were set in some eternal Thirties, beyond historical time.[28]

Such a movie or novel is a "symptom of the waning of our historicity."²⁹ This inability to distinguish between past, present, and future shows up at the individual level in a kind of schizophrenia. For the postmodern individual, events are fragmented and discontinuous.

McDonaldized systems generally lack a sense of history. People find themselves in settings that either defy attempts to be pinpointed historically or present a pastiche of many historical epochs. The best example of the latter is Disney World with its hodgepodge of past, present, and future worlds. Furthermore, visitors to McDonaldized settings tend to lack a sense of the passage of time. In many cases, the designers of the system intend this. The best examples are the shopping malls and the Las Vegas casinos, both of which lack visible clocks. However, not all aspects of the McDonaldized world create such timelessness, indicating their continuing modernity. For those who choose to eat in a fast-food restaurant, time has been made important (e.g., by signs giving a twenty-minute limit on the use of tables) to prevent them from lingering. On the other hand, the drive-through window seems part of some timeless web as people pass through it as one link of an unending chain of destinations.

Fifth, Jameson argues that a new technology is associated with postmodern society. Instead of productive technologies such as the automobile assembly line, he cites the dominance of *re*productive technologies, especially electronic media such as the television set and the computer. Rather than the "exciting" technology of the industrial revolution, these new technologies flatten all images and make each indistinguishable from all others. These "implosive" technologies of the postmodern era give birth to very different cultural products than the explosive technologies of the modern era.

While the McDonaldized systems do make use of some of the old-fashioned productive technologies (the assembly line, for example), they are dominated by reproductive technologies. That is, they reproduce over and over that which has been produced before. In chapter 2, I discussed how the fast-food restaurants have merely reproduced products, services, and technologies long in existence. What they produce are flattened, featureless products—the McDonald's hamburger—and services—the scripted interaction with the counterperson.

In sum, Jameson presents an image of postmodernity in which people are adrift and unable to comprehend the multinational capitalist system or the explosively growing culture and commodity market in which they live. As a paradigm of this world, and of each person's place in it, Jameson offers the example of Los Angeles' Hotel Bonaventure, designed by a famous postmodern architect, John Portman. People are unable to get their bearings in the hotel's lobby, an example of what Jameson calls *hyperspace*, an area where modern conceptions of space are useless in helping people orient themselves. This lobby is surrounded by four absolutely symmetrical towers containing the rooms. In fact, the hotel had to add color coding and directional signals because people had such difficulty getting their bearings in the hotel lobby as originally designed.

This situation in the lobby of the Bonaventure serves as a metaphor for people's inability to get their bearings in the multinational economy and cultural explosion of late capitalism. What they need are new kinds of maps. The need for such maps reflects Jameson's view that people have moved from a world defined temporally to one defined spatially. Indeed, the idea of hyperspace, and the example of the lobby of the Hotel Bonaventure, reflect the dominance of space in the postmodern world. Thus, for Jameson, the central problem today is that people have lost their ability to position themselves within postmodern space and to map that space.

Similarly, a McDonaldized world is disorienting and difficult to map. For instance, you can be in downtown Beijing and still eat at McDonald's and Kentucky Fried Chicken. Because space and the things associated with particular places are changing dramatically, people no longer know quite where they are and are in need of new guides. Excellent examples of hyperspace include the shopping mall, the large Las Vegas casino, and Disney World.

Thus, McDonaldization fits Jameson's five characteristics, but perhaps only because he sees postmodernity as simply a late stage of modernity. Because of this inability to draw a clear line, as well as other factors, some scholars reject the idea of a new, postmodern society. Says one, "Now I reject all this. I do not believe that we live in 'New Times,' in a 'postindustrial and postmodern age' fundamentally different from the capitalist mode of production globally dominant for the past two centuries."[30]

Clearly, while some characteristics of today's "postmodern" society differ dramatically from its "modern" predecessor, great continuity exists as well. McDonaldization shows no signs of disappearing and being replaced by new, postmodern forms. It is a highly rational modern phenomenon yielding, among other things, extremely rigid structures. Thus, McDonaldization constitutes a rejection of the thesis that we have moved on to a postmodern society in which such modern phenomena are quickly disappearing. Furthermore, McDonaldized systems exhibit many postmodern characteristics side by side with modern elements. In other words, the McDonaldizing world demonstrates *both* modernity and postmodernity.

Conclusion

No social institution lasts forever. While McDonaldization remains a powerful force in today's world, it, too, will pass from the scene. McDonaldized
systems will remain powerful until the nature of society has changed so
dramatically that they can no longer adapt to it. Even after it is gone,
McDonald's will be remembered for the dramatic impact it had, both positive and negative, on the United States and much of the rest of the world. In
chapter 2, I discussed bureaucracies, scientific management, and the assembly line as predecessors of McDonaldization. When McDonald's has, like
its predecessors, receded in importance or even passed from the scene, it
will be remembered as yet another precursor to what is likely to be a still
more rational world.

9

Frontiers of McDonaldization

Birth, Death, and Beyond

M cDonaldization has an inexorable quality, multiplying and extending itself continuously.[1] One could say that McDonaldization has
ceaselessly extended its boundaries, incessantly "pushed the envelope." This
is clear, as seen throughout this book, in many obvious ways. McDonald's
itself has spread throughout the United States and beyond,[2] with as much
or more business overseas than in the States. The fast-food and upscale
chains that emulate its methods have mushroomed. Many other types of
organizations have adapted the McDonald's model to their needs. Other
nations have developed indigenous versions of McDonald's, and some have
even turned the tables and exported them back to the United States.

In this chapter, however, I want to approach the expansionism of
McDonaldization in a very different, and even more startling, way.
McDonaldization first focused on a variety of things associated with *life*,
that is, the day-to-day aspects of living—food, drink, shelter, and so on.
Firmly ensconced in the process of living, McDonaldization has pressed
outward in both directions to encompass, where possible, both the beginning and the end of life—birth and death. As the postmodern theorist, Jean
Baudrillard, has put it, "The fundamental law of the social order [is] . . . the
progressive control of life and death."[3] Indeed, the process has moved beyond what would, on first glance, appear to be its absolute limits to encompass (again, where possible) what might be termed "prebirth" and
"postdeath." Thus, this chapter is devoted to what might be termed the
"colonization" of birth and its antecedents, and death and its aftermath, by
McDonaldization.[4]

As has been the custom in this book, I will not dwell on the many widely
publicized advantages associated with McDonaldizing birth and death.
Children have been born, and survived, who otherwise might have never
been born.[5] At the other end of the spectrum, modern medicine has saved

many people who otherwise might have perished. However, the problems associated with the McDonaldization of birth and death receive comparatively little attention. Even when treated, these problems are never presented in the broader context of a process such as McDonaldization. This context allows us to see that these problems are not isolated developments, but intimately related to a wide range of social changes.

Why McDonaldize birth and death? For one thing, after living itself, nothing is more important to people than their entrance into, and exit from, life. Given their importance, it is not surprising that birth and death have attracted the attention of those who benefit from McDonaldization.

Second, the processes of birth and death present many unpredictabilities that cause a great deal of anxiety. A modern, rational society would try to minimize these unpredictabilities. Among the unpredictabilities associated with birth are whether

+ a woman can get pregnant
+ a man can father a child
+ the mother or father carries genetic defects that can be passed on to offspring
+ the infant will be born with genetic defects
+ the pregnancy will be free of complications
+ a woman should carry her child to term or terminate the pregnancy
+ the mother and/or child will survive childbirth
+ the infant will be a boy or a girl
+ parents should have more children
+ society should seek to pass laws prohibiting certain births
+ society should prohibit abortion under some or all circumstances

A similar set of uncertainties accompany death:

+ whether or not to keep someone alive by mechanical means when there is no hope of recovery
+ how far to go in those efforts
+ whether or not there is a right to die
+ how to know and decide when someone is in fact dead
+ what ceremonies are needed when death occurs
+ how to dispose of the dead body

With McDonaldization, the unpredictabilities, ambiguities, and anxieties associated with birth and death can be reduced, albeit not eliminated. Yet, in the end, these efforts are likely to be limited, and in many cases thwarted altogether. As the physician, Sherwin Nuland, states in terms of death (and much the same could be said of birth), "Every life is different from any that has gone before it, and so is every death. The uniqueness of each of us extends even to the way we die."[6] In other words, some are trying to rationalize that which is, to at least some degree, ultimately unrationalizable. Yet people continue to press forward in an effort to rationalize as much as they can; to leave as nonrational or irrational as little of living, being born, and dying as possible. Nuland marvelously captures what people are up against:

> Cancer, far from being a clandestine foe, is in fact berserk with the malicious exuberance of killing. The disease pursues a continuous, uninhibited, circumferential, barn-burning expedition of destructiveness, in which it heeds no rules, follows no commands, and explodes all resistance in a homicidal riot of devastation. Its cells behave like members of a barbarian horde run amok—leaderless and undirected, but with a single-minded purpose: to plunder everything within reach.[7]

Similarly, cancer is described as an "uncontrolled mob of misfits," "a gang of perpetually wilding adolescents," and the "juvenile delinquents of cellular society."[8] If ever there was a daunting enemy of rationalization, cancer is it.

Finally, there are immense rewards in rationalizing as much of birth and death as possible. Ultimately, in subduing birth and death, people will be able to improve the quality of their lives. These rewards also bring great economic returns to those people and institutions that succeed in rationalizing various aspects of birth and death. Spurred by popular demand and the lure of great riches, many institutions seek to expand these frontiers of McDonaldization. One can almost visualize the storefront signs in the "McBirths" and "McDeaths" of the future: "Millions of birth defects avoided," or "Billions of deaths averted."

Birth, and Before: High-Tech Pregnancies and Designer Babies

In recent years a variety of steps have been taken to rationalize the process leading up to birth. For example, the problem of male impotence[9] has been attacked by the burgeoning impotence clinics (chains,[10] or soon-to-be chains) and their increasingly wide array of medicinal and mechanical nonhuman technologies. Many males are able to impregnate their partners and initiate pregnancies that otherwise might not occur. Similarly, infertility has been ameliorated by advances in the nonhuman technologies associated with artificial (more precisely, "donor"[11]) insemination, in vitro fertilization,[12] and so on. For those women who still cannot become pregnant or carry to term, surrogate mothers can do the job.[13] Even postmenopausal women now have the chance of becoming pregnant ("granny pregnancies").[14] These developments and many others have made having a child far more predictable for many women. Efficient, easy-to-use, home-pregnancy tests now take the ambiguity out of whether or not a woman is pregnant. There are also ovulation-predictor home tests to help women seeking pregnancy. [15]

One of the great unpredictabilities associated with becoming pregnant is whether a woman will conceive a girl or a boy. Sex-selection[16] clinics have opened in London and Hong Kong as the first of what may eventually become a chain of "Gender Choice Centres." Using a technique developed in the early 1970s, semen is filtered through albumen to separate sperm with male from sperm with female chromosomes. The woman is then artificially inseminated with the desired sperm. The chances of having a boy are 75%; a girl, 70%.[17] The U.S. Department of Agriculture is currently experimenting with sex selection among animals.[18] The sperm's DNA is dyed with a fluorescent compound then exposed to a laser. Because male (y-bearing) sperm have 3–4% less DNA, they fluoresce slightly less; therefore, computers can identify male sperm and separate them out. Ultimately, the hope is that "male" or "female" sperm can be used to tailor the sex of offspring to the needs and demands of the parents. This technology might lead to even greater predictability about sex of offspring than the techniques currently used at the Gender Choice Centres and therefore come to be used more widely.

Already at hand, amniocentesis can be used to determine whether a fetus is male or female. First used in 1968 for prenatal diagnosis, amniocentesis is a process whereby fluid is drawn from the amniotic sac, usually between the fourteenth and eighteenth weeks of pregnancy.[19] With amniocentesis, parents might choose to abort a pregnancy if the fetus is of the "wrong" sex. This is clearly a far less efficient technique than the others discussed because it occurs *after* conception. In fact, very few Americans (about 5% in one study) say that they *might* use abortion as a method of sex selection.[20] However, amniocentesis does allow parents to know long in advance what the sex of their child will be.

Concern about a baby's sex pales in comparison to the possibility of genetic defects. A variety of recently developed tests determine whether a fetus carries such genetic defects as Down's syndrome, hemophilia, Tay-Sachs, and sickle-cell disease. In addition to amniocentesis, these tests include chorionic villus sampling, maternal serum alpha-fetoprotein, and ultrasound. Chorionic villus sampling (CVS) is generally done earlier than amniocentesis, between the ninth and twelfth weeks of pregnancy, and involves taking a sample from the finger-like structures projecting from the sac that later becomes the placenta. These structures have the same genetic makeup as the fetus.[21] Maternal serum alpha-fetoprotein (MSAFP) is a simple blood test done in the sixteenth to eighteenth weeks of pregnancy. A high level of alpha-fetoprotein might indicate spina bifida; a low level, Down's syndrome. Derived from sonar, ultrasound provides an image of the fetus by bouncing high-frequency energy off it. It can reveal various genetic defects, as well as many other things (sex, gestational age, and so on). Many other technologies are also available, and others will undoubtedly be created.

If one or more of these tests indicates the existence of a genetic defect in the fetus, then abortion becomes an option for those parents willing to consider aborting a fetus with a genetic defect. Parents who choose this option are unwilling to inflict the pain and suffering of genetic abnormality or illness on the child and on the family. Eugenicists feel that it is not rational for a society to allow such children to be born and to create whatever irrationalities will accompany their birth. From a cost-benefit point of view (calculability), it is less costly to abort the defective fetuses than to allow infants to be born and survive for a number of years. Given such logic, the nonhuman technologies available can allow society to discover which fetuses are to be permitted to survive and which are not. The ultimate step here would be a societal ban on certain marriages and births, something that China is now considering. The goal of such law would be to reduce the number of sick or retarded children that burden the state.[22] As an indication of the progress of McDonaldization in the prebirth phase, the use of all the techniques mentioned has increased dramatically, with some (e.g., sonograms, MSAFP) already routine practices.[23]

These techniques, collectively leading to "high-tech baby making,"[24] can be used to produce "designer pregnancies"[25] and "designer babies."[26] In other words, parents can now reduce some of the unpredictabilities, incalculabilities, and inefficiencies of natural pregnancies and births. Parodying the jingle for one of the fast-food hamburger chains, as a parent you are more likely now to "have it your way."

The ability to produce designer babies will dramatically increase with progress in the Human Genome Project, the construction of a genetic map of human chromosomes.[27] Knowledge of where each gene is and what each does will allow scientists to develop still more diagnostic tests and therapeutic methods. This knowledge will also extend the ability to test fetuses, children, and prospective mates for genetic diseases. Such tests may lead people not to marry or those who are already married not to procreate. Another possibility (and fear) is that as the technology gets cheaper and becomes more widely available, people may be able to do the testing (we already have home pregnancy tests) and make a decision to abort in the isolation and privacy of their bedrooms.[28] Overall, human mating and procreation will come to be increasingly affected and controlled by these new nonhuman technologies.

The principles of rational consumer society have also extended into the prebirth process. As one observer put it, "Being able to specify your child's sex in advance leads to nightmare visions of ordering babies with detailed specifications, like cars with automatic transmission or leather upholstery."[29] Said a medical ethicist, "Choosing a child like we choose a car is part of a consumerist mentality, the child becomes a 'product' rather than a full human being."[30] In the terms of McDonaldization, by turning a baby into just another "product" to be engineered, manufactured, and commodified, people are in danger of dehumanizing the birth process.

Dehumanization is, of course, a crucial irrationality of rationality. In fact, Dr. Michelle Harrison, who served as a resident in obstetrics and gynecology, found hospital birth to be a "dehumanized process."[31] But there are many other irrationalities associated with the procedures just discussed. For one thing, fetal abnormalities are extremely rare; more than 98% of women tested receive good news.[32] However, the testing experience itself may have negative consequences:

> The test's focus on abnormality heightens women's fears for their babies' health. The late gestational age at which some prenatal procedures take place makes the experience even more disturbing. Some women try to avoid bonding with the baby or telling others about the pregnancy until they receive the test results. . . . The stress imposed by . . . 'the tentative pregnancy' is an unanticipated consequence, or byproduct, of prenatal testing.[33]

Barbara Rothman created the idea of the "tentative pregnancy":

> The tentatively pregnant woman has entered the pregnant status, she is a pregnant woman, but she knows she may not be carrying a baby

but a genetic accident, a mistake. The pregnancy may not be leading to a baby but to an abortion.[34]

Clearly, such uncertainty arising from prenatal testing can take a toll on pregnant women.

Fetal testing has also tended to shift the focus from the rights of the mother to those of the fetus. While ultrasonography enables fathers to see the fetus on a TV screen, it may serve to mediate and demystify the mother's relationship with it.[35] Then there is the specter of eugenics and the destruction of fetuses because they do not fit somebody's image of what a child should be.

More specifically, a number of the prenatal procedures carry with them a variety of risks. CVS has been associated with a somewhat elevated risk of miscarriage as well as with some birth defects, MSAFP testing can lead to false positives or false negatives, and an ultrasound test may reveal to the parents directly and without prior notice that the fetus is dead or that the pregnancy is not viable.

Of course, the march of McDonaldization will not stop with the testing of fetuses for sex and physical abnormalities. Some claim that similar tests may eventually gauge the personality of a fetus.[36] Presumably, this will make it possible for parents to push still further the idea of the designer baby by aborting fetuses with the "wrong" personality.

Rationalization is also manifest in the process of giving birth. One measure of this is the decline of midwifery, a very human and personal practice. In 1900, midwives attended about half of American births, but by 1986, they attended only 4%.[37] Today, however, midwifery has enjoyed a slight renaissance *because* of the dehumanization and rationalization of modern childbirth practices. When asked why they have sought out midwives, women complain about things such as the "callous and neglectful treatment by the hospital staff," "labor unnecessarily induced for the convenience of the doctor," and "unnecessary cesareans for the same reason."[38] The flip side of the decline of midwives is the increase in the control of the birth process by professional medicine,[39] especially obstetricians. It is they who are most likely to rationalize and dehumanize the birth process.

Then there is the bureaucratization of childbirth. Once done largely in the home, with female relatives and friends in attendance, the formerly "social childbirth" now takes place almost totally in hospitals, "alone among strangers."[40] In 1900, less than 5% of U.S. births took place in hospitals; by 1940, it was 55%; and by 1960, the process was all but complete, with nearly 100% of births occurring in hospitals.[41] The preeminence of bureaucracies,

Weber's paradigm of rationalization, reflects the rationalization of the birth process. In more recent years, hospital chains have emerged, modeled after my paradigm for the rationalization process—the fast-food restaurant chain—as birthing centers.

Over the years, hospitals and the medical profession have developed many standard, routinized (McDonaldized) procedures for handling childbirth. One of the best known was created by Dr. Joseph De Lee and widely followed through the first half of the twentieth century. De Lee viewed childbirth as a disease (a "pathologic process"), and his procedures were to be followed even in the case of low-risk births.[42]

First, the patient was to be placed in the lithotomy position, "lying supine with legs in air, bent and wide apart, supported by stirrups."[43] Second, the mother-to-be was to be sedated from the first stage of labor on. Third, an episiotomy[44] was to be performed to enlarge the area through which the baby must pass. Finally, forceps were to be used to make the delivery more efficient. Describing this type of procedure, one woman wrote, "Women are herded like sheep through an obstetrical assembly line, are drugged and strapped on tables where their babies are forceps delivered."[45]

De Lee's standard practice had most of the elements of McDonaldization—efficiency, predictability, control through nonhuman technology (the procedure itself, forceps, drugs, an assembly-line approach), and the irrationality of turning the human delivery room into an inhuman baby factory. The calculability that it lacked was added later in the form of Emanuel Friedman's "Friedman Curve." This curve prescribed three rigid stages of labor with, for example, the first stage allocated exactly 8.6 hours during which cervical dilation went from two to four centimeters.[46]

The use of various nonhuman technologies in the delivery of babies has tended to ebb and flow. The use of forceps, invented in 1588, reached a peak in the United States in the 1950s when as many as 50% of all births involved their use. However, forceps fell out of vogue—in the 1980s, only about 15% of all births employed forceps. Many methods of drugging mothers-to-be have been widely used. The electronic fetal monitor became popular in the 1970s. Today, ultrasonography is a popular technology.

Another worrisome technology associated with childbirth is the scalpel. For example, many doctors routinely perform episiotomies during delivery so that the opening of the vagina does not tear or stretch unduly during pregnancy. Often done to enhance the pleasure of future sex partners (and to ease the passage of the infant), episiotomies are quite debilitating and painful in the days immediately after birth. Dr. Michelle Harrison concludes, "It's the episiotomy, though, that bothers me so much. . . . I want those obstetricians to stop cutting open women's vaginas. Childbirth is not a surgical procedure."[47]

The scalpel is also a key tool in cesarean sections. A perfectly human process has come, in a large number of cases, to be controlled by this technology and those who wield it.[48] The first modern cesarean took place in 1882, but as late as 1970, only 5% of all births involved cesarean. The use skyrocketed in the 1970s and 1980s, reaching 25% of all births in 1987 in what has been described as a "national epidemic."[49] By 1989, the practice declined slightly to just under 24%. This decline reflects the growing concern over the epidemic of cesareans as well as the fact that the American College of Obstetricians formally abandoned the time-honored idea, "once a cesarean, always a cesarean," that is, the view that once a mother has a cesarean, all succeeding births must be by cesarean.

While clearly necessary in some cases, cesareans are being performed unnecessarily. First, historical data leads to the questions: Why the sudden need for so many more cesareans? Weren't cesareans just as necessary a few decades ago? Second, some data indicate that private patients who can pay are more likely to get cesareans than those on Medicaid (which reimburses far less) and *twice* as likely to get cesareans as indigent patients.[50] The rate of cesareans is linked to social class and income, with those in higher social classes and with more income more likely to have cesareans than those with less income and from the lower social classes.[51]

One explanation for the dramatic increase in cesareans is the fact that cesareans fit well with the growing McDonaldization of society. First, they are more predictable than the normal, often unpredictable, birth that can occur a few weeks (or even months) early or late. It is frequently noted that cesareans generally seem to be performed before 5:30 P.M. so that physicians can be home for dinner. Similarly, well-heeled women may choose a cesarean so that the unpredictabilities of natural childbirth do not interfere with careers or social demands. For both doctor and patient, the cesarean eliminates the array of unforeseeable problems that may arise during natural childbirth. Second, as a comparatively simple operation, the cesarean is more efficient than natural childbirth, which may involve many more unforeseen circumstances. Third, cesareans are more calculable, normally involving no less than twenty minutes or more than forty-five minutes, while the time required for a normal birth, especially a first birth, may be far more incalculable. Fourth, as seen, the cesarean procedure *is* a nonhuman technology that controls the normal birth process. Finally, irrationalities exist, including the risks associated with surgery—anesthesia, hemorrhage, blood replacement. Compared to a normal childbirth, those who have ce-

sareans may experience more physical problems and a longer period of re-
cuperation, and the mortality rate can be as much as twice as high. Then
there are the higher costs associated with cesareans. A 1986 study indicated
that physicians' costs were 68% higher and hospital costs 92% higher for
cesareans compared with natural childbirth.[52] Finally, and most important
in terms of the theory of McDonaldization, cesareans are dehumanizing
because a natural human process is transformed, often unnecessarily, into a
nonhuman or even inhuman process in which women endure a surgical
procedure. At the minimum, many of those who have cesareans are denied
unnecessarily the very human experience of vaginal birth. The wonders of
childbirth are reduced to the routines of a minor surgical procedure.

The moment that babies come into the world, they are greeted by a
calculable scoring system, Apgar. The babies receive scores of zero to two
on each of five factors (for example, heart rate, color), with ten being the
healthiest score. Most babies have scores between seven and nine after a
minute of birth, eight to ten after five minutes. Babies with scores of zero to
three are considered in very serious trouble. Harrison wonders why medical personnel don't ask about more subjective things, such as the infant's
curiosity and mood. She concludes,

> A baby doesn't have to be crying for us to know it is healthy. Hold a
> new baby. It makes eye contact. It breathes. It sighs. The baby has
> color. Lift it in your arms and feel whether it has good tone or poor,
> strong limbs or limp ones. The baby does not have to be on a cold
> table to have its condition measured.[53]

Death—Before, During, and Beyond: Conveyor-Belt Funerals

Now to the other frontier: the McDonaldization of death begins long before a person dies. It commences in the efforts by the medical system to
keep the person alive as long as possible. A few things are worth underscoring here. First, there is the increasing array of nonhuman technologies designed to keep people alive long after they would have expired had they
lived at an earlier time in history. In fact, some, perhaps many, are kept alive
who would not want to stay alive under those conditions that allow them to
survive (a clear irrationality of the rationality associated with technologies
designed to keep people alive). Unless the physicians are following an advance directive (a living will) stating such things as "do not resuscitate," or

"no heroic measures," people will lose control over their own death. This is also true of family members who in the absence of such directives must bow to the medical mandate to keep people alive as long as possible.

This leads to another central issue in the predeath phase—the focus of medicine on maximizing the quantity of days, weeks, or years a patient remains alive and the lack of emphasis on the quality of life during that extra time. This calculability is akin to the fast-food restaurant telling people how large its sandwiches are but saying nothing about their quality.

Computers play an increasingly important role in medical practice, including the treatment of dying patients. For example, some computer systems can assess a patient's chances of survival—90%, 50%, 10%, and so on. With a nonhuman technology spitting out such odds, the actions of human medical personnel may come to be increasingly determined by such technologies. Whether a person lives or dies, the rationing of life may come to depend increasingly on a computer program.

But who actually makes the decision? It seems increasingly likely that the decision on who lives and who dies will be left to another inhuman technology: the guidelines of the huge bureaucratic systems that control the computers.

Death itself has followed much the same path as birth. That is, it has been moved out of the home and beyond the control of the dying and their family and into the hands of medical personnel and hospitals.[54] Physicians have gained a large measure of control over death just as they won control over birth, with death, like birth, increasingly likely to take place in the hospital. In 1900, only 20% of deaths took place in hospitals; in 1949, it was up to 50%; by 1958, it was at 61%; and by 1977, it had reached 70%. By 1993 the number of hospital deaths was down slightly (65%), but to that must be added the increasing number of people who die in nursing homes (11%) and residences such as hospices (22%).[55] Thus, death has been bureaucratized, which means it has been rationalized, even McDonaldized. The latter is quite explicit in the growth of hospital chains and even chains of hospices, using principles derived from the fast-food restaurant, which are increasingly controlling death.

One result of all this control is the dehumanization of the very human process of death as people are increasingly likely to die (as they are likely to be born) impersonally in the presence of total strangers:

> A process of *depersonalization* has set in. A patient is every day less a human being and more a complicated challenge in intensive care. To most of the nurses and a few of the doctors who knew him [a patient]

before his slide into sepsis, there remains some of the person he was (or may have been), but to the consulting superspecialists . . . he is a case. . . . Doctors thirty years his junior call him by his first name. Better that, than to be called by the name of the disease or the number of the bed.[56] [Italics added]

This dehumanization is part of the process, according to Philippe Aries, by which the modern world has "banished death."[57] Here is the way Nuland describes it:

We seek ways to deny the power of death and the icy hold in which it grips human thought. Its constant closeness has always inspired traditional methods by which we consciously and unconsciously disguise its reality, such as folk tales, allegories, dreams, and even jokes. In recent generations, we have added something new: We have created the *method of modern dying*. Modern dying takes place in modern hospitals, where it can be hidden, cleansed of its organic blight, and finally packaged for modern burial. We can now deny the power not only of death but of nature itself.[58] [Italics added]

Similarly, paralleling "designer births," Jean Baudrillard has written of "designer deaths":

To streamline death at all costs, to varnish it, cryogenically freeze it, or condition it, put make-up on it, "design" it, to pursue it with the same relentlessness as grime, sex, bacteriological or radioactive waste. The make-up of death . . . "designed" according to the purest laws of . . . international marketing.[59]

Closely related to the growing power of physicians and hospitals over death, nonhuman technologies play an increasing role in the dying process. Technology has blurred the line between life and death by, for example, keeping people's hearts going even though their brains are dead. Medical personnel have also come to rely on technology to help them decide when it is acceptable to declare death. Dehumanization occurs here as people die alone amid machines rather than with their loved ones:

When people are asked how they wish to die, most respond something like this: quickly, painlessly, at home, surrounded by family and friends. Ask them how they expect to die, and the fear emerges: in the hospital, all alone, on a machine, in pain.[60]

Here is the way Nuland describes dehumanized death:

The beeping and squealing monitors, the hissings of respirators and pistoned mattresses, the flashing multicolored electronic signals—the whole technological panoply is background for the tactics by which we are deprived of the tranquility we have every right to hope for, and separated from those few who would not let us die alone. By such means, biotechnology created to provide hope serves actually to take it away, and to leave our survivors bereft of the unshattered final memories that rightly belong to those who sit nearby as our days draw to a close.[61]

However, even the best efforts of modern, rationalized medicine inevitably fail, and patients die. Surely, after death people are finally free of McDonaldization. But, has the postdeath process, too, been McDonaldized? The answer, of course, is yes, at least to some degree. For example, we are beginning to witness the change from family-owned to chains of funeral homes.[62] As of 1992, the largest chain, Service Corp. International, owned about 850 funeral homes and cemeteries.[63] Said one industry analyst with a seemingly inappropriate rosy outlook on death, "The golden era of the death-care industry is still ahead."[64] It is estimated that death is currently an $8-billion-a-year industry. Business is booming, with deaths, now at about 2.2 million a year, likely to rise to 2.6 million a year by 2010. The chains leaping into this lucrative and growing market often offer not only funeral services, but also cemetery property and merchandise such as caskets and markers. Modern installment payment plans have been instituted so that people can prearrange a funeral with as little as 20% down, with the balance financed over a two- to five-year period. The business has even begun to use advertising:

> You will now have a choice! Louisville's affordable funeral home is your best choice; professional services $995; metal caskets as low as $160; opening May 1, 1994.[65]

With this emphasis on low prices (calculability), the funeral business now appears to have its version of McDonald's "value meal."

The funeral business has apparently adopted still another lesson from the fast-food industry—that what it is really selling is "fun": "Somber boo hoo funerals with loved ones weeping at the grave seem to be going out of style."[66] One family, for example, planned a beach party memorial service. The Japanese, as usual doing the United States one better, are planning a death amusement park modeled after that key element of McDonaldized society, Disney World. An Osaka undertaker is already putting on quite a show:

A coffin on an electronically operated cart moves down a 50-meter hill, bathed in the light of laser beams and accompanied by chanting monks and the family of the deceased.

When it reaches the end of the hall, which was once a bowling alley, the coffin enters a semicircular tunnel, enveloped in a thick fog of dry ice, and disappears into the "other world."[67]

Cremations are generally more efficient than conventional funerals and burials. Because they tend to minimize ritual and sometimes have a kind of assembly-line quality, cremations can lead to "conveyor-belt funerals." Here is the way an authority on English funeral customs describes one cremation:

An unaccompanied funeral car glides noiselessly under the porte-cochere, the coffin is transferred to a stainless steel hors-d'oeuvre trolley and wheeled into the chapel, which looks more like a waiting room in a university college hospital than a dignified setting for the disposal of the dead. Ten minutes later, to the accompaniment of slurred canned music the curtains jerk their way noisily round the catafalque as the coffin sinks slowly through the floor.[68]

Cremations also tend to lend themselves to greater calculability than traditional funerals and burials. For example, like the fast-food signs urging customers to leave after twenty minutes, the City of London crematorium has the following sign: "Please restrict service to 15 minutes." Then there is the irrationality of highly rationalized cremations, which have tended to eliminate much of the human ceremony associated with a traditional funeral and burial. To the modern family, death can be "just an embarrassing moment in time, half an hour at the crematorium, an inspection of the wreaths and back to the office." Some have gone even farther and eliminated the funeral altogether: "You don't have to have a funeral at all. . . . Sometimes people will have a service afterwards with the cremated remains sitting on the altar in a little casket."[69]

Even the period after people die has been rationalized to some degree. For example, prearranged funerals allow people to have control over their affairs even after they are dead. Another example is the harvesting of the organs of the deceased to help others. The most extreme version of this is cryogenics. People have themselves, or perhaps just their heads, frozen so that they might be brought back to life when anticipated advances in the rationalization of life make such a thing possible. It should come as little surprise that Walt Disney was interested in cryogenics, and there are those who believe that he was frozen after his death in the hopes of being resuscitated some day.[70]

McDonaldization of birth and death has spawned a series of counterreactions, efforts to cope with the excesses of rationalization. For example, as a way to humanize birth, interest in midwives has grown. However, the greatest counterreaction has occurred as people have sought various ways to regain control over their deaths. Advance directives and living wills tell hospitals and medical personnel what they may or may not do during the dying process. Then there is the growth of suicide societies and books such as Derek Humphry's *Final Exit* that, among other things, give people instructions on how to kill themselves, on how to control their own deaths. Finally, there is the growing interest in euthanasia, most notably the work of "Dr. Death," Jack Kevorkian, whose goal is to give back to people control over their own deaths.

However, it is worth noting in closing that these counterreactions themselves have elements of McDonaldization. For example, Dr. Kevorkian uses a nonhuman technology, a "machine," to help people kill themselves. More generally, and strikingly, he is an advocate of a "rational policy" for the planning of death.[71] Thus, the rationalization of death is found even in the efforts to counter it.

Conclusion

If there were still any doubts about the extent of McDonaldization, this chapter should have put them to rest. The previous chapters have shown the innumerable ways in which our lives have been McDonaldized. Here we see that the forces behind McDonaldization have pushed the frontier back to include not only the birth process, but the steps leading up to birth. Similarly, the frontier has also been extended in the other direction to include not only the process of dying, but its aftermath as well. There seem to be no bounds to McDonaldization and no barriers strong enough to resist it, at least for very long.

10

A Practical Guide for Living in a McDonaldized Society

W hat can people do to cope with an increasingly McDonaldized world? The answer to that question depends, at least in part, on their attitudes toward McDonaldization.

Is the Cage Made of Velvet, Rubber, or Iron?

The image of an iron cage communicates a sense of coldness, hardness, of great discomfort. However, many people view the future as more of a "velvet cage" of McDonaldization. Though they might admit that McDonaldization is steadily encircling them, they find this quite comfortable. They like, even crave, the McDonaldized world and welcome its continued growth and proliferation. This is certainly a viable position and one especially likely to be adopted by those who have lived only in McDonaldized societies and have been reared since the advent of the McDonaldized world. The only world they know, McDonaldized society represents their standard of good taste and high quality. They can think of nothing better than an increasingly rationalized world, preferring a world uncluttered with many choices and options. They like the predictability of many aspects of their lives. They relish an impersonal world in which they interact with human and even nonhuman automatons. They seek to avoid, at least in the McDonaldized portions of their world, close human contact. For such people, who probably represent an increasingly large portion of the population, McDonaldization represents not a threat, but nirvana.

For many other people, McDonaldization is a rubber cage the bars of which can be stretched to allow adequate means for escape. Such people dislike many aspects of McDonaldization but find others quite appealing. Like those who see themselves in a velvet cage, these people may well like the efficiency, speed, predictability, and impersonality of McDonaldized systems and services. Such people may be busy and therefore appreciate obtaining a meal (or some other McDonaldized service) efficiently. However, they also realize the costs of McDonaldization and therefore seek to escape it when they can. Its efficiencies may even enhance their ability to escape from it. That is, getting a fast meal may allow them the time to luxuriate in other, nonrationalized activities. These are the types of people who on weekends and vacations go into the wilderness to camp the old-fashioned way; go mountain-climbing, spelunking, fishing, and hunting (without elaborate equipment), antique hunting, and museum browsing; and search out traditional restaurants, inns, and bed and breakfasts. Such people try to humanize their telephone answering machines with creative messages such as, "Sorry ain't home, don't break my heart when you hear the tone."[1] These are also the people who continue to bake, and prepare elaborate home-cooked meals, from scratch. Said one devotee of baking from scratch, "The hands-on hobby of bread baking clings to life for reasons that go beyond food. It's an experience and a process. . . . It's the getting there that's the payoff for me. I need to knead." Said another, "There's a magic to it, isn't there?"[2]

However, while the bars may seem like rubber, they are still there. For example, a company that sells prerecorded, humorous messages has come into existence to rationalize the escape route for those who prefer creative answering machine messages. Thus, people can now have a tape with an impressionist imitating Humphrey Bogart answer their phone: "Of all the answering machines in the world, you had to call this one."[3] Similarly, for many, home baking has been reduced to the use of bread-baking machines which, while they do not produce a very good loaf, "do everything but butter the bread."[4]

The third type of person believes that the McDonaldized cage is made of iron. Such a person is deeply offended by the process and sees few, if any, ways out. Unlike the second type of person, these people see escape routes (if they see them at all) providing only temporary respites that will soon fall under the sway of McDonaldization. They share the dark and pessimistic outlook of Max Weber and me, viewing the future as a "polar night of icy darkness and hardness."[5] These are the severest critics of McDonaldization and the ones who see less and less place for themselves in modern society.

Given these three types of people, this chapter offers actions open to each in a McDonaldized world. Clearly, the different types will choose different actions. People of the first type will do nothing but continue to frequent fast-food restaurants and their clones within other sectors of society and even actively seek to McDonaldize new, as yet unrationalized venues. Extremists of the third type may want to work for the radical transformation of McDonaldized society. This might involve efforts to return to a pre-McDonaldized world or to create a new non-McDonaldized world out of the rubble created by the fall of the golden arches.

This chapter argues neither for the passive acceptance nor for the overthrow of McDonaldized society. Rather it is directed primarily at those of the second and third types not totally happy about McDonaldization and interested in carving out a less rationalized life for themselves.

I begin by presenting a wide range of often successful efforts to modify McDonaldized systems and limit their negative effects. These efforts help make McDonaldized systems slightly more palatable. Second, I will discuss some efforts aimed at the creation of non-McDonaldized institutions. Third, I will discuss a few examples of other, more individual ways people can carve out nonrationalized niches for themselves. Finally, I will discuss a number of do's and don'ts for surviving in a McDonaldized society.

Modifying McDonaldized Institutions: Trying to Avoid Chock Full o' Nuts' Fate

One course of action open to those opposed to McDonaldization is to put pressure on McDonaldized institutions to reduce or eliminate their irrationalities. In fact, when people have pressured McDonaldized systems, these systems have responded by mitigating some of their worst excesses.

However, McDonaldized organizations only respond when there is enormous external pressure. Furthermore, the responses are necessarily limited because McDonaldized organizations can only go so far before they undermine the basic principles that have made them so successful. Thus, people can expect only minor modifications and reforms by McDonaldized organizations, primarily as a response to strong external pressure.

Fast-Food Restaurants

In spite of the fast-food restaurant's widespread acceptance, many people have attacked it on a variety of grounds. A few communities have fought hard, at times successfully, against the invasion of fast-food restaurants, against the garish signs and structures, traffic, noise, and rowdy nature of some of the clientele drawn to fast-food restaurants. Most generally, they have fought against the irrationalities and assaults on tradition that the fast-food restaurant represents. Thus, there exist communities highly attractive to fast-food chains (for example, Sanibel Island in Florida) in which there are few, if any, fast-food restaurants.

The resort village of Saugatuck, Michigan, fought McDonald's attempt to take over the site of a quaint old cafe called Ida Red's. Said one local businessman, "People can see McDonald's anywhere—they don't come to Saugatuck for fast food." The owner of a local inn seemed to recognize that the town was really resisting the broader process of rationalization: "It's the Howard Johnson's, the McDonald's, the malls of the world that we're fighting against. . . . You can go to a mall and not know what state you're in. We're a relief from all that."[6] Outside the United States, the resistance has often been even greater. The opening of the first McDonald's in Italy, for example, led to widespread protest involving several thousand people. The Italian McDonald's opened near the picturesque Piazza di Spagna in Rome adjacent to the headquarters of the famous fashion designer Valentino. One Roman politician claimed that McDonald's was "the principal cause of degradation of the ancient Roman streets."[7] More recently, protests against the opening of a McDonald's in the medieval main market square of Kráków, Poland led one critic to say,

> The activities of this firm are symbolic of mass industrial civilization and a superficial cosmopolitan way of life. . . . Many historic events happened in this place, and McDonald's would be the beginning of the cultural degradation of this most precious urban area.'[8]

In response to such protests and criticisms, and as an attempt to forestall them in the future, McDonald's is building outlets that fit better into the community and nation in which they are placed. Thus, a McDonald's in Miami's Little Havana has a Spanish-style roof and feels more like a hacienda. Another in Freeport, Maine, looks like a quaint New England inn.[9] The 12,000th restaurant, opened in 1991, stands in a restored 1860s white Colonial House on Long Island. The interior has a 1920s look.[10] McDonald's managing director of Polish operations said, "We took a 14th-century building that was devastated and restored it to its natural beauty."[11]

Although McDonald's has been forced to mute and adapt its physical symbols and structure in light of various criticisms, few communities have successfully kept its franchises out completely. Similarly, small communities have usually been unsuccessful[12] in keeping Wal-Mart stores out even though they usually devastate local businesses when they move in[13] and hurt the communities on the rare occasions when they depart.[14]

In addition to Wal-Mart, other McDonaldized businesses have encountered similar opposition. For example, in San Francisco recently, Blockbuster ran into opposition from local businesses that blocked, at least for a time, the opening of a new outlet. Said the owner of a local video store, "Blockbuster is using predatory methods to kill off the smaller stores. If we get Blockbuster, then McDonald's, Boston Chicken and Sizzler are next, and you can say bye-bye neighborhood."[15]

As you saw in chapter 7, fast-food restaurants have also begun to alter their menus as a result of the numerous criticisms of nutritionists. Even Johnny Carson picked up on this, labeling the McDonald's burger "McClog the Artery."[16] By far the most notable and visible critic of fast-food fare has been Phil Sokoloff and his nonprofit organization, National Heart Savers Association. In 1990, for example, Sokoloff took out full-page advertisements in the *New York Times* and twenty-two other major newspapers with the headline, "The Poisoning of America." The ads singled out McDonald's for serving food high in fat and cholesterol. When Sokoloff first began running such ads in 1988, McDonald's responded to them by calling them "reckless, misleading, the worst kind of sensationalism."[17] But Sokoloff persisted, and in July 1990 he ran ads with the lead, "McDonald's, Your Hamburgers Still Have Too Much Fat! And Your French Fries *Still* are Cooked with Beef Tallow." With surveys showing that people were reducing their patronage of fast-food restaurants, McDonald's and other chains buckled. By the end of July 1991, Burger King, Wendy's, and McDonald's announced that they would use vegetable oils to cook french fries. Said Sokoloff, "I couldn't be happier. Millions of ounces of saturated fat won't be clogging the arteries of American people."[18] (However, recent research has shown that french fries cooked in vegetable oil generally have as much artery-clogging fat as those cooked in beef tallow.[19])

McDonald's has begun to respond more broadly to these criticisms; people will undoubtedly see less fat, salt, and sugar in future products. In late 1990, McDonald's unveiled its Lean Deluxe burger. Instead of the Quarter Pounders' twenty grams of fat and 410 calories, the Lean Deluxe burger offers ten grams of fat and 310 calories. Although still far from a diet food, the Lean Deluxe reflects McDonald's responsiveness on this issue. In 1991, McDonald's went even further and introduced the McLean Deluxe hamburger with about 9% fat (still considered far too high by many nutritionists), less than half the fat in a typical McDonald's burger. (Other chains sell hamburgers with as much as 25% fat.) To accomplish this, McDonald's adds carrageen, a seaweed extract, to the McLean Deluxe. This additive binds water to the meat, preventing it from being too dry because of its lower fat content. To make up for the loss of flavor, McDonald's adds natural beef flavoring to the mix.

Other chains have not been quick to jump on the low-fat bandwagon. Said one Hardee's spokesperson, "We're not going to sell a water-and-seaweed burger."[20] Burger King experimented with Weight Watchers products for awhile in the early 1990s, but soon halted that effort. After having come under attack for the fat and calories in at least some of its food, in early 1995 Taco-Bell announced a new line of products, "Border Lights." These have about half the fat and one-fifth fewer calories than regular menu items. To accomplish this, Taco Bell uses leaner meat, low-fat cheese, and non-fat sour cream.[21]

Some fast-food chains have responded to these kinds of criticisms in a far broader way. For example, a small chain of Mexican restaurants on the West Coast, "Macheezmo Mouse," uses the slogan, "Fresh-Fit-Fast." It specializes in low-fat, low-calorie dishes that are baked, steamed, or grilled instead of fried. The menu includes nutritional information on each item. A corporate executive calls it "fast food for smart people."[22]

McDonald's is also showing signs of responding to environmentalists, creating packaging less harmful to the environment.[23] In late 1990, McDonald's began eliminating its polystyrene "clamshell" hamburger box. The box had been attacked by environmentalists because the production of the boxes generated pollutants and, more important, the boxes lingered for decades in landfills or on the sides of roads. A paper wrapping with a cellophane-like outer wrapper took their place. In 1991, Hardee's announced that it would use recycled polystyrene in its packages. Said one environmentalist, "I think that the public is pressuring these people into taking positive steps."[24]

In fact, the responses to complaints by communities, nutritionists, and environmentalists indicate that the fast-food restaurant is quite an adaptable institution, although all these adaptations remain within the broad confines of rationality. Thus, for example, there seems to be little that can be done about the poor quality of the food. This fact is reflected in a diner opened by McDonald's, the Golden Arch Cafe, in Hartsville, Tennessee, which is modeled after old-time diners and sells things such as cola floats and Salisbury steak dinners with two vegetables. The diner includes traditional "chrome-glass decor, neon lights, spinseat counter stools, cozy booths, and a jukebox that blares '50s and '60s hits."[25] McDonald's is experimenting with the return to the diner so it can operate in very small towns. The belief is that diners are more likely than fast-food outlets to be viable economically in small towns. However, the opening of the diner does not seem to have done anything to improve the quality of the food:

> Not until your meal arrives does the restaurant reveal its origins in the fast-food industry: virtually everything reeks of processing. On a recent visit, scraps of stale-tasting catfish were all but invisible in their heavy orange breading; the mashed potatoes had the slightly bitter flavor that bespeaks dehydrated and reconstituted; the pork "cutlet" was perfectly shaped, oblong, dry and flabby, and heaped with a pale, salty gravy so congealed you could have eaten it with a fork—if you could have eaten it. Apart from a breakfast biscuit, which tasted fresh, the baked goods were heavy and doughy. A dessert called banana pudding came with sliced bananas tucked into it, but otherwise had the artificial, perfume-sweet flavor of a packaged pudding mix. Only the fried chicken was, as described, "real." If you strip off its greasy, acrid coat, you get an acceptable dish; what's more, the startling sight of a plain, honest piece of chicken is enough to bring tears to your eyes. Now *that's* nostalgia.[26]

Despite the poor quality of the food, the diner was jammed, at least as of a few months after its opening.

Another limitation of the fast-food restaurant's adaptability is that it must offer a simple and short menu. Over the years, McDonald's has experimented with, and even expanded on, its menu, but only within narrow boundaries. For instance, at one time, McDonald's concluded that a variety of simple breakfast foods following its traditional model (for example, the Egg McMuffin) could be offered in the morning to increase business. In a similar expansion, they added a few desserts to the menu. One franchisee expressed concern about a decline in his outlet's business during Lent. The result was the Filet-O-Fish sandwich, ultimately adopted with great success by the McDonald's chain.

Faced with the growth of the fried-chicken business, McDonald's introduced Chicken McNuggets. Confronted by people wanting healthier meals, it offered salads, then carrot and celery sticks. For those who complain about the boring sameness of the fare, McDonald's has experimented with foods such as the McRib sandwich and the Breakfast Burrito. McDonald's is even test marketing McGrits in some of its southern markets.[27] Some McDonald's franchises have invested in ovens and are now selling pizza.[28] While their menu is not nearly as limited today as it was in the 1950s (now, many outlets offer thirty-three items), the diner in search of variety will not find it at

McDonald's. The physical limitations of the restaurants and the limited skill of the workers make it impossible for the fast-food restaurant to offer more than a short menu of simple foods.

However, in expanding its fare, McDonald's may be losing sight of the simple line of products that made it so successful. The success of chicken, Mexican, and pizza chains has led McDonald's to sell such products. One might even find subs, oatmeal, soup, or cappuccino at a local McDonald's. This diversification stands in contrast to the position taken by the President of Subway, "We've stayed very simple with the menu while others have diversified, which can cause operational and quality problems."[29] While the addition of diverse foods will undoubtedly lead to additional business, it could cause McDonald's these kinds of problems. Furthermore, expansion could endanger McDonald's distinctive niche in the fast-food market. If McDonald's loses its identity, is it destined to fail?

McDonald's has adapted in other ways: Some people have actually complained about the disappearance of the old-fashioned huge golden arches, and at least one McDonald's franchise has responded by bringing them back. On the other side, in response to complaints from upscale clientele about a dehumanizing dining environment, a McDonald's in Manhattan's financial district offers Chopin on a grand piano, chandeliers, marble walls, fresh flowers, a doorman, and hosts who show people to their tables. The golden arches are virtually invisible. However, besides a few classy additions to the menu (espresso, cappuccino, tarts), the menu is largely the same as in all other McDonald's (albeit with slightly higher prices). Said one recent visitor, underscoring the continuity between this franchise and all others, "A smashing place, and the best thing is you can still eat with your fingers."[30]

In fact, McDonald's has been forced to pick up the pace of innovation because it has endured periods of flat and even declining sales and falling stock prices. Their twelve restaurants in Bakersfield, California, experimented with a credit-card system—McCharge. To compete with the home delivery of pizzas, other McDonald's experimented with McDelivery.[31] McDonald's has even been forced to accept a practice contemporary capitalistic firms are notoriously unwilling to engage in—price competition. Until recently, McDonald's followed the modern practice of competing on the basis of advertising rather than price. But with its American sales and profits declining in the late 1980s, and other fast-food restaurants succeeding on the basis of price, McDonald's had to adapt. This development was ushered in by Taco Bell in the late 1980s when it introduced a "value menu"— tacos and other items for fifty-nine cents. Price competition allowed Taco Bell to attract new customers without violating the basic principle of keeping its menu short and simple. As a result, Taco Bell became, at least for a time, the best-performing fast-food chain in the United States (although it has recently suffered some setbacks[32]). Reluctantly, McDonald's began to offer discounts on food with fifty-nine-cent burgers and soft drinks.[33]

McDonald's is certainly not the only fast-food restaurant to adapt to changing conditions. For example, Burger King has experimented with mobile restaurants, Burger Kings on wheels. As the fast-food business grows more and more competitive, people can expect the pace of innovation and experimentation to increase.[34]

What keeps the fast-food business on its toes is the knowledge that food fashions change; even the giant franchises can find themselves on the brink of bankruptcy. By 1990, the Chock Full o' Nuts chain of coffee shops in New York City was left with only one outlet; at its peak in the 1960s, it comprised about eighty restaurants. Its nutty cheese sandwich, "cream cheese and chopped nuts on dark raisin bread wrapped in plain, waxed paper" has been described as "the original fast food."[35] Then there is Howard Johnson's (HoJo's), once a franchise leader with about 1,000 outlets, now reduced to just eighty-five locations. Said an expert on restaurant chains, "In the '60s, they were the No. 1 chain. . . . They could have had the whole world at their fingertips, but they sat on it. . . . They were stuck in the 1950s and 1960s. Howard Johnson's just sat there with its ice cream and clams."[36]

While McDonald's is in no immediate danger of going the way of Chock Full o' Nuts or HoJo's, it has shown signs of trouble. Besides several years of slow sales and low share prices, McDonald's has had to face Mexican fast-food sales growing at more than twice the sales rate of hamburgers, with pizza sales increasing at slightly less than twice that rate.[37] In addition, such upscale franchises as Red Lobster are exhibiting greater profitability. Further, many people are moving away from the high-fat, high-sodium, high-calorie food served at McDonald's. Given these and other problems, McDonald's will clearly continue to change and evolve. In fact, it may even have begun to surrender at least some of the fundamental rational principles that made it such a success and such a revolutionary force.

One issue that fast-food restaurants have shown little inclination to deal with is dehumanizing working conditions. Burger King, for example, has fought hard against unionization to avoid, at least in part, improving such conditions.[38] As long as there is a steady supply of people willing to work in such settings for even just a few months, McDonald's will not do much about their working conditions. In some locales, McDonald's has faced an inadequate supply from its traditional labor pool—teenagers. Rather than alter and improve the work to attract teenagers and keep them on the job longer, McDonald's has responded by broadening its hiring net and seeking out teenagers who live in distant communities, hiring disabled adults, and bringing older employees, often retirees, into a program called "McMasters."[39] In the past, McDonald's would not hire older people because management believed that they would find the low wages and nature of the work intolerable. However, many older workers, such as those permanently laid off from dying or declining "smokestack industries" such as steel, are desperate enough for work that they will tolerate these conditions. Kinder-Care also hires older people to make up for the shortage in younger workers. In fact, one expert said, "For old people who need to be needed, it [Kinder-Care] sure beats working in McDonald's."[40]

McDonald's will most likely not significantly alter its working conditions until it can no longer find a steady supply of new workers. Even then, it may simply move toward eliminating human employees rather than humanizing the work. If so, customers can expect to see more automation and robotization in the fast-food restaurants of the future.

Modifying the Auto Assembly Line in Sweden

Other elements of McDonaldizing society have changed in response to their critics, the best example being the automobile industry and its assembly-line technology. The automobile companies have sought, often only after considerable external pressure, to reduce some of the worst irrationalities associated with the automobile. Under pressure from environmentalists, the automobile companies have done a few things to help reduce air pollution from automobiles. When also pressed by the government and severe competition from abroad, the industry made automobiles smaller and more fuel efficient.

However, the greatest irrationality of the automobile assembly line, at least from the point of view of this book, is the unreasonable character of working on it. As seen earlier, the demands of the high speed of the line and the ultraspecialization of the jobs made the work alienating and dehumanizing. For many years, workers and their unions pressed the automobile companies to improve the nature of the work. However, the companies did very little except perhaps pay workers more. With plenty of people available and eager to replace disgruntled workers on the assembly line, companies faced little real pressure to humanize the work.

However, in the 1960s and 1970s, especially in Sweden, a number of factors helped lead to significant humanization of assembly-line work.[41]

Many Swedish workers did not like work on the automobile assembly line. Their distaste was even greater because they tended to be more highly educated and to have higher aspirations than their American counterparts. They showed their greater distaste through high levels of absenteeism, tardiness, sabotage, and turnover. However, Swedish industrialists could not, like their counterparts in the United States, ignore these problems, especially turnover. With little unemployment in Sweden in the 1960s, it was difficult, if not impossible, to replace workers who quit their jobs. Thus, the Swedes were forced to take steps to reduce the dehumanizing and alienating aspects of work on the assembly line.

The Swedish automobile companies, such as Saab and especially Volvo, greatly modified the assembly line to eliminate its worst excesses. The single long line was divided into subsections, each handled by a relatively small work group of about twenty-five to thirty workers. A sense of community was engendered among the members of the work group. Instead of performing highly specialized tasks, each member of the group was allowed to perform a number of more complex tasks. Workers could also trade jobs. Instead of being told which tasks to do and how to do them, work groups and their members could decide for themselves, within limits. These changes met with some considerable success, at least initially.

In the United States, there was considerable interest in these humanizing reforms; however, with the absence of the pressure caused by the low unemployment rate in Sweden, very few actual changes took place until many years later. And then, the changes came about not to humanize work, but to compete better with the Japanese automobile industry.

Creating "Reasonable" Alternatives: Sometimes You Really Do Have to Break the Rules

The excesses of McDonaldization have led to the birth and development of various alternatives that tend to reject rationalization. These alternative organizations do not put a premium on the efficient production of goods and services or the efficient processing of customers. Instead of large quantities, they focus on high-quality products. They revel in the unpredictabilities of their products and services. Instead of nonhuman technologies, they tend to employ more skilled human beings who practice their crafts relatively unconstrained by external controls. Hence, these are not McDonaldized settings for workers or customers.

Alternatives to rationalized settings exist in businesses and other social institutions. Food co-ops offer an alternative to the supermarket,[42] specializing in vegetarian and health foods. The food is healthier than that in supermarkets, the shoppers are often members of the co-op and therefore actively involved in its management, and the employees are frequently more involved in and committed to their work.

In education, alternatives to highly rational state universities are small schools such as Hampshire College[43] of Amherst, Massachusetts, which has the motto, "Where It's Okay to Go Outside the Lines." (The fast-food restaurants are not above using similar mottos; for example, Burger King uses "Sometimes You Gotta Break the Rules," even though that's the last thing it wants people to do.) At such colleges there are no specialized majors or grade-point averages.

As nonrationalized institutions become successful, pressures mount to McDonaldize them. Then, the issue becomes how to avoid rationalization. For example, one thing to avoid is too much expansion. At some point, any institution will grow so large that it requires increasingly rational principles to function. With larger size comes another danger—franchising, which almost by definition brings with it rationalization. Because greater size and franchising hold out the almost overpowering lure of greater profits, the entrepreneurs behind a nonrationalized business must always keep the reasons for creating such a business in the forefront of their thinking. They must also keep in mind their obligations to the customers who frequent them because they are not McDonaldized. However, as creatures of a capitalist society, they might well succumb to greater profitability and allow their businesses to expand or to be franchised. If they did, I would hope they would use their profits to begin new nonrationalized enterprises.

Three specific examples of efforts to resist McDonaldization are discussed below. The first two in particular show successful resistance and its pitfalls. That is, as they became successful because of their opposition to McDonaldization, these businesses were drawn into McDonaldizing their products and operations and thereby undermined that which made them successful.

Marvelous Market: "Crunchy Crusts and Full Taste"

Marvelous Market is a good example of a relatively nonrational, reasonable business in Washington, D.C.[44] I hasten to add that from its inception even it did not eschew all aspects of the rational model. It is a take-out market, emphasizing that its foods can be picked up "quickly" and used to prepare an "effortless" dinner. Thus, even a business developed in reaction to McDonaldization cannot totally ignore the demands of a society grown accustomed to the fast-food system.

However, Marvelous Market was primarily oriented toward reason rather than rationality, most notably in its emphasis on quality rather than quantity. Here is the way its newsletter talked about food: "Cuisine is not just a way of cooking; it is a way of life. Food is much more than the answer to hunger. Food triggers moods and memories, reveals needs and desires, releases tensions and stimulates creativity."[45] (Compare this to what fast-food restaurants have to say.) The main product at Marvelous Market is bread:

> I [the owner] moved to Washington in 1961, and was told right away, "There is no good bread in Washington." I have heard that flat sentence over the years, thousands of times, probably. It is said commonly by people talking wistfully about the old days.
>
> I don't expect to hear it any longer. The old days have arrived.
>
> Marvelous Market's breads have crunchy crusts and full tastes. . . .
>
> Every day you will find round loaves of walnut bread and rye with currants, great batards of sourdough, chewy country loaves with big holes, bread with rosemary and black olives, baguettes baked once before lunch and, so that they will be perfectly fresh for dinner, again at 4pm.
>
> This bread may be a little startling to people accustomed to . . . soft pre-sliced loaves wrapped in plastic bags. You have not tasted breads like this before; they are . . . addictive.

Marvelous Market's newsletter concludes, "We are most of all determined to sell foods with great taste."

Marvelous Market was not an efficient operation. Its foods were unpredictable. Customers dealt with people rather than automatons or robots. Says Marvelous Market, "You will find a friendly store where the bakers and cooks talk and explain, and work on new recipes for breads and foods."

Stores and shops like this have existed all along, although fast-food outlets have forced many out of business. What is new is the birth of shops specifically created to provide an alternative for people fed up with the excesses of McDonaldization. But, can this countermovement ever become anything more than a minor phenomenon that exists within the interstices of the marketplace?

For a variety of reasons, I think that places like Marvelous Market are doomed to be restricted to isolated pockets of the McDonaldized society. For one thing, the growth of such places is restricted by their very nature.

Their expansion is limited, because with increasing size come ever greater threats to quality. And not many people have the skills and inclinations needed to open places like Marvelous Market. For another, a population reared from infancy on fast foods will likely regard fast-food products as the ultimate in quality. The McDonald's hamburger bun, not the "batard," is apt to be that generation's standard of quality. Thus, for example, one mother of a four-year-old said, "One day I hope that Kevin will appreciate my cooking. . . . But for now, I can't even compete with a Big Mac and fries."[46] Finally, and most important, if such markets and shops really show signs of taking over a significant share of the market, the forces of McDonaldization will notice and seek to transform them into rationalized systems that can be franchised around the world. For instance, Gulf and Western or some other large conglomerate could buy out Marvelous Market, rationalize its products (much as Kentucky Fried Chicken did to poor old Colonel Sanders's recipes), and create a worldwide chain of Marvelous Markets—at that point, no longer an alternative to McDonaldization, but part of the process.

Marvelous Market quickly became a phenomenal success in the Washington area. Because sales grew so dramatically, the market soon had to limit bread purchases to two loaves per person and close for several hours during the day because it could not handle the demand. The owner ordered new, larger ovens, opened another bakery devoted solely to production and not sales, bought a truck to dispense bread at various locations in the Washington area, and began selling his breads to supermarkets and restaurants. As this expansion took place, the owner claimed that his market continued to emphasize quality: "And certainly we're trying to attend to quality, refusing to increase our output faster than we can, refusing to give up our hand-shaping, pulling off our shelves each week hundreds of pounds of bread that don't meet our standards." However, in my view, and the view of many other customers, the quality of the bread *did* suffer; for example the store sold more burned loaves. The demand for quantity seemed to cause the quality to deteriorate.

In light of these problems, the owner published an open letter to his customers on November 9, 1991, on the opening of his new bakery. On the one hand, the letter recognized that in various ways growth had created irrationalities:

> We are in transition . . .
>
> In the process we have offended some of you because the *quality of our bread has been erratic*, and we haven't adhered to our schedule of breads . . .

On some days of the week, like Saturday, we *run out of products* before you can come. Many of you who might wish to be on the courts playing tennis or at the firm billing clients, now *stand in line* Saturday mornings. . . .

Moreover, although you have been fairly tolerant over the months in *quality variations*, we have been offended by them consistently. [Italics added.]

On the other hand, the owner promised that expansion would not mean a decline in quality (and other irrationalities):

So we built a large new bakery, putting into it the best equipment capable of producing our kinds of breads. It is *not automated* equipment; we make breads in the other bakery just as we make them here, *slowly, by hand.* . . . we'll be able to get *far more quality and consistency* in our breads.

In addition, we managed to attract as leader of the new bakery . . . one of the premier bakers of the country. . . .

For those who think that we are going to follow the course of other Washington bakeries which began with promise and then compromised, it's not going to happen here. [Italics added.]

Clearly aware of the dangers of rationalizing his operation, the owner of Marvelous Market tried to avoid them while he greatly expanded the market's business. However, he failed. Today, Marvelous Market is in bankruptcy. There is talk that the business is to be sold, bringing an end to the saga of Marvelous Market. The rapid rise and descent of Marvelous Market represents *both* the attractiveness of offering an alternative to McDonaldization and the almost irresistible pressures to McDonaldize such an operation once it has become successful.

Ben & Jerry's: "Caring Capitalism"

A far more established and well-known alternative to a highly rationalized business is the Ben & Jerry's ice-cream company with headquarters in Waterbury, Vermont.[47] With a $12,000 initial investment, Ben & Jerry's began selling ice cream on May 5, 1978 in a refurbished gas station. Neither Ben Cohen nor Jerry Greenfield had any real experience in the business. They set out to sell a high-quality product at a low price. In fact, Ben had a "fanatical commitment to producing a high-quality product."[48] That quality is characterized by the high fat content of the ice cream and the large chunks of add-ins. However, the use of large chunks did not arise from some rational decision-making process, but rather from Ben's inability to distinguish subtle flavors. The commitment to high quality is reflected in the way Super Fudge Chunk ice cream was created in 1985:

> [Ben] came up with a formula that called for liquid chocolate syrup to be pumped into our regular chocolate mix. The result was an ice cream that was incredibly rich, fudgy, and intensely flavorful. For add-ins, Ben settled on white and dark chocolate chunks, chocolate-covered almonds, pecans and walnuts. . . . He set the specs so that the total amount of chunks, by weight and volume, would be 40 percent more than we used in any other flavor. It was by far the most expensive product we'd ever made, but that was of absolutely no consequence to Ben, who never let concerns about cost of goods distract him during the creative process. If it tasted great, Ben figured we'd make money on it.[49]

The first shop was anything but rational. The frequently long lines at the counters reflected its inefficiency. Unpredictability arose in variations in the scoop size and inconsistent service. Calculability was almost nonexistent. Two months after opening, the shop was closed and a sign posted: "'We're closed today so we can figure out if we're making any money.'"[50] From the beginning, and to some degree even now, the technology was primitive and exerted minimal control over employees. In contrast to rationalized, McDonaldized businesses,

> Ben and Jerry came to describe their business as being 'funky,' which to them meant honest, no frills, handmade, and homemade. It was on the opposite end of the spectrum from slick, refined, polished, or packaged.[51]

In a conscious effort to differentiate itself from the cold impersonality of rationalized businesses, Ben & Jerry's has sought to be known as the "company that cares." Unlike most of its rationalized alternatives, Ben & Jerry's cares not only about quality, but also about its workers and the environment. The company policy until 1995 was that executives may earn no more than five times the earnings of the lowest-paid worker. Practicing "caring capitalism," the company commits 7.5% of its pretax earnings to its foundation, which makes grants to organizations "committed to imaginative social change"; pays premiums for milk to assist Vermont's ailing family farms; and purchases blueberries from local Indians, peaches from black Georgia farmers, and nuts from the natives of the Amazonian rain forest.

Its corporate shareholder meetings involve not only the usual election of directors, but also such nontraditional activities as videotaping messages to Congress promoting shareholders' favorite causes.

Ben & Jerry's avoids and limits environmental damage caused by corporate activities. The company recycles plastic and cardboard, uses recycled paper in its offices, and conserves energy. Ben & Jerry's even acknowledges that its main product, its superpremium ice cream, endangers the health of at least some people. Its 1990 annual report stated that "ice cream has nutritional value, despite its high fat and sugar content. People who should not eat it for health reasons are free to choose not to eat it."[52] More concretely, in recent years the company has begun to market actively both light ice-milk and low-fat and nonfat frozen yogurt. These products reflect Ben & Jerry's concern for health (although it continues to actively market its super premium ice cream and to give each of its employees three free pints of ice cream *per day*). They also reflect an increasingly health-conscious public growing resistant to high-fat ice cream.

The company has also sought to avoid some of the effects of McDonaldization on its employees. Employees do not wear uniforms or follow scripts; in fact, to this day, Ben & Jerry's has "embraced diverse lifestyles, people could dress the way they wanted, and you could personalize your workplace however you saw fit."[53] Ben and Jerry themselves have customarily come to work in T-shirts and sneakers. Employees apparently adore their jobs. Workers can exercise at least some choice over the tasks they will perform on any given day. The company has a "joy gang," which seeks to take some of the drudgery out of work. One can watch "the employees cheerfully yuk it up during a public tour of the pastel-colored Waterbury facility"; an executive answering machine might tell a caller that the officer is unavailable because he or she is "off doing transcendental meditation"[54]; and a letter I received from the Ben & Jerry's public relations officer was signed by the "P.R. Info Queen." Then there are the many employee benefits, such as free massages, free health-club membership, profit sharing, and child care. Said one worker, "It's what a job should be." One journalist describes it as "the friendliest of employee-friendly firms."[55]

However, from the beginning, Ben & Jerry's has shown signs of McDonaldization. For example, there was early concern with the inconsistent size of the scoops and periodic efforts to rationalize the process. In one effort, later abandoned because of its inefficiency, they used scales to weigh the cones. The first Ben & Jerry's franchised "scoop shop" opened in Vermont in 1981; the first out-of-state franchise opened in 1983. By early 1995, there were 100 scoop shops primarily in the United States, but also in Israel, Canada, and Russia[56]. To meet demand, others, under license to the company, began to produce some of Ben & Jerry's ice cream. Sales, profits, and the number of employees grew dramatically. As early as 1982, Jerry was conscious of the rationalization underway: "We'd started as this homemade ice cream parlor and evolved into a sort of a manufacturing plant. . . . Where it used to be that we made every batch of ice cream and scooped every cone, now there were people buying our ice cream who had never met Ben or Jerry."[57] Jerry left the company but returned a few years later to seek to combine economic success with the values that had built the company in the first place.

Having achieved international success, the company made a conscious policy to limit growth. In contrast to the growth-conscious leaders of virtually all McDonaldized businesses, "Ben never bought into the argument that a business that wasn't growing was dying."[58] The company has limited franchise growth, with only twenty more scoop shops today than in 1989, and has focused on improving its ties to existing franchisees. Similarly, it has slowed the growth in the number of employees. A consultant was hired to improve both job and product quality.[59] A new plant under construction will return all ice cream production to the company, thereby eliminating the dangers of allowing licensees to manufacture the ice cream.

Patricia Aburdene, coauthor (with John Naisbitt) of *Megatrends 2000*, saw Ben & Jerry's as "most certainly . . . the new model of the corporate form that we will see created in the 1990s and into the 21st century."[60] This view stands in contrast to my own, that the highly rationalized McDonald's and *not* the determinedly nonrationalized Ben & Jerry's will most likely continue to serve as the primary corporate model. At the minimum, to represent a viable alternative, Ben & Jerry's must continue to be vigilant and demonstrate that it can both be successful and ward off McDonaldization over the long haul.

Recent developments offer little comfort to the opponents of McDonaldization. In early 1995, Ben & Jerry's share prices had dropped about two-thirds from their all-time high; total sales for 1994 were expected to be only slightly higher than those for 1993; and the company lost almost five million dollars in the fourth quarter of 1994,[61] the company's first loss since it became publicly owned in 1984.

The result of the recent search for a new president and chief executive officer is telling. Consistent with its "funky" image, the company began a contest, "Yo! I'm Your C.E.O.," and 20,000 people responded to the call for 100-word essays explaining why they should get the job. In the end, however, the company turned its back on the contestants and its funky corporate image, and employed a mainstream executive "headhunter." This effort eventually led to the hiring of an experienced businessman, Robert Holland, Jr., to run the company. Only after his appointment did he submit a poem as his entry in the "contest." The way he was chosen is only part of the problem. For example, when he was introduced, he announced that his objective for Ben & Jerry's was "to go from $150 million to a half-billion or more" in revenues.[62] Such a policy stands in contrast to Ben's position of slow growth and, if successful, promises to bring an unprecedented degree of McDonaldization to Ben & Jerry's. It is also worth noting that to recruit the new executive, the company bypassed its restrictions on pay differences and offered him a base salary of $250,000 a year.

B&B's: Alternatives to "McBed, McBreakfasts"

Another example of a nonrationalized alternative is the bed-and-breakfast (B&B). In fact, one news report on B&Bs was entitled, "B&Bs Offer Travelers Break from McBed, McBreakfast."[63] B&Bs are private homes that rent out rooms to travelers and offer them home-style hospitality and a breakfast in the morning. Traditionally, the hosts live in the home while they operate it, taking a personal interest in the guests. Although many existed long before, B&Bs began to boom at the beginning of the 1980s.[64] Some travelers had grown weary of the cold impersonality of rationalized motel rooms and sought out, instead, the types of nonrationalized accommodations offered by B&Bs. Said one visitor to a B&B, "It was marvelous. . . . The innkeepers treated us like family. It was so comfortable and friendly and charming and romantic."[65]

But success, once again, has brought with it the signs of McDonaldization. The range of amenities offered is expanding, and the prices rising. It is getting harder to distinguish B&Bs from inns or small hotels. Owners increasingly no longer live in the B&B but hire managers to run things for them. Said one observer, "Your best B&B's are those where the owner is on the premises. . . . When the owner leaves and hires a manager, bad things start happening. Dust balls start accumulating under the beds, the coffee gets stale, and the toast is burnt."[66] In other words, quality suffers. With the expansion of B&Bs, the American Bed and Breakfast Association came into existence in 1981, and guidebooks about B&Bs proliferated. Now inspections are being undertaken, standards developed, and a rating system implemented. In other words, efforts are underway to rationalize the burgeoning B&B industry.

Carving out a Nonrationalized Niche: Life in the Skunk Works

Although you might open a business like Marvelous Market or start a bed-and-breakfast as a way of carving a nonrationalized niche for yourself, few people can or want to assay such an undertaking. This section offers a few illustrations of more easily achieved ways to carve out nonrationalized niches in rationalized systems. It will focus on the work world; however, similar niches can be carved in every other social institution.

The ability to carve out such a niche tends to be related to one's position in the occupational hierarchy. Those in high-ranking occupations have a greater ability to create such niches than those in lower-status occupations. Physicians, lawyers, accountants, architects, and the like in private practice have the capacity to create such an environment for themselves. Within large organizations, those at the top have the greatest power to resist rationalization. The general (unwritten) rule for most organizational higher-ups seems to be to impose rationality on others while keeping their own work as nonrational as possible. Rationalization is something to be imposed on others, especially those with little power. However, some people in lower-ranking occupations are also in a position to be largely free of rationalization. For example, taxi drivers, because they work primarily on their own, are free to construct a nonrationalized work life. They can go where they want, choose their passengers, and eat and take breaks when they wish. Similar possibilities exist for nightguards and maintenance workers in automated factories. Those who work on their own or in relative isolation within an organization are in a better position to create a nonrationalized work environment. Nonetheless, higher-status occupations offer people the most opportunities to create nonrationalized niches.

Take the position of a tenured senior college professor at a large state university (no names, please) as an extreme example of a position that enables the creation of a nonrationalized work life in an otherwise highly rational university bureaucracy. This semester, for example, our professor teaches on Monday afternoons from 3:00 to 4:15 and evenings from 6:30 to 9:00 and on Wednesday afternoons from 3:00 to 4:15. In addition, office hours (about two hours a week), an occasional faculty meeting (one hour, once a month), and an occasional committee meeting are the only other work hours determined by the university. The professor will often be on campus at other times, but for various appointments arranged at her convenience. Furthermore, the preset class hours run for only thirty weeks, or two full semesters, each year, leaving the other twenty-two weeks virtually free. Thus, for only a few hours a week and a little more than half the year does she have to be at any particular place doing any particular thing at any particular time. In other words, her work time is almost totally nonrationalized.

If she wanted, as a tenured full professor, she could idle her days away. However, she chooses not to do that; instead she occupies herself with professional activities, such as writing books and articles. But how, when, and what she writes is totally nonrationalized: in the middle of the night or early in the morning; on a word processor, a yellow pad, or even a stone tablet; about McDonaldization or the latest demographic trends. She can write clad in a business suit or in her bathrobe. She can take a break when she likes, go for daily walks with her dog, or listen to her favorite book-on-tape whenever she pleases. In short, her work life is almost totally nonrationalized.

It is possible to find such nonrationalized work in other types of organizations, at least to some degree. For example, some high-tech organizations have created and encouraged the use of "skunk works," where people can be insulated from routine organizational demands and do their work as they see fit.[67] Skunk works emphasize creativity and innovation, not conformity. Thomas Peters and Robert Waterman describe them as singularly nonrational, even irrational, work settings:

> They were creating almost radical *decentralization and autonomy*, with its attendant *overlap, messiness* around the edges, *lack of coordination*, *internal competition*, and somewhat *chaotic* conditions, in order to breed the entrepreneurial spirit. They had *forsworn* a measure of *tidiness* in order to achieve regular innovation.[68] [Italics added.]

The italicized terms in the preceding quotation would all be considered nonrational or irrational from the point of view of a McDonaldized society.

Nonrationalized times and places tend to be conducive to creativity. It is difficult to be creative in the face of incessant, externally imposed, and repetitive demands. Thus, working in a nonrationalized setting serves not only the individual, but many employers and society as well. All need a steady influx of creative new ideas and products, which are far less likely to emanate from rigidly controlled bureaucratic settings than they are from skunk works.

Even in highly rationalized organizations, people can carve out a range of nonrationalized work spaces and times. For example, by finishing routine tasks quickly, a worker would leave himself or herself time to engage in nonrationalized, albeit work-related, activities. I am not suggesting that it is easy to find nonrationalized occupations or to carve out nonrationalized space within McDonaldized organizations, and I am not suggesting that everyone can do it all the time. But it is possible for some people, some of the time, to carve out nonrationalized niches for themselves.

I would not want to push this idea too far. First, rationalized organizations must provide both what is needed to do creative work and the outlets for that work. In other words, nonrationalized niches of creativity need the support of rationalized systems. Second, no large-scale organization can exist composed of nothing but such niches. The result would be organizational chaos. Third, not everyone wants to work in such nonrationalized niches; indeed many people prefer their work days to be highly routinized. Fourth, not everyone is capable of operating in a nonrationalized niche. Thus, I am not arguing for a work world composed of nothing but creative occupational spaces. However, I do assert the need for more nonrationalized niches in an otherwise highly rationalized world.

Individual Responses to McDonaldization: Subverting the Process

Beyond actions within the work world, those uncomfortable with or opposed to McDonaldization can challenge it in other ways. People who view the rationalized cage as rubber or iron may choose to extract the best of what the McDonaldized world has to offer without succumbing to its dangers and excesses. This will not be easy to do, because the lure of McDonaldized institutions is great, and it is easy to become a devotee of, and enmeshed in, rationalized activities. Thus, those who use rationalized systems for what they have to offer need to keep the dangers of McDonaldization always in the forefront of their thinking. But, being able to get a bank balance in the middle of the night, to avoid hospital emergency rooms by having minor problems cared for at "McDoctors," and to lose weight quickly and safely at Jenny Craig, among many other conveniences, are all attractive possibilities for most people. The secret is clearly to be able to take advantage of the best that the McDonaldized world has to offer without becoming imprisoned in that world.

How can people do this? For one thing, they can use McDonaldized systems *only* when such use is unavoidable, or when what they have to offer cannot be matched by nonrationalized systems. To help limit their use, perhaps we should put warning labels on the front doors of McDonaldized systems much like those found on cigarette packs:

WARNING!

Sociologists have found that habitual use of McDonaldized systems is hazardous to your physical and psychological well-being and to society as a whole.

Above all, people should avoid the routine and systematic use of McDonaldized systems. To avoid the iron cage, they must seek out nonrationalized alternatives whenever possible. Such a search for these niches is difficult and time-consuming. It is far easier to use the various aspects of McDonaldized society than it is to find and use nonrationalized alternatives. Avoiding McDonaldization requires hard work and vigilance.

The most extreme step would be to pack up and leave the highly McDonaldized society of the United States. However, many, if not most, other societies have embarked on the rationalization process or are about to. Thus, a move to another society might buy people some time, but eventually, McDonaldization would have to be confronted, this time in a less familiar context.

A less extreme step would be to create nonrationalized enterprises. Not only good in themselves, such enterprises can offer much success, since there will always be people (I hope) who will frequent these enterprises as a manifestation of their undying gratitude for the existence of alternatives to McDonaldization. Thus, the founding and frequenting of nonrationalized enterprises in niches throughout society can help people cope with the excesses of rationalization.

The following list contains other actions individuals can take to cope with McDonaldization.[69] Some of these suggestions are offered "tongue-in-cheek," although the reader should not lose sight of the fact that McDonaldization is an extremely serious problem.

- For those of you who can afford it, avoid living in apartments or tract houses. Try to live in an atypical environment, preferably one you have built yourself or have had built for you. If you must live in an apartment or a tract house, humanize and individualize it.

- Avoid daily routine as much as possible. Try to do as many things as possible in a different way from one day to the next.

- More generally, do as many things as you can for yourself. If you must use services, frequent nonrationalized, nonfranchised establishments. For example, lubricate your own car. If you are unwilling or unable to do so, have it done at your local, independent gasoline station. Do not, at all costs, frequent one of the franchised lube businesses.

- Instead of popping into H & R Block at income-tax time, hire a local accountant, preferably one who works out of an office in his or her home.

- Similarly, the next time a minor medical or dental emergency leads you to think of a "McDoctor" or a "McDentist," resist the temptation and go instead to your neighborhood doctor or dentist, preferably one in solo practice.

- The next time you need a pair of glasses, use the local store-front optometrist rather than the Pearle Vision Center, for example.

- Avoid Hair Cuttery, SuperCuts, and other hair-cutting chains; go instead to a local barber or hairdresser.

- At least once a week, pass up lunch at McDonald's and frequent a local cafe or deli. For dinner, again at least once a week, stay at home, unplug the microwave, avoid the freezer, and cook a meal from scratch.

- To really shake up the clerk at the department store, use cash rather than your credit card.

- Send back to the post office all junk mail, especially that addressed to "occupant" or "resident."

- The next time a computer phones you, gently place the phone on the floor, thereby allowing the disembodied voice to drone on, occupying the line so that others will not be bothered by such calls for a while.

- When dialing a business, always choose the "voice mail" option that permits you to speak to a real person.

- Never buy artificial products such as Molly McButter and Butter Buds.

- Seek out restaurants that use real china and metal utensils; avoid those that use materials such as styrofoam that adversely affect the environment.

- Organize groups to protest abuses by McDonaldized systems. As you have seen, these systems do adapt to such protests. If you work in such a system, organize your coworkers to create more humanized working conditions.

- If you must frequent a fast-food restaurant, dine at one, such as Macheezmo Mouse Mexican Cafe, that has demonstrated sensitivity to the dangers of McDonaldization.

- If you are a regular at McDonald's, try to get to know the counterpeople. Also, do what else you can to humanize it. In fact, during the breakfast hours, customers have done just that, "subverting the process." Instead of hastening through their meal, many breakfast customers, especially among the elderly, form informal "breakfast clubs" and "come every day of the week to read their papers, chat, drink coffee, and gobble down an Egg McMuffin."[70] If breakfasts can be de-McDonaldized, why not other meals? Other aspects of the fast-food experience?

- Read *The New York Times* rather than *USA TODAY* once a week. Similarly, watch PBS news once a week with its three long stories rather than the network news shows with their numerous snippets.

- More generally, watch as little television as possible. If you must watch TV, choose PBS. If you must watch one of the networks, turn off the sound and avert your eyes during commercials. After all, most commercials are sponsored by enterprises that tout the virtues of rationalization.

- Avoid most finger foods. If you must eat finger foods, make them homemade sandwiches and fresh fruits and vegetables.

- On your next vacation, go to only one locale and get to know it and its inhabitants well.

- Never enter a domed stadium or one with artificial grass; make periodic pilgrimages to Fenway Park in Boston and Wrigley Field in Chicago.

- Avoid classes with short-answer tests graded by computer. If a computer-graded exam is unavoidable, make extraneous marks and curl the edges of the exam so that the computer cannot deal with it.

- Seek out small classes; get to know your professors.

- Go to no movies that have roman numerals after their names.

Regina Schrambling has developed a variety of strategies similar to those in the previous list for dealing with the health threats (especially Salmonella) posed by the rationalization of food production.[71] Interestingly, Schrambling recognizes that returning to the prerationalized raising of chickens is not the answer. She argues that the "lifestyles" of such chickens, including "worm-grubbing," led to the possibility of Salmonella even in the prerationalized days of chicken production. Nevertheless, she prefers to shop at farmers' markets and buy chickens raised the older way. She buys her eggs "in hand-packed boxes from the same New York State farmer." In her view such eggs are fresher and cleaner than mass-produced eggs. She also purchases cantaloupes from farmers' markets and refuses to buy them in supermarkets because they have been in transit so long that there is an increased risk of spoilage and disease. Though rationalization has allowed people to eat fruits and vegetables year-round, it creates costs and dangers. As she puts it, they have been raised "in countries where we would never dare drink the water, where pesticides banned here are used freely." Thus, of course, she only buys fruits and vegetables during their local seasons.

More generally, Schrambling argues that people need to understand the limited seasons for fruits and vegetables:

> We would remember that the strawberry crop is really as fleeting as fireflies, that sweet corn waits for no one; it's best when eaten within hours of leaving the stalk. There's nothing like the farmers' market in January, with only potatoes and squash and apples for sale, to give a deep new appreciation of nature's cycles.

Because of this, people need to understand that "we can't have all of the food all of the time."[72]

Schrambling's position seems reasonable, even laudable, but the forces of McDonaldization continue to press forward, overcoming the kinds of boundaries she articulates. For example, science has recently discovered that genetically altered tomatoes can be prevented from producing the gas that causes them to ripen.[73] This permits the tomatoes, and potentially many other fruits and vegetables, to be left on the vine until maturity instead of being picked early as is often the case, shipped great distances without refrigeration, stored for weeks, and then ripened through exposure to ethylene gas when the retailer wishes to put them up for sale. Thus, if this technique proves viable commercially, people will, contrary to Schrambling, have many fruits and vegetables, and even cut flowers, "all the time." Similarly, the strawberry crop may now not be as "fleeting" as Schrambling says. The Driscoll strawberry, grown in Watsonville, California ("the strawberry capital of the world"), is big, glossy, and, most important, available [because of the favorable climate] all year round. Surprisingly, Driscoll strawberries "actually have some flavor, too."[74]

It is particularly important that steps be taken to prevent children from becoming mindless supporters of McDonaldization.

◆ Instead of using a "McChild"-care center, leave your child with a responsible neighbor interested in earning some extra money.

◆ Keep your children away from television as much as possible and encourage them to participate in creative games. It is especially important that they not be exposed to the steady barrage of commercials from rationalized institutions, especially on Saturday morning cartoon shows.

◆ Lead efforts to keep McDonaldization out of the school system.

◆ If you can afford it, send your child to a small, non-McDonaldized educational institution.

◆ Above all, when possible, avoid taking your children to fast-food restaurants or their clones in other domains. If no alternatives are present (for example, you're on a highway and the only options are various fast-food chains), consider blindfolding your child until the ordeal is over. (Remember, some of these suggestions are only half serious.)

Conclusion

There *are* steps that can be taken to cope with McDonaldization. However, I hold little hope that such actions, even if they were all to be employed by many people, would reverse the trend toward McDonaldization. But, despite this apparent inevitability, I think the struggle is worthwhile. First, it will mitigate the worst excesses of McDonaldized systems. Second, it will lead to the discovery, creation, and use of more niches where people who are so inclined can escape McDonaldization for at least a part of their day or even a larger portion of their lives. Finally, and perhaps most important, the struggle itself is ennobling. As a general rule, such struggles are nonrationalized, individual and collective activities. It is in such struggles that people can express genuinely human reason in a world that in virtually all other ways has set up rationalized systems to deny people this expression.

Although I have emphasized the irresistibility of McDonaldization throughout this book, my fondest hope is that I am wrong. Indeed, a major motivation behind this book is to alert readers to the dangers of McDonaldization and to motivate them to act to stem its tide. I hope that people can resist McDonaldization and create instead a more reasonable, more human world.

A few years ago, McDonald's was sued by the famous French chef, Paul Bocuse, for using his picture on a poster without his permission. Enraged, Bocuse said, "How can I be seen promoting this tasteless, boneless food in which everything is soft." Nevertheless, Bocuse seemed to acknowledge the inevitability of McDonaldization: "There's a need for this kind of thing . . . and trying to get rid of it seems to me to be as futile as trying to get rid of the prostitutes in the Bois de Bologne."[75] Lo and behold, two weeks later, it was announced that the Paris police had cracked down on prostitution in the Bois de Bologne. Said a police spokesperson, "There are none left." Thus, just as chef Bocuse was wrong about the prostitutes, perhaps I am wrong about the irresistibility of McDonaldization. Yet, before I grow overly optimistic, it should be noted that "everyone knows that the prostitutes will be back as soon as the operation is over. In the spring, police predict, there will be even more than before."[76] Similarly, it remains likely that no matter how intense the opposition, the future will bring with it more rather than less McDonaldization. Even if this proves to be the case, it is my hope that you will follow some of the advice outlined in this chapter for protesting and mitigating the worst effects of McDonaldization. Faced with Max Weber's iron cage and image of a future dominated by the polar night of icy darkness and hardness, I hope that if nothing else, you will consider the words of the poet Dylan Thomas: "Do not go gentle into that good night. . . . Rage, rage against the dying of the light."[77]

Endnotes

Chapter 1

1. For a similar but narrower viewpoint to the one expressed here, see Benjamin R. Barber. "Jihad Vs. McWorld." *The Atlantic Monthly*, March 1992, pp. 53–63.

2. These and other data on McDonald's come from its most recent (1993) annual report, *The Annual*.

3. Cynthia Rigg. "McDonald's Lean Units Beef up NY Presence." *Crain's New York Business*, October 31, 1994, p. 1.

4. The source for this information is Pepsico, Inc.'s 1993 Annual Report, p. 18.

5. Mark Albright. "INSIDE JOB: Fast-Food Chains Serve a Captive Audience." *St. Petersburg Times*, January 15, 1995, p. 1H.

6. Bill McDowall. "The Global Market Challenge." *Restaurants & Institutions*, vol. 104, no. 26, November 1, 1994, pp. 52ff.

7. Eben Shapiro in "Overseas Sizzle for McDonald's." *New York Times*, April 17, 1992, pp. D1, D4.

8. "Investors with Taste for Growth Looking to Golden Arches." *Tampa Tribune*, January 11, 1995, Business and Finance, p. 7.

9. Valerie Reitman. "India Anticipates the Arrival of the Beefless Big Mac." *Wall Street Journal*, October 20, 1993, pp. B1, B3.

10. Alison Leigh Cowan. "Unlikely Spot for Fast Food." *New York Times*, April 29, 1984, section 3, p. 5.

11. Philip Elmer-Dewitt. "Anita the Agitator." *Time*, January 25, 1993, pp. 52ff; Eben Shapiro. "The Sincerest Form of Rivalry." *New York Times*, October 19, 1991, pp. 35, 46.

12. Timothy Egan. "Big Chains Are Joining Manhattan's Toy Wars." *New York Times*, December 8, 1990, p. 29

13. Stacey Burling. "Health Club . . . For Kids." *Washington Post*, November 21, 1991, p. D5.

14. Tamar Lewin. "Small Tots, Big Biz." *New York Times Magazine*, January 19, 1989, p. 89.

15. Paul Gruchow. "Unchaining America: Communities Are Finding Ways to Keep Independent Entrepreneurs in Business." *Utne Reader*, January–February 1995, p. 17.

16. Paul Gruchow. "Unchaining America: Communities Are Finding Ways to Keep Independent Entrepreneurs in Business." *Utne Reader*, January–February 1995, pp. 17–18.

17. McDonald's Corporation Customer and Community Relations.

18. E. R. Shipp. "The McBurger Stand That Started It All." *New York Times*, February 27, 1985, section 3, p. 3.

19. "Wedge of Americana: In Moscow, Pizza Hut Opens 2 Restaurants." *Washington Post*, September 12, 1990, p. B10.

20. Jeb Blount. "Frying Down to Rio." *Washington Post/Business*, May 18, 1994, pp. F1, F5.

21. Marshall Fishwick, Ed. *Ronald Revisited: The World of Ronald McDonald*. Bowling Green, OH: Bowling Green University Press, 1983.

22. John F. Harris. "McMilestone Restaurant Opens Doors in Dale City." *Washington Post*, April 7, 1988, p. DI.

23. Conrad Kottak. "Rituals at McDonald's," in Marshall Fishwick (ed.). *Ronald Revisited: The World of Ronald McDonald*. Bowling Green, OH: Bowling Green University Press, 1983, pp. 52–58.

24. Bill Keller. "Of Famous Arches, Beeg Meks and Rubles." *New York Times*, January 28, 1990, section 1, pp. 1, 12.

25. William Severini Kowinski. *The Malling of America: An Inside Look at the Great Consumer Paradise*. New York: William Morrow, 1985, p. 218.

26. Stephen M. Fjellman. *Vinyl Leaves: Walt Disney World and America*. Boulder, CO: Westview Press, 1992. In another example of other countries creating their own McDonaldized systems and exporting them, Japan's Sega Enterprises is planning to open the first Segaworld indoor urban theme park in London in 1996; see "A Sega Theme Park for Piccadilly Circus." *New York Times*, February 14, 1995, p. D5.

27. Bob Garfield. "How I Spent (and Spent and Spent) My Disney Vacation." *Washington Post*, July 7, 1991, p. B5. See also Margaret J. King.

"Empires of Popular Culture: McDonald's and Disney," in Marshall Fishwick (ed.). *Ronald Revisited: The World of Ronald McDonald*. Bowling Green, OH: Bowling Green University Press, 1983, pp. 106–119.

28. Steven Greenhouse. "The Rise and Rise of McDonald's." *New York Times*, June 8, 1986, section 3, p. 1.

29. Richard L. Papiernik. "Mac Attack?" *Financial World*, April 12, 1994, p. 30.

30. Laura Shapiro. "Ready for McCatfish?" *Newsweek*, October 15, 1990, pp. 76–77; N. R. Kleinfeld. "Fast Food's Changing Landscape." *New York Times*, April 14, 1985, section 3, pp. 1, 6.

31. Louis Uchitelle. "That's Funny, Those Pickles Don't Look Russian." *New York Times*, February 27, 1992, p. A4.

32. Nicholas D. Kristof. "'Billions Served' (and That Was Without China)." *New York Times*, April 24, 1992. p. A4.

33. Cynthia Rigg. "McDonald's Lean Units Beef up NY Presence." *Crain's New York Business*, October 31, 1994, p. 1.

34. Carole Sugarman. "Dining Out on Campus." *Washington Post/Health* February 14, 1995, p. 20.

35. Gilbert Chan. "Fast Food Chains Pump Profits at Gas Stations." *Fresno Bee*, October 10, 1994, p. F4.

36. Edwin McDowell. "Fast Food Fills Menu for Many Hotel Chains." *New York Times*, January 9, 1992, pp. D1, D6.

37. "Fast-Food Flights." *Phoenix Gazette*, November 25, 1994, p. D1.

38. Mark Albright. "INSIDE JOB: Fast-Food Chains Serve a Captive Audience." *St. Petersburg Times*, January 15, 1995, p. 1H.

39. Mike Berry. "Redoing School Cafeterias to Favor Fast-Food Eateries." *Orlando Sentinel*, January 12, 1995, p. 11.

40. Paul Farhi. "Domino's Is Going to School." *Washington Post*, September 21, 1990, p. F3.

41. "Grade 'A' Burgers." *New York Times*, April 13, 1986, pp. 12, 15.

42. George Anders. "McDonald's Methods Come to Medicine As Chains Acquire Physicians' Practices." *Wall Street Journal*, August 24, 1993, pp. B1, B6.

43. Peter Prichard. *The Making of McPaper: The Inside Story of USA TODAY*. Kansas City, MO: Andrews, McMeel and Parker, 1987.

44. I would like to thank Lee Martin for bringing this case (and menu) to my attention.

45. Peter Prichard. *The Making of McPaper: The Inside Story of USA TODAY*. Kansas City, MO: Andrews, McMeel and Parker, 1987, pp. 232–233.

46. Howard Kurtz. "Slicing, Dicing News to Attract the Young." *Washington Post*, January 6, 1991, p. Al.

47. Nicholas D. Kristof. "Court Test Is Likely on Dial-a-Porn Service Game." *New York Times*, October 15, 1986, section 1, p. 16.

48. Cited in Robin Leidner. *Fast Food, Fast Talk: Service Work and the Routinization of Everyday Life*. Berkeley: University of California Press, 1993, p. 9.

49. Martin Gottlieb. "Pornography's Plight Hits Times Square." *New York Times*, October 5, 1986, section 3, p. 6.

50. Max Weber. *Economy and Society*. Totowa, NJ: Bedminster Press, 1921/1968; Stephen Kalberg. "Max Weber's Types of Rationality: Cornerstones for the Analysis of Rationalization Processes in History." *American Journal of Sociology* 85(1980):1145–1179.

51. Ian Mitroff and Warren Bennis. *The Unreality Industry: The Deliberate Manufacturing of Falsehood and What It Is Doing to Our Lives*. New York: Birch Lane Press, 1989, p. 142.

52. Robin Leidner has developed the idea of scripts in her book, *Fast Food, Fast Talk: Service Work and the Routinization of Everyday Life*. Berkeley: University of California Press, 1993.

53. The idea of recipes comes from the work of Alfred Schutz. See, for example, *The Phenomenology of the Social World*. Evanston, IL: Northwestern University Press, 1932/1967.

54. Robin Leidner. *Fast Food, Fast Talk: Service Work and the Routinization of Everyday Life*. Berkeley: University of California Press, 1993, p. 82.

55. Experimental robots of this type already exist.

56. Robert J. Samuelson. "In Praise of McDonald's." *Washington Post*, November 1, 1989, p. A25.

57. I would like to thank my colleague, Stan Presser, for suggesting that I enumerate the kinds of advantages listed on these pages.

58. Edwin M. Reingold. "America's Hamburger Helper." *Time*, June 29, 1992, pp. 66–67.

59. It should be pointed out that the words *rational, rationality,* and *rationalization* are being used differently here and throughout the book than they are ordinarily employed. For one thing, people usually think of these terms as being largely positive; something that is rational is usually considered to be good. However, they are used here in a generally negative way. The positive term in this analysis is genuinely human "reason" (for example, the ability to act and work creatively), which is seen as being denied by inhuman, rational systems such as the fast-food restaurant. For another, the term *rationalization* is usually associated with Freudian theory as a way of explaining away some behavior, but here it describes the increasing pervasiveness of rationality throughout society. Thus, in reading this book, you must be careful to interpret the terms in these ways rather than in the ways they are conventionally employed.

60. Timothy Egan. "In Land of French Fry, Study Finds Problems." *New York Times*, February 7, 1994, p. A10.

61. Alan Riding. "Only the French Elite Scorn Mickey's Debut." *New York Times*, April 13, 1992, p. A13.

62. George Stauth and Bryan S. Turner. "Nostalgia, Postmodernism and the Critique of Mass Culture." *Theory, Culture and Society* 5(1988):509–526; Bryan S. Turner. "A Note on Nostalgia." *Theory, Culture and Society* 4(1987):147–156.

63. Lee Hockstader. "No Service, No Smile, Little Sauce." *Washington Post*, August 5, 1991, p. A12.

64. Douglas Farah. "Cuban Fast Food Joints Are Quick Way for Government to Rally Economy." *Washington Post*, January 24, 1995, p. A14.

65. In this sense, this resembles Marx's critique of capitalism. Marx was not animated by a romanticization of precapitalist society, but rather by the desire to produce a truly human (communist) society on the base provided by capitalism. Despite this specific affinity to Marxist theory, this book is, as you will see, premised far more on the theories of Max Weber.

Chapter 2

1. Though the precursors discussed throughout this chapter do not exhaust the rationalized institutions that predate McDonald's, they are the most important for understanding McDonald's and McDonaldization.

2. This discussion of Weber's ideas is based on Max Weber. *Economy and Society*. Totowa, NJ: Bedminster Press, 1921/1968.

3. Weber called the latter substantive rationality in order to distinguish it from formal rationality.

4. Ronald Takaki. *Iron Cages: Race and Culture in 19th-Century America*. New York: Oxford University Press, 1990, p. ix.

5. Harvey Greisman. "Disenchantment of the World." *British Journal of Sociology* 27(1976): 497–506.

6. Zygmunt Bauman. *Modernity and the Holocaust*. Ithaca, NY: Cornell University Press, 1989, p. 149.

7. Zygmunt Bauman. *Modernity and the Holocaust*. Ithaca, NY: Cornell University Press, 1989, p. 8.

8. As you will see in chapter 3, the fast-food restaurants enhance their efficiency by getting customers to perform (without pay) a variety of their tasks.

9. Zygmunt Bauman. *Modernity and the Holocaust*. Ithaca, NY: Cornell University Press, 1989, p. 103.

10. Zygmunt Bauman. *Modernity and the Holocaust*. Ithaca, NY: Cornell University Press, 1989, p. 89.

11. Zygmunt Bauman. *Modernity and the Holocaust*. Ithaca, NY: Cornell University Press, 1989, p. 8.

12. Zygmunt Bauman. *Modernity and the Holocaust*. Ithaca, NY: Cornell University Press, 1989, p. 102.

13. Feingold, cited in Zygmunt Bauman. *Modernity and the Holocaust*. Ithaca, NY: Cornell University Press, 1989, p. 136.

14. Frederick W. Taylor. *The Principles of Scientific Management*. New York: Harper & Row, 1947.

15. George Ritzer and Terri LeMoyne. "Hyperrationality: An Extension of Weberian and Neo-Weberian Theory," in George Ritzer. *Metatheorizing in Sociology*. Lexington, MA: Lexington Books, 1991, pp. 93–115.

16. Ester Reiter. *Making Fast Food*. Montreal and Kingston: McGill-Queen's University Press, 1991, pp. 112–114.

17. Henry Ford. *My Life and Work*. Garden City, NY: Doubleday, Page, and Co., 1922; James T. Flink. *The Automobile Age*. Cambridge, MA: MIT Press, 1988.

18. Bruce A. Lohof. "Hamburger Stand Industrialization and the Fast-Food Phenomenon," in Marshall Fishwick (ed.). *Ronald Revisited: The World of Ronald McDonald*. Bowling Green, OH: Bowling Green University Press, 1983, p. 30; see also Ester Reiter. *Making Fast Food*. Montreal and Kingston: McGill-Queen's University Press, 1991, p. 75.

19. Marshall Fishwick. "Cloning Clowns: Some Final Thoughts," in Marshall Fishwick (ed.). *Ronald Revisited: The World of Ronald McDonald*. Bowling Green, OH: Bowling Green University Press, 1983, pp. 148-151. For more on the relationship described in the same paragraph between the automobile and the growth of the tourist industry, see James T. Flink. *The Automobile Age*. Cambridge, MA: MIT Press, 1988.

20. James T. Flink. *The Automobile Age*. Cambridge, MA: MIT Press, 1988; see also Alfred P. Sloan, Jr. *My Years at General Motors*. Garden City, NY: Doubleday, 1964.

21. "Levitt's Progress." *Fortune*, October 1952, pp. 155ff.

22. Richard Perez-Pena. "William Levitt, 86, Suburb Maker, Dies." *New York Times*, January 29, 1994, p. 26.

23. "The Most House for the Money." *Fortune*, October 1952, p. 152.

24. "The Most House for the Money," *Fortune*, October 1952, p. 153.

25. Herbert Gans. *The Levittowners: Ways of Life and Politics in a New Suburban Community*. New York: Pantheon Books, 1967, p. 13.

26. Patricia Dane Rogers. "Building . . ." *Washington Post/Home*, February 2, 1995, pp. 12, 15.

27. Richard E. Gordon, Katherine K. Gordon, and Max Gunther. *The Split Level Trap*. New York: Gilbert Geis Associates, 1960.

28. Georgia Dullea. "The Tract House As Landmark." *New York Times*, October 17, 1991, pp. Cl, C8.

29. Herbert Gans. *The Levittowners: Ways of Life and Politics in a New Suburban Community*. New York: Pantheon Books, 1967, p. 432.

30. William Severini Kowinski. *The Malling of America: An Inside Look at the Great Consumer Paradise*. New York: Morrow, 1985.

31. Kara Swisher. "A Mall for America?" *Washington Post/Business*, June 30, 1991, pp. H1, H4.

32. Janice L. Kaplan. "The Mall Outlet for Cabin Fever." *Washington Post/Weekend*, February 10, 1995, p. 53.

33. William Severini Kowinski. *The Malling of America: An Inside Look at the Great Consumer Paradise*. New York: Morrow, 1985, p. 25.

34. Ray Kroc. *Grinding It Out*. New York: Berkeley Medallion Books, 1977; Stan Luxenberg. *Roadside Empires: How the Chains Franchised America*. New York: Viking, 1985; and John F. Love. *McDonald's: Behind the Arches*. Toronto: Bantam Books, 1986.

35. John F. Love. *McDonald's: Behind the Arches*. Toronto: Bantam Books, 1986, p. 18.

36. John F. Love. *McDonald's: Behind the Arches*. Toronto: Bantam Books, 1986, p. 20.

37. John F. Love. *McDonald's: Behind the Arches*. Toronto: Bantam Books, 1986, pp. 68–69.

38. Like McDonald's Hamburger University, Burger King set up its own Burger King University in 1978; see Ester Reiter. *Making Fast Food*. Montreal and Kingston: McGill-Queen's University Press, 1991, p. 68.

39. John F. Love. *McDonald's: Behind the Arches*. Toronto: Bantam Books, 1986, pp. 141–142.

Chapter 3

1. Herbert Simon. *Administrative Behavior* (2nd ed.). New York: Free Press, 1957.

2. Ray Kroc. *Grinding It Out*. New York: Berkeley Medallion Books, 1977, p. 8.

3. Max Boas and Steve Chain. *Big Mac: The Unauthorized Story of McDonald's*. New York: E. P. Dutton, 1976, pp. 9–10.

4. Max Boas and Steve Chain. *Big Mac: The Unauthorized Story of McDonald's*. New York: E. P. Dutton, 1976, pp. 9–10.

5. Ray Kroc. *Grinding It Out*. New York: Berkeley Medallion Books, 1977, pp. 96–97.

6. Arthur Kroker, Marilouise Kroker, and David Cook. *Panic Encyclopedia: The Definitive Guide to the Postmodern Scene*. New York: St. Martin's Press, 1989, p. 119.

7. Barnaby J. Feder. "McDonald's Finds There's Still Plenty of Room to Grow." *New York Times*, January 9, 1994, p. 5.

8. Michael Lev. "Raising Fast Food's Speed Limit." *Washington Post*, August 7, 1991, p. DI.

9. They already have McDonaldized the process of breeding, raising, and slaughtering chickens (see chapter 6).

10. Henry Ford. *My Life and Work*. Garden City, NY: Doubleday, 1922, p. 72.

11. Thomas R. Ide and Arthur J. Cordell. "Automating Work." *Society 31*, 1994, p.68.

12. Martin Parker and David Jary. "The McUniversity: Organization, Management and Academic Subjectivity." *Organization 2* (1995): 1–19.

13. George Ritzer and David Walczak. "The Changing Nature of American Medicine." *Journal of American Culture 9* (1987): 43–51.

14. Julia Wallace. "Dr. Denton Cooley—Star of 'The Heart Surgery Factory.'" *Washington Post*, July 19, 1980, p. A6.

15. "Moving Right Along," *Time*, July 1, 1985, p.44.

16. Robert Zussman. "The Medical Profession, Health Care Reform and the Welfare State," in Craig Calhoun and George Ritzer (eds.). *PRIMIS*. New York: McGraw-Hill, 1995.

17. Frederick W. Taylor. *The Principles of Scientific Management*. New York: Harper & Row, 1947, pp. 6–7.

18. Frederick W. Taylor. *The Principles of Scientific Management*. New York: Harper & Row, 1947, p. 117.

19. Henry Ford. *My Life and Work*. Garden City, NY: Doubleday, 1922, p. 80.

20. Michael Miller. "Professors Customize Textbooks, Blurring Roles of Publisher, Seller and Copy Shop." *Wall Street Journal*, August 16, 1990, pp. B1, B4.

21. Jeffrey Hadden and Charles E. Swann. *Primetime Preachers: The Rising Power of Televangelism*. Reading, MA: Addison-Wesley, 1981.

22. John Tagliabue. "Indulgences by TV." *New York Times*, December 19, 1985, section 1, p. 8.

23. Daniel Boorstin. *The Image: Guide to Pseudo-Events in America*. New York: Harper Colophon, 1961, p. 135.

24. Ian Mitroff and Warren Bennis. *The Unreality Industry: The Deliberate Manufacturing of Falsehood and What It Is Doing to Our Lives*. New York: Birch Lane Press, 1989, p. 12.

25. Barry Meier. "Need a Teller? Chicago Bank Plans a Fee." *Washington Post*, April 27, 1995, pp. D1, D23.

26. Thomas R. Ide and Arthur J. Cordell. "Automating Work." *Society 31*(1994):65ff.

27. James Barron. "Please Press 2 for Service; Press ? for an Actual Human." *New York Times*, February 17, 1989, pp. A1, B2.

28. Michael Schrage. "Calling the Technology of Voice Mail into Question." *Washington Post*, October 19, 1990, p. F3.

29. National Public Radio's "Morning Edition," October 3, 1990.

30. "The Microwave Cooks Up a New Way of Life." *Wall Street Journal*, September 19, 1989, p. B1; "Microwavable Foods—Industry's Response to Consumer Demands for Convenience." *Food Technology 41*(1987): 52–63.

31. "Microwavable Foods—Industry's Response to Consumer Demands for Convenience." *Food Technology 41*(1987):54.

32. Eben Shapiro. "A Page from Fast Food's Menu." *New York Times*, October 14, 1991, pp. Dl, D3.

33. Stan Luxenberg. *Roadside Empires: How the Chains Franchised America*. New York: Viking, 1985.

34. I would like to thank Dora Giemza for the insights on page 53 into Nutri/System. See also "Big People, Big Business: The Overweight Numbers Rising, Try Nutri/System." *Washington Post/Health*, October 10, 1989, p. 8.

35. William Severini Kowinski. *The Malling of America: An Inside Look at the Great Consumer Paradise*. New York: Morrow, 1985, p. 61.

36. It should be noted that supermarkets have sought to make shopping more efficient by institutionalizing ten-item limit, no-checks-accepted lines for consumers who might otherwise frequent the convenience stores.

37. Kara Swisher. "Companies Unveil 'Scanfone' Shopping Service." *Washington Post*, April 16, 1992, pp. B1, B15.

38. George Ritzer. *Expressing America: A Critique of the Global Credit Card Society*. Thousand Oaks, CA: Pine Forge Press, 1995.

39. Mark Potts. "Blockbuster Struggles with Merger Script." *Washington Post/Washington Business*, December 9, 1991, p. 24; Eben Shapiro. "Market Place: A Mixed Outlook for Blockbuster." *New York Times*, February 21, 1992, p. D6.

40. Don L. Boroughs. "Pressing Fast-Forward." *U.S. News & World Report*, May 16, 1994, pp. 53ff; "A Blockbuster New Idea for Grown-up Entertainment." *Chicago Tribune*, November 18, 1994, p. 1.

41. Steve Fainaru. "Endangered Species: Will the Corner Video Store Disappear in the Interactive Age?" *Boston Globe*, January 16, 1994, p. A1.

42. Stephen Fjellman. *Vinyl Leaves: Walt Disney World and America*. Boulder, CO: Westview Press, 1992.

43. Michael Harrington. "To the Disney Station." *Harper's*, January 1979, pp. 35–39.

44. Lynn Darling. "On the Inside at Parks a la Disney." *Washington Post*, August 28, 1978, p. A10.

45. For suggesting to me some of the points about McDonaldization and health clubs made on this page, I would like to thank Steve Lankenau.

46. Another dimension of McDonaldization, exercise machines also offer a high degree of calculability, with many of them registering miles run, level of difficulty, and calories burned.

Chapter 4

1. Just as quality is equated with quantity, quality is also equated with other aspects of McDonaldization such as "standardization and predictability." See Ester Reiter. *Making Fast Food*. Montreal and Kingston: McGill-Queen's University Press, p. 107.

2. In addition, as you will see in chapter 10, protests against these garish signs helped lead to their virtual disappearance.

3. This emphasis on quantity in a McDonaldized society is not restricted to fast-food restaurants. Continuing their emulation of the fast-food business, manufacturers are bringing out products for the home such as Campbell Soup Company's Big Start home breakfasts. In another example, United Airlines boasts that it serves more cities than any other airline.

4. Philip Elmer-DeWitt. "Fat Times." *Time*, January 16, 1995, pp. 60–65.

5. Barbara W. Tuchman. "The Decline of Quality." *New York Times Magazine*, November 2, 1980, p. 38. For example, United Airlines does not tell people anything about the quality of their numerous flights, such as the likelihood that their planes will be on time.

6. Marion Clark. "Arches of Triumph." *Washington Post/Book World*, June 5, 1977, p. G6.

7. A. A. Berger. "Berger Vs. Burger: A Personal Encounter," in Marshall Fishwick (ed.). *Ronald Revisited: The World of Ronald McDonald*, Bowling Green, OH: Bowling Green University Press, 1983, p. 126.

8. Max Boas and Steven Chain. *Big Mac: The Unauthorized Story of McDonald's*. New York: Dutton, 1976, p. 121.

9. Max Boas and Steven Chain. *Big Mac: The Unauthorized Story of McDonald's*. New York: Dutton, 1976, p. 117.

10. "Taco Bell Delivers Even Greater Value to its Customers by Introducing Big Fill Menu." *Business Wire*, November 2, 1994.

11. Ester Reiter. *Making Fast Food*, Montreal and Kingston: McGill-Queen's University Press, p. 84.

12. Ester Reiter. *Making Fast Food*, Montreal and Kingston: McGill-Queen's University Press, p. 85.

13. Stan Luxenburg. *Roadside Empires: How the Chains Franchised America*. New York. Viking, 1985, pp. 73–74

14. Stan Luxenburg. *Roadside Empires: How the Chains Franchised America*. New York. Viking, 1985, p. 80

15. Stan Luxenburg. *Roadside Empires: How the Chains Franchised America*. New York. Viking, 1985, pp. 84–85

16. Robin Leidner. *Fast Food, Fast Talk: Service Work and the Routinization of Everyday Life*. Berkeley: University of California Press, 1993, p. 60.

17. Susan Gervasi. "The Credentials Epidemic." *Washington Post*, August 30, 1990, p. D5.

18. Iver Peterson. "Let that Be a Lesson: Rutgers Bumps a Well-Liked but Little-Published Professor." *New York Times*, May 9, 1995, p. B1.

19. Kenneth Cooper. "Stanford President Sets Initiative on Teaching." *Washington Post*, March 3, 1991, p. A12.

20. Kenneth Cooper. "Stanford President Sets Initiative on Teaching." *Washington Post*, March 3, 1991, p. A12.

21. Dan Colburn. "Unionizing Doctors: Physicians Begin Banding Together to Fight for Autonomy and Control over Medical Care." *Washington Post/Health*, June 19, 1985, p. 7.

22. Frederick W. Taylor. *The Principles of Scientific Management*. New York: Harper & Row, 1947, p. 42.

23. Frederick W. Taylor. *The Principles of Scientific Management*. New York: Harper & Row, 1947, p. 138.

24. Frank Mankiewicz and Joel Swerdlow. *Remote Control: Television and the Manipulation of American Life*. New York: Time Books, 1978, p. 219.

25. Erik Larson. "Watching Americans Watch TV." *The Atlantic Monthly*, March 1992, p. 66; see also Peter J. Boyer. "TV Turning to People Meters to Find Who Watches What." *New York Times*, June 1, 1987, pp. A1, C16.

26. Jennifer L. Stevenson. "PBS Is a Roost for Canceled 'I'll Fly Away.'" *The San Diego Union-Tribune*, August 11, 1993, p. E10.

27. Sports are not alone in this; the political parties have shortened and streamlined their conventions to accommodate the needs and demands of television.

28. Allen Guttman. *From Ritual to Record: The Nature of Modern Sports*. New York: Cambridge University Press, 1978, p. 47.

29. Allen Guttman. *From Ritual to Record: The Nature of Modern Sports*. New York: Cambridge University Press, 1978, p. 51.

30. However, specialization in baseball has more than compensated for this and it is undoubtedly the case that people now see more rather than less use of relief pitchers. Indeed, there are now very specialized relief roles—the "long reliever" who comes in early in the game, the "closer" who finishes off a game in which his team is ahead, and relievers who specialize in getting out left- or right-handed batters.

31. Kathleen Jamieson. *Eloquence in an Electronic Age: The Transformation of Political Speechmaking*. New York: Oxford University Press, 1988; see also Marvin Kalb. "TV, Election Spoiler." *New York Times*, November 28, 1988. p. A25.

32. Kathleen Jamieson. *Eloquence in an Electronic Age: The Transformation of Political Speechmaking*. New York: Oxford University Press, 1988, p. 11.

33. Sam Marullo. *Ending the Cold War at Home: From Militarism to a More Peaceful World Order*. New York: Lexington Books, 1993.

34. Stuart Flexner. *I Hear America Talking*. New York: Simon & Schuster, 1976, p. 142.

35. N. R. Kleinfeld. "The Ever-Fatter Business of Thinness." *New York Times*, September 7, 1986, section 3, pp. 1ff.

36. Official Nutri/System publications.

37. Peter Prichard. *The Making of McPaper: The Inside Story of USA Today*. Kansas City, MO: Andrews, McMeel and Parker, 1987, p. 8.

38. That the newspaper can be read in a single sitting at a fast-food restaurant reminds me of the line in the movie *The Big Chill*, spoken by Michael (played by Jeff Goldblum), who writes for a magazine resembling *People*: "Where I work we only have one editorial rule: You can't write anything longer than the average person can read during the average crap."

39. Peter Prichard. *The Making of McPaper: The Inside Story of USA Today*. Kansas City, MO: Andrews, McMeel and Parker, 1987, pp. 113, 196.

40. Shoshana Zuboff. *In the Age of the Smart Machine: The Future of Work and Power*. New York: Basic Books, 1988.

Chapter 5

1. W. Baldamus. "Tedium and Traction in Industrial Work," in David Weir (ed.). *Men and Work in Modern Britain*. London: Fontana, 1973, pp. 78–84.

2. Robin Leidner. *Fast Food, Fast Talk: Service Work and the Routinization of Everyday Life*. Berkeley: University of California Press, 1993, pp. 45–47, 54.

3. Cited in Robin Leidner. *Fast Food, Fast Talk: Service Work and the Routinization of Everyday Life*. Berkeley: University of California Press, 1993, p. 82.

4. Margaret King. "McDonald's and the New American Landscape." *USA TODAY*, January 1980, p. 46.

5. Conrad Kottak. "Rituals at McDonald's," in Marshall Fishwick (ed.). *Ronald Revisited: The World of Ronald McDonald*. Bowling Green, OH: Bowling Green University Press, 1983, pp. 52–58.

6. Robin Leidner. *Fast Food, Fast Talk: Service Work and the Routinization of Everyday Life*. Berkeley: University of California Press, 1993.

7. Leidner reports that employees are encouraged to vary the process in order to reduce the customers' feelings of depersonalization. But at the franchise in which she worked, limits were placed on even this.

8. Roy Rogers had been taken over by Hardee's, but declining sales by franchises using the Hardee's name has led some outlets to return to using the Roy Rogers name. See Paul Farhi. "Roy Rogers to the Rescue of Hardee's." *Washington Post*, February 21, 1992, pp. Fl, F3.

9. Robin Leidner. *Fast Food, Fast Talk: Service Work and the Routinization of Everyday Life*. Berkeley: University of California Press, 1993.

10. Robin Leidner. *Fast Food, Fast Talk: Service Work and the Routinization of Everyday Life*. Berkeley: University of California Press, 1993, p. 6.

11. Robin Leidner. *Fast Food, Fast Talk: Service Work and the Routinization of Everyday Life*. Berkeley: University of California Press, 1993, p. 135.

12. Robin Leidner. *Fast Food, Fast Talk: Service Work and the Routinization of Everyday Life*. Berkeley: University of California Press, 1993.

13. Robin Leidner. *Fast Food, Fast Talk: Service Work and the Routinization of Everyday Life*. Berkeley: University of California Press, 1993, pp. 220, 230.

14. Robin Leidner. *Fast Food, Fast Talk: Service Work and the Routinization of Everyday Life*. Berkeley: University of California Press, 1993.

15. I will have more to say about this aspect of McDonaldization in chapter 7.

16. Robin Leidner. *Fast Food, Fast Talk: Service Work and the Routinization of Everyday Life*. Berkeley: University of California Press, 1993, p. 10.

17. Robin Leidner. *Fast Food, Fast Talk: Service Work and the Routinization of Everyday Life*. Berkeley: University of California Press, 1993, p. 25.

18. Robin Leidner. *Fast Food, Fast Talk: Service Work and the Routinization of Everyday Life*. Berkeley: University of California Press, 1993.

19. Harrison M. Trice and Janice M. Beyer. *The Cultures of Work Organizations*. Englewood Cliffs, NJ: Prentice-Hall, 1993.

20. Dick Schaaf. "Inside Hamburger University." *Training*, December 1994, pp. 18–24.

21. Robin Leidner. *Fast Food, Fast Talk: Service Work and the Routinization of Everyday Life*. Berkeley: University of California Press, 1993, p. 58.

22. Robin Leidner. *Fast Food, Fast Talk: Service Work and the Routinization of Everyday Life*. Berkeley: University of California Press, 1993, p. 58.

23. Henry Mitchell. "Wonder Bread, Any Way You Slice It." *Washington Post*, March 22, 1991, p. F2.

24. Stanley Joel Reiser. *Medicine and the Reign of Technology*. Cambridge, England: Cambridge University Press, 1978, p. ix.

25. Robin Leidner. *Fast Food, Fast Talk: Service Work and the Routinization of Everyday Life*. Berkeley: University of California Press, 1993, pp. 107, 108.

26. John Powers. "Tales of Hoffman." *Washington Post Sunday Arts*, March 5, 1995, p. G6.

27. The information in this section comes from an official Disney publication.

28. Lynn Darling. "On the Inside at Parks a la Disney." *Washington Post*, August 28, 1978, p. A10.

29. Lynn Darling. "On the Inside at Parks a la Disney." *Washington Post*, August 28, 1978, p. A10.

30. Cited in Stephen J. Fjellman. *Vinyl Leaves: Walt Disney World and America*. Boulder, CO: Westview, 1992, p. 226.

31. Andrew Beyer. "Lukas Has the Franchise on Almighty McDollar." *Washington Post*, August 8, 1990, pp. Fl, F8.

32. William Severini Kowinski. *The Malling of America: An Inside Look at the Great Consumer Paradise*. New York: Morrow, 1985, p. 27.

33. Iver Peterson. "Urban Dangers Send Children Indoors to Play; A Chain of Commercial Playgrounds Is One Answer for Worried Parents." *New York Times*, January 1, 1995, section 1, p. 29.

34. Jan Vertefeuille. "Fun Factory: Kids Pay to Play at the Discovery Zone and While That's Just Fine with Many Parents, It Has Some Experts Worried." *Roanoke Times & World News*, December 8, 1994, Extra, pp. 1ff.

35. William Serrin. "Let Them Eat Junk." *Saturday Review*, February 2, 1980, p. 18.

36. Similarly, Busch Gardens offers European attractions, such as a German-style beer hall, without having its clientele leave the predictable confines of the United States and the even more predictable surroundings of the modern amusement park.

37. At the opening of the Istanbul Hilton, Conrad Hilton said, "Each of our hotels . . . is a 'little America'." This quotation is from Daniel J. Boorstin. *The Image: A Guide to Pseudo-Events in America*. New York: Harper Colophon, 1961, p. 98.

38. Beth Thames. "In the Mists of Memory, Sun Always Shines on Family Camping." *New York Times*, July 9, 1986, p. C7.

39. Dirk Johnson. "Vacationing at Campgrounds Is Now Hardly Roughing It." *New York Times*, August 28, 1986, p. B1.

40. "Country-Club Campgrounds." *Newsweek*, September 24, 1984, p. 90.

41. Dirk Johnson. "Vacationing at Campgrounds Is Now Hardly Roughing It." *New York Times*, August 28, 1986, p. B1.

42. Malvina Reynolds' lyrics on page 98 are reprinted by permission of Schroder Music Co., ASCAP, copyright 1962.

Chapter 6

1. Richard Edwards. *Contested Terrain: The Transformation of the Workplace in the Twentieth Century*. New York: Basic Books, 1979.

2. Richard Edwards. *Contested Terrain: The Transformation of the Workplace in the Twentieth Century*. New York: Basic Books, 1979.

3. In recent years, the shortage of a sufficient number of teenagers to keep turnover-prone fast-food restaurants adequately stocked with employees has led to a widening of the traditional labor pool of fast-food restaurants. The fast-food restaurant seeks to maximize control even over the work behavior of adults, as I have previously discussed in chapter 5.

4. Michael Lev. "Raising Fast Food's Speed Limit." *Washington Post*, August 7, 1991, pp. D1, D4.

5. Ray Kroc. *Grinding It Out*. New York: Berkeley Medallion Books, 1977, pp. 131–132.

6. William R. Greer. "Robot Chef's New Dish: Hamburgers." *New York Times*, May 27, 1987, p. C3.

7. William R. Greer. "Robot Chef's New Dish: Hamburgers." *New York Times*, May 27, 1987, p. C3.

8. Michael Lev. "Taco Bell Finds Price of Success (59 cents)." *New York Times*, December 17, 1990, p. D9.

9. Calvin Sims. "Robots to Make Fast Food Chains Still Faster." *New York Times*, August 24, 1988, p. 5.

10. Chuck Murray. "Robots Roll from Plant to Kitchen." *Chicago Tribune/Business*, October 17, 1993, pp. 3ff; "New Robots Help McDonald's Make Fast Food Faster." *Business Wire*, August 18, 1992.

11. Chuck Murray. "Robots Roll from Plant to Kitchen." *Chicago Tribune/Business*, October 17, 1993, pp. 3ff.

12. "Disenchanted Evenings." *Time*, September 3, 1990, p. 53.

13. Ester Reiter. *Making Fast Food*. Montreal and Kingston: McGill-Queens University Press, p. 86.

14. Stan Luxenberg. *Roadside Empires: How the Chains Franchised America*. New York: Viking, 1985.

15. Harold Gracey. "Learning the Student Role: Kindergarten As Academic Boot Camp," in Dennis Wrong and Harold Gracey (eds.). *Readings in Introductory Sociology*. New York: Macmillan, 1967, pp. 243–254.

16. Charles E. Silberman. *Crisis in the Classroom: The Remaking of American Education*. New York: Random House, 1970, p. 122.

17. Charles E. Silberman. *Crisis in the Classroom: The Remaking of American Education*. New York: Random House, 1970, p. 125.

18. Charles E. Silberman. *Crisis in the Classroom: The Remaking of American Education*. New York: Random House, 1970, p. 137.

19. "The McDonald's of Teaching." *Newsweek*, January 7, 1985, p. 61.

20. "The McDonald's of Teaching." *Newsweek*, January 7, 1985, p. 61.

21. William Stockton. "Computers that Think." *New York Times Magazine*, December 14, 1980, p. 48.

22. Frederick W. Taylor. *The Principles of Scientific Management*. New York: Harper & Row, 1947, p. 59.

23. Henry Ford. *My Life and Work*. Garden City, NY: Doubleday, 1922, p. 103.

24. Robin Leidner. *Fast Food, Fast Talk: Service Work and the Routinization of Everyday Life*. Berkeley: University of California Press, 1993, p. 105.

25. William Serrin. "Let Them Eat Junk." *Saturday Review*, February 2, 1980, p. 23.

26. Martha Duffy. "The Fish Tank on the Farm." *Time*, December 3, 1990, pp. 107–111.

27. Peter Singer. *Animal Liberation: A New Ethic for Our Treatment of Animals*. New York: Avon Books, 1975.

28. Peter Singer. *Animal Liberation: A New Ethic for Our Treatment of Animals*. New York: Avon Books, 1975, pp. 96–97.

29. Peter Singer. *Animal Liberation: A New Ethic for Our Treatment of Animals*. New York: Avon Books, 1975, pp. 105–106.

30. Peter Singer. *Animal Liberation: A New Ethic for Our Treatment of Animals*. New York: Avon Books, 1975, p. 123.

31. "Super Soup Cooks Itself." *Scholastic News*, January 4, 1991, p. 3.

32. Eben Shapiro. "Ready, Set, Scan that Melon." *New York Times*, June 14, 1990, pp. D1, D8.

33. When the scanners were instituted at my local market, management announced that it was issuing markers to customers who were interested in writing the price on each item. This, again, is consistent with the trend toward getting the consumer to do work historically done by others, in this case by grocery clerks who worked deep into the night to

mark each item. In any case, the markers did not last long, since few hurried shoppers had the desire to put in several additional minutes a day as grocery clerks.

34. Eben Shapiro. "Ready, Set, Scan that Melon." *New York Times,* June 14, 1990, pp. D1, D8.

35. William Severini Kowinski. *The Malling of America: An Inside Look at the Great Consumer Paradise.* New York: Morrow, 1985, p. 359.

36. Virginia A. Welch. "Big Brother Flies United." *Washington Post/Outlook* March 5, 1995, p. C5.

37. Virginia A. Welch. "Big Brother Flies United." *Washington Post/Outlook* March 5, 1995, p. C5.

38. Gary Langer. "Computers Reach Out, Respond to Human Voice." *Washington Post,* February 11, 1990, p. H3.

39. Gary Langer. "Computers Reach Out, Respond to Human Voice." *Washington Post,* February 11, 1990, p. H3.

40. Jill Smolowe. "Read This!!!!!!!!" *Time,* November 26, 1990, pp. 62ff.

41. Michael Schrage. "'Personalized' Publishing: Confusing Information with Intimacy." *Washington Post,* November 23, 1990, p. B13.

42. Jeffrey Hadden and Charles E. Swann. *Prime Time Preachers: The Rising Power of Televangelism.* Reading, MA: Addison-Wesley, 1981.

43. E. J. Dionne, Jr. "The Vatican Is Putting Video to Work." *New York Times,* August 11, 1985, section 2, p. 27.

44. Raymond Kurzweil. *The Age of Intelligent Machines.* Cambridge, MA: MIT Press, 1990.

Chapter 7

1. Negative effects other than the ones discussed here, such as racism and sexism, cannot be explained by this process. See Ester Reiter. *Making Fast Food.* Montreal and Kingston: McGill-Queen's University Press, 1991, p. 145.

2. Paul Farhi. "McDonald's Customers: Made-to-Order Audience." *Washington Post,* November 19, 1991, pp. B1, B5.

3. Michael Schrage. "The Pursuit of Efficiency Can Be an Illusion." *Washington Post,* March 20, 1992, p. F3.

4. Richard Cohen. "Take a Message—Please!" *Washington Post Magazine*, August 5, 1990, p. 5.

5. Peter Carlson. "Who Put the Sunshine in the Sunshine Scent?" *Washington Post Magazine*, December 16, 1990, p. 21.

6. Peter Perl. "Fast Is Beautiful." *Washington Post Magazine*, May 24, 1992, p. 26.

7. Bob Garfield. "How I Spent (and Spent and Spent) My Disney Vacation." *Washington Post/Outlook*, July 7, 1991, p. B5.

8. Both quotations are from "Fast Food Speeds Up the Pace." *Time*, August 26, 1985, p. 60.

9. John Bowman. "Playing Around: Local Leaps and Bounds to Close in Wake of Discovery Zone Buying Chain." *Business First—Louisville*, January 9, 1995, section 1, p.4.

10. Stephen Levine. "McDonald's Makes a Play to Diversify." *Washington Post*, August 30, 1991, pp. GI, G4.

11. Yomiuri Shimbun. "Golden Arches Better-Known in Japan." *The Daily Yomiuri*, January 26, 1995, p. 17. Here, Shimbun also states that McDonald's owns 20% of the Japanese operations of Toys"Я"Us.

12. "Allying Toys and Fast Foods." *New York Times*, October 8, 1991, p. D15.

13. Stan Luxenberg. *Roadside Empires: How the Chains Franchised America*. New York: Viking, 1985, p. 116.

14. Burger King does the same thing to its fries. See Ester Reiter. *Making Fast Food*. Montreal and Kingston: McGill-Queen's University Press, 1991, p. 65.

15. Allen Shelton. "Writing McDonald's, Eating the Past: McDonald's As a Postmodern Space." (unpublished).

16. Peter Carlson. "Who Put the Sunshine in the Sunshine Scent?" *Washington Post Magazine*, December 16, 1990, p. 20.

17. Michael Ryan. "Fast Food Vs. Supermarkets." *Parade*, November 13, 1988, p. 6.

18. Neil Postman. *Amusing Ourselves to Death: Public Discourse in the Age of Show Business*. New York: Viking, 1985, p. 3.

19. William Severini Kowinski. *The Malling of America: An Inside Look at the Great Consumer Paradise*. New York: Morrow, 1985.

20. William Severini Kowinski. *The Malling of America: An Inside Look at the Great Consumer Paradise*. New York: Morrow, 1985, p. 371.

21. Jack Schnedler. "Mastering Mall of America: Full-Throttle Day of Shop-Hopping Tames Minnesota's Mighty Monster." *Chicago Sun-Times/Travel*, February 6, 1994, pp. 1ff.

22. Kara Swisher. "A Mall for America?" *Washington Post/Business*, June 30, 1991, pp. H1, H4.

23. Ian Mitroff and Warren Bennis. *The Unreality Industry: The Deliberate Manufacturing of Falsehood and What It Is Doing to Our Lives*. New York: Birch Lane Press, 1989, p. 12.

24. Daniel Boorstin. *The Image: A Guide to Pseudo-Events in America*. New York: Harper Colophon, 1961.

25. Ian Mitroff and Warren Bennis. *The Unreality Industry: The Deliberate Manufacturing of Falsehood and What It Is Doing to Our Lives*. New York: Birch Lane Press, 1989.

26. Joel Achenbach. "The Age of Unreality." *Washington Post*, November 22, 1990, pp. Cl, C14.

27. Maryellen Spencer. "Can Mama Mac Get Them to Eat Spinach?" in Marshall Fishwick (ed.). *Ronald Revisited: The World of Ronald McDonald*. Bowling Green, OH: Bowling Green University Press, 1983, pp. 85–93.

28. Regina Schrambling. "The Curse of Culinary Convenience." *New York Times*, September 10, 1991, p. A19.

29. Regina Schrambling. "The Curse of Culinary Convenience." *New York Times*, September 10, 1991, p. A19.

30. Eric Lipton. "Visit to Groomer's Takes Deadly Turn." *Washington Post*, March 31, 1995, p. B1.

31. Tim Luke. "Postcommunism in the USSR: The McGulag Archipelago." *Telos 84*(1990):33–42.

32. Max Boas and Steve Chain. *Big Mac: The Unauthorized Story of McDonald's*. New York: NAL, 1976.

33. Ester Reiter. *Making Fast Food*. Montreal and Kingston: McGill-Queen's University Press, 1991, pp. 150, 167.

34. Leidner disagrees with this, arguing that McDonald's "workers expressed relatively little dissatisfaction with the extreme routinization." See Robin Leidner. *Fast Food, Fast Talk: Service Work and the Routinization of Everyday Life*. Berkeley: University of California Press, 1993, p. 134. One could ask, however, whether this indicates a McDonaldizing society in which people, accustomed to the process, simply accept it as an inevitable part of their work.

35. Robin Leidner. *Fast Food, Fast Talk: Service Work and the Routinization of Everyday Life*. Berkeley: University of California Press, 1993, p. 30.

36. Bob Garfield. "How I Spent (and Spent and Spent) My Disney Vacation." *Washington Post/Outlook*, July 7, 1991, p. 5.

37. One exception to the general rule discussed here that diners do not linger is the tendency for retirees to use McDonald's as a social center, especially over breakfast or coffee.

38. Ester Reiter. *Making Fast Food*. Montreal and Kingston: McGill-Queen's University Press, 1991, p. 95.

39. Nicholas von Hoffman. "The Fast-Disappearing Family Meal." *Washington Post*, November 23, 1978, p. C4.

40. Margaret Visser. "A Meditation on the Microwave." *Psychology Today*, December 1989, pp. 38ff.

41. "The Microwave Cooks Up a New Way of Life." *Wall Street Journal*, September 19, 1989, p. B1.

42. Margaret Visser. "A Meditation on the Microwave." *Psychology Today*, December 1989, p. 40.

43. Margaret Visser. "A Meditation on the Microwave." *Psychology Today*, December 1989, p. 42.

44. Margaret Visser. "A Meditation on the Microwave." *Psychology Today*, December 1989, p. 42.

45. Ellen Goodman. "Fast-Forwarding Through Fall." *Washington Post*, October 5, 1991, p. A19.

46. Leonard Sloane. "Buying by Catalogue Is Easy: Timely Delivery May Not Be." *New York Times*, April 25, 1992, p. 50.

47. William H. Honan. "Professors Battling Television Technology." *New York Times*, April 4, 1995, p. D24.

48. Carl H. Lavin. "Automated Planes Raising Concerns." *New York Times*, August 12, 1989, pp. 1, 6.

49. Mark Dowie. "Pinto Madness." *Mother Jones*, September/October 1977, pp. 24ff.

50. Henry Ford. *My Life and My Work*. Garden City, NY: Doubleday Page & Co., 1922, pp. 105, 106.

51. Studs Terkel. *Working*. New York: Pantheon, 1974, p. 159.

52. Barbara Garson. *All the Livelong Day*. Harmondsworth, England: Penguin, 1977, p. 88.

53. Studs Terkel. *Working*. New York: Pantheon, 1974, p. 175.

54. For a review of the literature on this issue, see George Ritzer and David Walczak. *Working: Conflict and Change* (3rd ed.). Englewood Cliffs, NJ: Prentice-Hall, 1986, pp. 328–372.

Chapter 8

1. Ester Reiter. *Making Fast Food*. Montreal and Kingston: McGill-Queen's University Press, 1991, p. 165.

2. Molly O'Neill. "The Lure and Addiction of Life on Line." *New York Times*, March 8, 1995, pp. C1, C8.

3. However, the technology gives people the power to ignore them or delete them instantaneously.

4. Daniel Bell. *The Coming of Post-Industrial Society: A Venture in Social Forecasting*. New York: Basic Books, 1973.

5. Jerald Hage and Charles H. Powers. *Post-Industrial Lives: Roles and Relationships in the 21st Century*. Newbury Park, CA: Sage, 1992.

6. Jerald Hage and Charles H. Powers. *Post-Industrial Lives: Roles and Relationships in the 21st Century*. Newbury Park, CA: Sage, 1992, p. 10.

7. Steven L. Goldman, Roger N. Nagel, and Kenneth Preiss. "Why Seiko Has 3,000 Watch Styles." *New York Times*, October 9, 1994, p. 9; Steven L. Goldman, Roger N. Nagel, and Kenneth Preiss. *Agile Competitors and Virtual Organizations: Strategies for Enriching the Customer*. New York: Van Nostrand Reinhold, 1995.

8. Jerald Hage and Charles H. Powers. *Post-Industrial Lives: Roles and Relationships in the 21st Century*. Newbury Park, CA: Sage, 1992, p. 50.

9. Simon Clarke. "The Crisis of Fordism or the Crisis of Social Democracy?" *Telos* 8(1990):71–98.

10. Pierre Bourdieu. *Distinction: A Social Critique of the Judgment of Taste*. Cambridge, MA: Harvard University Press, 1984.

11. Alex Witchel. "By Way of Canarsie, One Large Hot Cup of Business Strategy." *New York Times*, December 14, 1994, pp. C1, C8.

12. Alex Witchel. "By Way of Canarsie, One Large Hot Cup of Business Strategy." *New York Times*, December 14, 1994, p. C8.

13. For more on postmodernism, see Jean Baudrillard. *Symbolic Exchange and Death*. London: Sage, 1976/1993; Fredric Jameson. "Postmodernism,

or the Cultural Logic of Late Capitalism." *New Left Review* 146(1984): 53–92; Frederic Jameson. *Postmodernism, or The Cultural Logic of Late Capitalism*. Durham, NC: Duke University Press, 1991; Jean-Francois Lyotard. *The Postmodern Condition: A Report on Knowledge*. Minneapolis, MN: University of Minnesota Press, 1984. For a good overview, see Steven Best and Douglas Kellner. *Postmodern Theory: Critical Interrogations*. New York: Guilford Press, 1991.

14. See chapter 12 of George Ritzer. *Modern Sociological Theory* (4th ed.). New York: McGraw-Hill, forthcoming; for a more extensive discussion see George Ritzer. *Postmodern Social Theory*. New York: McGraw-Hill, forthcoming.

15. Arthur Kroker, Marilouise Kroker, and David Cook. *Panic Encyclopedia: The Definitive Guide to the Postmodern Scene*. New York: St. Martin's Press, 1989, p. 119.

16. Allen Shelton. "Writing McDonald's, Eating the Past: McDonald's as a Postmodern Space." (unpublished).

17. Smart argues that rather than viewing modernism and postmodernism as epochs, people can see them as engaged in a long-running and ongoing set of relationships with postmodernity continually pointing out the limitations of modernity. See Barry Smart. *Postmodernity*. London: Routledge, 1993.

18. Allen Shelton. "Writing McDonald's, Eating the Past: McDonald's as a Postmodern Space." (unpublished).

19. David Harvey. *The Condition of Postmodernity: An Enquiry into the Origins of Cultural Change*. Oxford, England: Basil Blackwell, 1989, p. 189.

20. David Harvey. *The Condition of Postmodernity: An Enquiry into the Origins of Cultural Change*. Oxford, England: Basil Blackwell, 1989, pp. 284, 293. Shelton also places great emphasis on time-space compression, but he associates it with postmodernism and disassociates it from modernism.

21. Fredric Jameson. "Postmodernism, or the Cultural Logic of Late Capitalism." *New Left Review* 146(1984):53–92; *Postmodernism, or The Cultural Logic of Late Capitalism*. Durham, NC: Duke University Press, 1991.

22. Fredric Jameson. "Postmodernism, or the Cultural Logic of Late Capitalism." *New Left Review* 146(1984):78.

23. Fredric Jameson. "Postmodernism, or the Cultural Logic of Late Capitalism." *New Left Review* 146(1984):66.

24. Fredric Jameson. "Postmodernism, or the Cultural Logic of Late Capitalism." *New Left Review 146*(1984):64.

25. Fredric Jameson. "Postmodernism, or the Cultural Logic of Late Capitalism." *New Left Review 146*(1984):76.

26. Postmodern intensity also occurs when "the body is plugged into the new electronic media." See Martin Donougho. "Postmodern Jameson," in Douglas Kellner (ed.). *Postmodernism, Jameson, Critique.* Washington, DC: Maisonneuve Press, 1989, p. 85.

27. Fredric Jameson. "Postmodernism, or the Cultural Logic of Late Capitalism." *New Left Review 146*(1984):65–66, 71.

28. Fredric Jameson. "Postmodernism, or the Cultural Logic of Late Capitalism." *New Left Review 146*(1984):68.

29. Fredric Jameson. "Postmodernism, or the Cultural Logic of Late Capitalism." *New Left Review 146*(1984):68.

30. Alex Callinicos. *Against Postmodernism: A Marxist Critique.* New York: St. Martin's Press, 1990, p. 4.

Chapter 9

1. Lest I be accused of anthropomorphizing and reifying McDonaldization, it is actually people and their agencies that push the process.

2. Bill McDowall. "The Global Market Challenge." *Restaurants & Institutions,* vol. 104, no. 26, November 1, 1994, pp. 52ff.

3. Jean Baudrillard. *Symbolic Exchange and Death.* London: Sage 1976/1993, p. 172.

4. This idea comes from the work of the contemporary German theorist, Jurgen Habermas, who has focused on what he calls the colonization of the life world. See Jurgen Habermas. *The Theory of Communicative Action: Vol. 2, Lifeworld and System: A Critique of Functionalist Reason.* Boston: Beacon Press, 1987.

5. Somewhat more controversial is the idea that other children have not been born, have been aborted, and therefore a life of agony to them and their loved ones has been avoided.

6. Sherwin B. Nuland. *How We Die: Reflections on Life's Final Chapter.* New York: Knopf, 1994, p. 3.

7. Sherwin B. Nuland. *How We Die: Reflections on Life's Final Chapter*. New York: Knopf, 1994, p. 207.

8. Sherwin B. Nuland. *How We Die: Reflections on Life's Final Chapter*. New York: Knopf, 1994, p. 208.

9. Lenore Tiefer, "The Medicalization of Impotence: Normalizing Phallocentrism." *Gender and Society* 8(1994):363–377.

10. Cheryl Jackson. "Impotence Clinic Grows Into Chain." *The Tampa Tribune/Business and Finance*, February 18, 1995, p. 1.

11. Annette Baran and Reuben Pannor. *Lethal Secrets: The Shocking Consequences and Unresolved Problems of Artificial Insemination*. New York: Warner Books, 1989.

12. Paula Mergenbagen DeWitt. "In Pursuit of Pregnancy." *American Demographics*, May 1993, pp. 48ff.

13. Diederika Pretorius. *Surrogate Motherhood: A Worldwide View of the Issues*. Springfield, IL: Charles C. Thomas, 1994.

14. "A New Mama, Aged 62." *Daily Mail* (London), July 19, 1994, p. 12.

15. Angela Cain. "Home-Test Kits Fill an Expanding Health Niche." *The Times Union-Life and Leisure* (Albany, NY), February 12, 1995, p. 11.

16. Neil Bennett (ed). *Sex Selection of Children*. New York: Academic Press, 1983.

17. "Selecting Sex of Child." *South China Morning Post*, March 20, 1994, p. 15.

18. Matt Ridley. "A Boy or a Girl: Is It Possible to Load the Dice?" *Smithsonian* 24 (June 1993):113–123.

19. Rayna Rapp. "The Power of 'Positive' Diagnosis: Medical and Maternal Discourses on Amniocentesis," in Donna Bassin, Margaret Honey, and Meryle Mahrer Kaplan (eds.). *Representations of Motherhood*. New Haven, CT: Yale University Press, 1994, pp. 204–219.

20. Aliza Kolker and B. Meredith Burke. *Prenatal Testing: A Sociological Perspective*. Westport, CT: Bergin and Garvey, 1994, p. 158.

21. Aliza Kolker and B. Meredith Burke. *Prenatal Testing: A Sociological Perspective*. Westport, CT: Bergin and Garvey, 1994; Ellen Domke and Al Podgorski. "Testing the Unborn: Genetic Test Pinpoints Defects, But Are There Risks?" *Chicago Sun-Times*, April 17, 1994, p. C5.

22. Mike Chinoy. CNN News. February 8, 1994.

23. However, some parents do resist the rationalization introduced by fetal testing. See Shirley A. Hill. "Motherhood and the Obfuscation of Medical Knowledge." *Gender and Society 8*(1994): 29–47.

24. Annette Baran and Reuben Pannor. *Lethal Secrets: The Shocking Consequences and Unresolved Problems of Artificial Insemination.* New York: Warner Books, 1989, p. 162.

25. Aliza Kolker and B. Meredith Burke. *Prenatal Testing: A Sociological Perspective.* Westport, CT: Bergin and Garvey, 1994, p. 16.

26. Janet Daley. "Is Birth Ever Natural?" *The Times* (London), March 16, 1994, p. 18.

27. Joan H. Marks. "The Human Genome Project: A Challenge in Biological Technology," in Gretchen Bender and Timothy Druckery (eds.). *Culture on the Brink: Ideologies of Technology.* Seattle, WA: Bay Press, 1994, pp. 99–106; R. C. Lewontin. "The Dream of the Human Genome," in Gretchen Bender and Timothy Druckery (eds.). *Culture on the Brink: Ideologies of Technology.* Seattle, WA: Bay Press, 1994, pp. 107–127.

28. Matt Ridley. "A Boy or a Girl: Is It Possible to Load the Dice?" *Smithsonian 24*(June, 1993):123.

29. Janet Daley. "Is Birth Ever Natural?" *The Times* (London), March 16, 1994, p. 18.

30. Matt Ridley. "A Boy or a Girl: Is It Possible to Load the Dice?" *Smithsonian 24*(June, 1993):123.

31. Michelle Harrison. *A Woman in Residence.* New York: Random House, 1982, p. 91.

32. Much of this is drawn from Aliza Kolker and B. Meredith Burke. *Prenatal Testing: A Sociological Perspective.* Westport, CT: Bergin and Garvey, 1994.

33. Aliza Kolker and B. Meredith Burke. *Prenatal Testing: A Sociological Perspective.* Westport, CT: Bergin and Garvey, 1994, p. 7.

34. Barbara Katz Rothman. *The Tentative Pregnancy.* New York: Viking, 1986, p. 101.

35. Margarete Sandelowski. "Separate, But Less Equal: Fetal Ultrasonography and the Transformation of Expectant Mother/Fatherhood." *Gender and Society 8*(June 1994):230–245.

36. Piontelli, cited in Aliza Kolker and B. Meredith Burke. *Prenatal Testing: A Sociological Perspective.* Westport, CT: Bergin and Garvey, 1994, p. 1.

37. Jessica Mitford. *The American Way of Birth.* New York: Plume, 1993.

38. Jessica Mitford. *The American Way of Birth*. New York: Plume, 1993, p. 13.

39. Catherine Kohler Riessman. "Women and Medicalization: A New Perspective," in P. Brown (ed.). *Perspectives in Medical Sociology*. Prospect Heights, IL: Waveland Press, 1989, pp. 190–220.

40. Judith Walzer Leavitt. *Brought to Bed: Childbearing in America, 1750–1950*. New York: Oxford University Press, 1986, p. 190.

41. Judith Walzer Leavitt. *Brought to Bed: Childbearing in America, 1750–1950*. New York: Oxford University Press, 1986, p. 190.

42. Paula A. Treichler. "Feminism, Medicine, and the Meaning of Childbirth," in Mary Jacobus, Evelyn Fox Keller, and Sally Shuttleworth. *Body Politics: Women and the Discourses of Science*, New York: Routledge, 1990, pp. 113–138.

43. Jessica Mitford. *The American Way of Birth*. New York: Plume, 1993, p. 59.

44. An episiotomy is an incision from the vagina toward the anus to enlarge the opening needed for a baby to pass.

45. Jessica Mitford. *The American Way of Birth*. New York: Plume, 1993, p. 61.

46. Jessica Mitford. *The American Way of Birth*. New York: Plume, 1993, p. 143.

47. Michelle Harrison. *A Woman in Residence*. New York: Random House, 1982, p. 113.

48. Jeanne Guillemin. "Babies by Cesarian: Who Chooses, Who Controls?" in P. Brown (ed.). *Perspectives in Medical Sociology*. Prospect Heights, IL: Waveland Press, 1989, pp. 549–558.

49. L. Silver and S.M. Wolfe. *Unnecessary Cesarian Sections: How to Cure a National Epidemic*. Washington, DC: Public Citizen Health Research Group, 1989.

50. Randall S. Stafford. "Alternative Strategies for Controlling Rising Cesarian Section Rates." *JAMA*, February 2, 1990, pp. 683–687.

51. Jeffrey B. Gould, Becky Davey, and Randall S. Stafford. "Socioeconomic Differences in Rates of Cesarian Sections." *The New England Journal of Medicine*, vol. 321, no.4, July 27, 1989, pp. 233–239; F.C. Barros, et al. "Epidemic of Caesarian Sections in Brazil." *The Lancet*, July 20, 1991, pp. 167–169.

52. Randall S. Stafford. "Alternative Strategies for Controlling Rising Cesarian Section Rates." *JAMA*, February 2, 1990, pp. 683–687.

53. Michelle Harrison. *A Woman in Residence*. New York: Random House, 1982, p.86.

54. Although, more recently, insurance and hospital practices have led to more deaths in nursing homes or even at home.

55. Sherwin B. Nuland. *How We Die: Reflections on Life's Final Chapter*. New York: Knopf, 1994, p. 255; National Center for Health Statistics, *Vital Statistics of the United States, 1992–1993, Volume II—Mortality, Part A.* Hyattsville, MD: Public Health Service, 1995.

56. Sherwin B. Nuland. *How We Die: Reflections on Life's Final Chapter*. New York: Knopf, 1994, p.149.

57. Philippe Aries. *The Hour of Our Death*. New York: Knopf, 1981.

58. Sherwin B. Nuland. *How We Die: Reflections on Life's Final Chapter*. New York: Knopf, 1994, p. xv.

59. Jean Baudrillard. *Symbolic Exchange and Death*. London: Sage, 1976/1993, p. 180.

60. Nancy Gibbs. "Rx for Death." *Time*, May 31, 1993, p.34.

61. Sherwin B. Nuland. *How We Die: Reflections on Life's Final Chapter*. New York: Knopf, 1994, p.254.

62. James Corcoran. "Chain Buys Funeral Home in Mt. Holly." *Burlington County Times* (New Jersey), January 26, 1992; Kathy Finn. "Funeral Trends Favor Stewart IPO." *New Orleans City Business*, September 9, 1991, p. 23.

63. Holt Hackney. "Caskets on the Installment Plan." Trend Magazines, Inc., Business Dateline, Florida Trend, October, 1993 [Internet].

64. Brian Edwards. "Scaring up Profits: Knocking at Death's Door Can Pay Off." *Chicago Tribune*, October 29, 1993, p. 15.

65. Marvin Greene. "New Ad Raises Curiosity of Funeral-Home Directors." *Louisville Courier Journal*, April 12, 1994, p. D4.

66. Ellen McCarthy. "Today's Upbeat Funerals: Balloons, Not Boo Hoos." *San Francisco Chronicle*, September 12, 1991, p. C1.

67. Waka Hamada. "Aging Society Giving Birth to "Death" Business." *Japan Economic Newswire*, September 5, 1991.

68. Elizabeth Grice. "The Last Show on Earth." *The Times* (London), January 11, 1992, p. 10.

69. Elizabeth Grice. "The Last Show on Earth." *The Times* (London), January 11, 1992, pp. 10, 11.

70. Stephen M. Fjellman. *Vinyl Leaves: Walt Disney World and America*. Boulder, CO: Westview Press, 1992, pp. 116, 418.

71. Ellen Goodman. "Kevorkian Isn't Helping 'Gentle Death.'" *Newsday*, August 4, 1992, p. 32.

Chapter 10

1. Vic Sussman. "The Machine We Love to Hate." *Washington Post Magazine*, June 14, 1987, p.33.

 2. Kirk Johnson. "Bread: Satisfying a Need to Knead." *New York Times*, February 8, 1995, p. C1.

 3. Vic Sussman. "The Machine We Love to Hate." *Washington Post Magazine*, June 14, 1987, p.33.

 4. Tanya Wenman Steel. "Have Time to Bake? What a Luxury!" *New York Times*, February 8, 1995, p. C4.

 5. Weber, cited in Hans Gerth and C. Wright Mills (eds.). *From Max Weber*. New York: Oxford University Press, 1958, p. 128.

 6. Isabel Wilkerson. "Midwest Village; Slow-Paced, Fights Plan for Fast-Food Outlet." *New York Times*, July 19, 1987, pp. 1, 16.

 7. Mary Davis Suro. "Romans Protest McDonald's." *New York Times*, May 5, 1986, p. C20.

 8. Jane Perlez. "A McDonald's? Not in Their Medieval Square," *New York Times*, May 23, 1994, p. A4.

 9. "Eating Out Is In, and the Chains Add Variety to Lure New Diners." *Time*, August 26, 1985, pp. 60–61.

10. Anthony Ramirez. "In the Orchid Room . . . Big Macs." *New York Times*, October 30, 1990, pp. DI, D5.

11. Jane Perlez. "A McDonald's? Not in Their Medieval Square." *New York Times*, May 23, 1994, p. A4.

12. In one notable exception, the entire state of Vermont has thus far been kept free of Wal-Marts. See Paul Gruchow. "Unchaining America: Communities Are Finding Ways to Keep Independent Entrepreneurs in Business." *Utne Reader*, January–February 1995, pp. 17–18.

13. Peter Pae. "Retail Giant Rattles the Shops on Main Street." *Washington Post*, February 12, 1995, p. B3.

14. Peter Kilborn. "When Wal-Mart Pulls Out, What's Left?" *New York Times/Business*, March 5, 1995, pp. 1, 6.

15. Steve Ginsberg. "Blockbusted: Neighborhood Merchants Produce Summer Flop." *San Francisco Business Times*, September 2, 1994, section 1, p. 3.

16. Anthony Ramirez. "When Fast Food Goes on a Diet." *Washington Post*, March 19, 1991, pp. D1, D7.

17. Marian Burros. "Fast-Food Chains Try to Slim Down." *New York Times*, April 11, 1990, pp. CI, C10.

18. Leon Jaroff. "A Crusader from the Heartland." *Time*, March 25, 1991, pp. 56, 58.

19. Marian Burros. "Eating Well." *New York Times*, March 2, 1994, p. C4.

20. Anthony Ramirez. "When Fast Food Goes on a Diet." *Washington Post*, March 19, 1991, pp. D1, D7.

21. Ross Kerber and Greg Johnson. "Getting Leaner." *Los Angeles Times*, February 9, 1995, p. D1.

22. Anthony Ramirez. "When Fast Food Goes on a Diet." *Washington Post*, March 19, 1991, p. D1, D7.

23. John Holusha. "McDonald's Expected to Drop Plastic Burger Box." *Washington Post*, November 1, 1990, pp. A1, D19; John Holusha. "Packaging and Public Image: McDonald's Fills a Big Order." *New York Times*, November 2, 1990, pp. Al, D5.

24. Warren Brown. "Hardee's to Introduce Recycled Plastic in Area." *Washington Post*, March 22, 1991, pp. B1, B3.

25. Phil West. "Cafe's Decor, Not-So-Fast Food Evoke McMemories." *Washington Times*, August 30, 1990, p. Cl.

26. Laura Shapiro. "Ready for McCatfish." *Newsweek*, October 15, 1990, pp. 76–77.

27. "Y'All Have Some McGrits." *The Bergen Record* (Hackensack, NJ), May 19, 1994, p. B2.

28. Randy Diamond. "That's Italian! McDonald's Putting Pizza on the Menu." *The Bergen Record* (Hackensack, NJ), October 21, 1993, p. C14.

29. Rajan Chaudry. "America Rates Its Favorite Chains." *Restaurants & Institutions*, vol. 104, no. 3, February 1, 1994, pp. 48ff.

30. Ron Alexander. "Big Mac with Chopin, Please." *New York Times*, August 12, 1990, p. 42.

31. Theresa Howard. "McD hits the road with 'McDelivery.'" *Nation's Restaurant News*, November 8, 1993, p. 1.

32. Ross Kerber and Greg Johnson. "Getting Leaner." *Los Angeles Times*, February 9, 1995, p. D1.

33. Richard Martin. "Bakersfield McD Units Test Credit Card System for Business Customers." *Nation's Restaurant News*, November 18, 1985, p. 3; Paul Baran and Paul M. Sweezy. *Monopoly Capital: An Essay on the American Economic and Social Order*. New York: Monthly Review Press, 1966; Michael Lev. "Taco Bell Finds Price of Success (59¢)." *New York Times*, December 17, 1990, pp. D1, D9; and Michael Lev. "California McDonald's to Cut Menu Prices." *New York Times*, December 21, 1990, p. D3.

34. Eric Schmitt. "Burger King on Wheels." *New York Times*, November 23, 1985, pp. 35, 37.

35. Eric Maykuth. "Chock Full o' Nuts Restaurants Are Dying Quietly." *Washington Post*, September 16, 1990, p. H16.

36. Anna D. Wilde. "Just Like Ice Cream in the Sun: HoJo's Dominance Has Melted Away." *Patriot Ledger*, August 13, 1994, p. B25.

37. Data on Taco Bell and Pizza Hut come from PepsiCo Inc.'s 1993 annual report.

38. Ester Reiter. *Making Fast Food*. Montreal and Kingston: McGill-Queen's University Press, 1991, pp. 70ff.

39. James Brooke. "Two McDonald's in Darien Do Their Hiring in Bronx." *New York Times*, July 13, 1985, section 1, p. 24; Michael Winerip. "Finding a Sense of McMission in McNuggets." *New York Times*, August 23, 1988, section 2, p. 1; "McDonald's Seeks Retirees to Fill Void." *New York Times*, December 20, 1987, section 1, p. 54; Jennifer Kingson. "Golden Years Spent Under Golden Arches." *New York Times*, March 6, 1988, section 4, p. 26.

40. Glenn Collins. "Wanted: Child-Care Workers, Age 55 and Up." *New York Times*, December 15, 1987, section 1, p. 1.

41. George Ritzer. "Implications of and Barriers to Industrial Democracy in the United States and Sweden," in Irving Louis Horowitz (ed.). *Equity, Income and Policy: A Comparative Developmental Context*. New York and London: Praeger, 1977, pp. 49–69.

42. Andrew Malcolm. "Bagging Old Rules to Keep a Food Co-op Viable." *New York Times*, November 8, 1991, p. B7.

43. Other examples include St. Mary's College in Maryland and Evergreen State College in Washington.

44. For other examples of shops such as Marvelous Market, see Marian Burros. "Putting the Pleasure Back into Grocery Shopping." *New York Times*, February 21, 1987, section 1, p. 54.

45. This quotation, as well as others in this section, are drawn from Marvelous Market's occasional newsletters.

46. "Eating Out Is In, and the Chains Add Variety to Lure New Diners." *Time*, August 26, 1985, p. 60.

47. Fred 'Chico' Lager. *Ben & Jerry's: The Inside Scoop*. New York: Crown, 1994; Suzanne Alexander. "Oh, Wow, Man: Let's, Like, Hear from the Auditors." *Wall Street Journal*, June 28, 1991, pp. Al, A6.

48. Fred 'Chico' Lager. *Ben & Jerry's: The Inside Scoop*. New York: Crown, 1994, p. 148.

49. Fred 'Chico' Lager. *Ben & Jerry's: The Inside Scoop*. New York: Crown, 1994, p. 133.

50. Fred 'Chico' Lager. *Ben & Jerry's: The Inside Scoop*. New York: Crown, 1994, p. 28.

51. Fred 'Chico' Lager. *Ben & Jerry's: The Inside Scoop*. New York: Crown, 1994, p. 36.

52. Ben & Jerry's 1990 annual report, p. 7.

53. Fred 'Chico' Lager. *Ben & Jerry's: The Inside Scoop*. New York: Crown, 1994, p. 145.

54. Two preceding quotations from Maxine Lipner. "Ben & Jerry's: Sweet Ethics Evince Social Awareness." *COMPASS Readings*, July 1991, pp. 26–27.

55. Two preceding quotations from Carol Clurman. "More than Just a Paycheck." *USA WEEKEND*, January 19–21, 1990, p. 4.

56. Glenn Collins. "Organization Man for Ben & Jerry's." *New York Times*, February 2, 1995, pp. D1, D7.

57. Maxine Lipner. "Ben & Jerry's: Sweet Ethics Evince Social Awareness." *COMPASS Readings*, July 1991, p. 25.

58. Fred 'Chico' Lager. *Ben & Jerry's: The Inside Scoop*. New York: Crown, 1994, p. 164.

59. Eric J. Wiffering. "Trouble in Camelot." *Business Ethics* 5(1991):16, 19.

60. Patricia Aburdene. "Paycheck." *USA WEEKEND*, January 19–21, 1990, p. 4.

61. "Digest." *Washington Post*, March 4, 1995, p. D1.

62. Glenn Collins. "Organization Man for Ben & Jerry's." *New York Times*, February 2, 1995, p. D7.

63. June R. Herold. "B&B's Offer Travelers Break from McBed, McBreakfast." *Business First—Columbus*, 5, 15: 1, p.1.

64. Betsy Wade. "B & B Book Boom." *Chicago Tribune*, July 28, 1991, pp. C16ff.

65. Paul Avery. "Mixed Success for Bed-Breakfast Idea." *New York Times*, July 28, 1991, pp. 12NJ, 8.

66. Eric N. Berg. "The New Bed and Breakfast." *New York Times*, October 15, 1989, pp. 5ff.

67. Thomas J. Peters and Robert H. Waterman. *In Search of Excellence: Lessons from America's Best-Run Companies*. New York: Harper & Row, 1982.

68. Thomas J. Peters and Robert H. Waterman. *In Search of Excellence: Lessons from America's Best-Run Companies*. New York: Harper & Row, 1982, p. 201.

69. For a similar effort, see Neil Postman. *Technopoly*. New York: Knopf, 1992, pp. 183ff.

70. Peter Perl. "Fast Is Beautiful." *Washington Post Magazine*, May 24, 1992, pp. 10ff; Allen Shelton."Writing McDonald's, Eating the Past: McDonald's As a Postmodern Space." (unpublished), p. 47.

71. Regina Schrambling. "The Curse of Culinary Convenience." *New York Times*, September 10, 1991, p. A19.

72. All quotations in this paragraph are from Regina Schrambling. "The Curse of Culinary Convenience." *New York Times*, September 10, 1991, p. A19.

73. Warren Leary. "Researchers Halt Ripening of Tomato." *New York Times*, October 19, 1991, p. 7.

74. John Tierney. "A Patented Berry Has Sellers Licking Their Lips." *New York Times*, October 14, 1991, p. A8.

75. Roger Cohen. "Faux Pas by McDonald's in Europe." *New York Times*, February 18, 1992, p. D1.

76. Two quotes from Sharon Waxman. "Paris's Sex Change Operation." *Washington Post*, March 2, 1992, p. B1.

77. Dylan Thomas. *The Collected Poems of Dylan Thomas*. "Do Not Go Gentle into That Good Night." New York: New Directions, 1952, p. 128.

Bibliography

Rather than repeating the citations listed in the end notes, I would like to use this section to cite some of the major academic works that served as resources for this book. There are three categories of such resources. The first is the work of Max Weber, especially that dealing with rationalization. The second is the work of various neo-Weberians who have modified and expanded upon Weber's original ideas. Finally, there is a series of works that focus on specific aspects of our McDonaldized society.

Works by Max Weber

Max Weber. *The Protestant Ethic and the Spirit of Capitalism*. New York: Scribner's, 1904–1905/1958.

Max Weber. "Religious Rejections of the World and Their Directions." In H. H. Gerth and C. W. Mills, eds. *From Max Weber: Essays in Sociology*. New York: Oxford University Press, 1915/1958, pp. 323–359.

Max Weber. "The Social Psychology of the World Religions." In H. H. Gerth and C. W. Mills, eds. *From Max Weber: Essays in Sociology*. New York: Oxford University Press, 1915/1958, pp. 267–301.

Max Weber. *The Religion of China: Confucianism and Taoism*. New York: MacMillan, 1916/1964.

Max Weber. *The Religion of India: The Sociology of Hinduism and Buddhism*. Glencoe, IL: Free Press, 1916–1917/1958.

Max Weber. *The Rational and Social Foundations of Music*. Carbondale, IL: Southern Illinois University Press, 1921/1958.

Max Weber. *Economy and Society*, volumes 1 through 3, Totowa, NJ: Bedminster Press, 1921/1968.

Max Weber. *General Economic History*. New Brunswick, NJ: Transaction Books, 1927/ 1981.

Works by Neo-Weberians

Rogers Brubaker. *The Limits of Rationality: An Essay on the Social and Moral Thought of Max Weber*. London: Allen and Unwin, 1984.

Randall Collins. "Weber's Last Theory of Capitalism: A Systematization." *American Sociological Review* 45(1980):925–942.

Randall Collins. *Weberian Sociological Theory*. Cambridge: Cambridge University Press, 1985.

Arnold Eisen. "The Meanings and Confusions of Weberian 'Rationality.'" *British Journal of Sociology* 29(1978):57–70.

Harvey Greisman. "Disenchantment of the World." *British Journal of Sociology* 27(1976):497–506.

Harvey Greisman and George Ritzer. "Max Weber, Critical Theory and the Administered World." *Qualitative Sociology* 4(1981):34–55.

Jurgen Habermas. *The Theory of Communicative Action*. Vol. 1, *Reason and the Rationalization of Society*. Boston: Beacon Press, 1984.

Stephen Kalberg. "Max Weber's Types of Rationality: Cornerstones for the Analysis of Rationalization Processes in History." *American Journal of Sociology* 85(1980):1145–1179.

Stephen Kalberg. "The Rationalization of Action in Max Weber's Sociology of Religion." *Sociological Theory* 8(1990):58–84.

Stephen Kalberg. *Max Weber's Comparative Historical Sociology*. Chicago: University of Chicago Press, 1994.

Donald Levine. "Rationality and Freedom: Weber and Beyond." *Sociological Inquiry* 51(1981):5–25.

Arthur Mitzman. *The Iron Cage: A Historical Interpretation of Max Weber*. New York: Grosset and Dunlap, 1969.

Wolfgang Mommsen. *The Age of Bureaucracy*. New York: Harper and Row, 1974.

George Ritzer. "Professionalization, Bureaucratization and Rationalization: The Views of Max Weber." *Social Forces* 53(1975):627–634.

George Ritzer and David Walczak. "Rationalization and the Deprofessionalization of Physicians." *Social Forces* 67(1988):1–22.

George Ritzer and Terri LeMoyne. "Hyperrationality." In George Ritzer, *Metatheorizing in Sociology*. Lexington, MA: Lexington Books, 1991, pp. 93–115.

Guenther Roth and Reinhard Bendix, eds. *Scholarship and Partisanship: Essays on Max Weber*. Berkeley: University of California Press, 1971.

Lawrence Scaff. *Fleeing the Iron Cage: Culture, Politics, and Modernity in the Thought of Max Weber*. Berkeley: University of California Press, 1989.

Wolfgang Schluchter. *The Rise of Western Rationalism: Max Weber's Developmental History*. Berkeley: University of California Press, 1971.

Alan Sica. *Weber, Irrationality and the Social Order*. Berkeley: University of California Press, 1988.

Ronald Takaki. *Iron Cages: Race and Culture in 19th-Century America*. New York: Oxford University Press, 1990.

Works on Various Aspects of a McDonaldizing Society

Zygmunt Bauman. *Modernity and the Holocaust*. Ithaca, New York: Cornell University Press, 1989.

Daniel Bell. *The Coming of Post-Industrial Society: A Venture in Social Forecasting*. New York: Basic Books, 1973.

Max Boas and Steve Chain. *Big Mac: The Unauthorized Story of McDonald's*. New York: E. P. Dutton, 1976.

Daniel Boorstin. *The Image: Guide to Pseudo-Events in America*. New York: Harper Colophon, 1961.

Pierre Bourdieu. *Distinction: A Social Critique of the Judgment of Taste*. Cambridge, MA: Harvard University Press, 1984.

Simon Clarke. "The Crisis of Fordism or the Crisis of Social Democracy?" *Telos* *83*(1990):71–98.

Richard Edwards. *Contested Terrain: The Transformation of the Workplace in the Twentieth Century*. New York: Basic Books, 1979.

Marshall Fishwick, ed. *Ronald Revisited: The World of Ronald McDonald*. Bowling Green: Bowling Green University Press, 1983.

Stephen M. Fjellman. *Vinyl Leaves: Walt Disney World and America*. Boulder: Westview Press, 1992.

James T. Flink. *The Automobile Age*. Cambridge: MIT Press, 1988.

Henry Ford. *My Life and Work*. Garden City, NY: Doubleday, Page, and Co., 1922.

Herbert Gans. *The Levittowners: Ways of Life and Politics in a New Suburban Community*. New York: Pantheon Books, 1967.

Barbara Garson. *All the Livelong Day*. Harmondsworth, England: Penguin, 1977.

Steven L. Goldman, Roger N. Nagel, and Kenneth Preiss. *Agile Competitors and Virtual Organizations: Strategies for Enriching the Customer*. New York: Van Nostrand Reinhold, 1995.

Richard E. Gordon, Katharine K. Gordon, and Max Gunther. *The Split Level Trap*. New York: Gilbert Geis Associates, 1960.

Harold Gracey. "Learning the Student Role: Kindergarten as Academic Boot Camp." In Dennis Wrong and Harold Gracey, eds. *Reading in Introductory Sociology*. New York: MacMillan, 1967.

Allen Guttmann. *From Ritual to Record: The Nature of Modern Sports*. New York: Cambridge University Press, 1978.

Jeffrey Hadden and Charles E. Swann. *Primetime Preachers: The Rising Power of Televangelism*. Reading, MA: Addison-Wesley, 1981.

Jerald Hage and Charles H. Powers. *Post Industrial Lives: Roles and Relationships in the 21st Century*. Newbury Park, CA: Sage, 1992.

David Harvey. *The Condition of Postmodernity: An Enquiry into the Origins of Cultural Change*. Oxford: Basil Blackwell, 1989.

Kathleen Jamieson. *Eloquence in an Electronic Age: The Transformation of Political Speechmaking*. New York: Oxford University Press, 1988.

Aliza Kolker and B. Meredith Burke. *Prenatal Testing: A Sociological Perspective*. Westport, CT: Bergin and Garvey, 1994.

William Severini Kowinski. *The Malling of America: An Inside Look at the Great Consumer Paradise*. New York: William Morrow, 1985.

Ray Kroc. *Grinding It Out*. New York: Berkeley Medallion Books, 1977.

Raymond Kurzweil. *The Age of Intelligent Machines*. Cambridge, MA: MIT Press, 1990.

Fred 'Chico' Lager. *Ben & Jerry's: The Inside Scoop*. New York: Crown Publishers, 1994.

Robin Leidner. *Fast Food, Fast Talk: Service Work and the Routinization of Everyday Life*. Berkeley: University of California Press, 1993.

John F. Love. *McDonald's: Behind the Arches*. Toronto: Bantam Books, 1986.

Stan Luxenberg. *Roadside Empires: How the Chains Franchised America*. New York: Viking, 1985.

Jean-François Lyotard. *The Postmodern Condition: A Report on Knowledge*. Minneapolis, MN: The University of Minnesota Press, 1984.

Frank Mankiewicz and Joel Swerdlow. *Remote Control: Television and the Manipulation of American Life*. New York: Time Books, 1978.

Jessica Mitford. *The American Way of Birth*. New York: Plume, 1993.

Ian Mitroff and Warren Bennis. *The Unreality Industry: The Deliberate Manufacturing of Falsehood and What it Is Doing to Our Lives*. New York: Birch Lane Press, 1989.

Sherwin B. Nuland. *How We Die: Reflections on Life's Final Chapter*. New York: Knopf, 1994.

Martin Parker and David Jary. "The McUniversity: Organization, Management and Academic Subjectivity." *Organization* 2(1995):319–337.

Thomas J. Peters and Robert H. Waterman. *In Search of Excellence: Lessons from America's Best-Run Companies.* New York: Harper & Row, 1982.

Neil Postman. *Amusing Ourselves to Death: Public Discourse in the Age of Show Business.* New York: Viking, 1985.

Neil Postman. *Technopoly: The Surrender of Culture to Technology.* New York: Knopf, 1992.

Peter Prichard. *The Making of McPaper: The Inside Story of USA Today.* Kansas City, MO: Andrews, McMeel and Parker, 1987.

Stanley Joel Reiser. *Medicine and the Reign of Technology.* Cambridge: Cambridge University Press, 1978.

Ester Reiter. *Making Fast Food.* Montreal and Kingston: McGill-Queen's University Press, 1991.

George Ritzer. "The McDonaldization of Society." *Journal of American Culture* 6(1983):100–107.

George Ritzer and David Walczak. "The Changing Nature of American Medicine." *Journal of American Culture* 9(1987):43–51.

George Ritzer. *Expressing America: A Critique of the Global Credit Card Society.* Newbury Park, CA: Pine Forge Press, 1995.

Charles E. Silberman. *Crisis in the Classroom: The Remaking of American Education.* New York: Random House, 1970.

Peter Singer. *Animal Liberation: A New Ethics for Our Treatment of Animals.* New York: Avon Books, 1975.

Alfred P. Sloan, Jr. *My Years at General Motors.* Garden City, NY: Doubleday, 1964.

Frederick W. Taylor. *The Principles of Scientific Management.* New York: Harper and Row, 1947.

Shoshana Zuboff. *In the Age of the Smart Machine: The Future of Work and Power.* New York: Basic Books, 1988.

Acknowledgments

We gratefully acknowledge the following for permission to reprint quotes:

Associated Press for "Cafe's Decor, Not-So-Fast-Food Evoke McMemories," P. West, 30 August 1990, *The Washington Times*. Copyright 1990 The Associated Press, reprinted by permission.

The Boston Globe for "Endangered Species: Will the Corner Video Store Disappear in the Interactive Age?" S. Fainaru, 16 January 1994, *The Boston Globe*. Copyright 1994 The Boston Globe, reprinted by permission.

Janet Daley for "Is Birth Ever Natural?" J. Daley, 16 March 1994, *The Times*. Copyright 1994 Janet Daley. Reprinted by permission.

Dow Jones & Company, Inc. for "The Microwave Cooks Up a New Way of Life," 19 September 1989, *The Wall Street Journal*. Reprinted by permission of The Wall Street Journal, ©1989 Dow Jones & Company, Inc. All Rights Reserved Worldwide.

Brian Edwards for "Scaring Up Profits: Knocking on Death's Door Can Pay Off," B. Edwards, 29 October 1993, *The Chicago Tribune*. Copyright 1993 Brian Edwards, reprinted by permission.

Financial World Partners for "Mac Attack?" R. Papiernik, 12 April 1994, *Financial World*. Copyright 1994 Financial World Partners, reprinted by permission.

Elizabeth Grice for "The Last Show on Earth," E. Grice, 11 January 1992, *The Times*. Copyright 1992 Elizabeth Grice. Reprinted by permission.

David Higham Associates for "Do Not Go Gentle into that Good Night," D. Thomas, 1952, *The Poems*, London: JM Dent. Copyright 1995 David Higham Associates, reprinted by permission.

Louisville Courier-Journal for "New Ad Raises Curiosity of Funeral Home Directors," M. Greene, 12 April 1994, *The Courier-Journal*. Copyright 1994 The Courier-Journal, reprinted by permission.

Newsweek, Inc. for "The McDonald's of Teaching," 7 January 1985 and "Ready for McCatfish," L. Shapiro, 15 October 1990, *Newsweek Magazine*. Copyright ©1985, 1990 Newsweek, Inc. All rights reserved. Reprinted by permission.

New Left Review for "Postmodernism, or, the Cultural Logic of Late Capitalism," 1984, *New Left Review 146*, p. 64. Copyright 1984 New Left Review, reprinted by permission.

The New York Times for "Unlikely Spot for Fast Food," A. Cowan, 29 April 1984; "Big Chains Joining Manhattan's Toy Wars," T. Egan, 8 December 1990; "McBurger

Time Warner, Inc. for "Disenchanted Evenings," 3 September 1990; "Fast Food Speeds Up the Pace," 26 August 1985; "Rx For Death," N. Gibbs, 31 May 1993; "A Crusader from the Heartland," L. Jaroff, 25 March 1991; "Eating Out Is In, and the Chains Add Variety to Lure New Diners," 26 August 1985, *Time Magazine.* Copyright ©1985/90/91/93 Time Warner Inc. Reprinted by permission.

USA Today Magazine for "McDonald's and the New American Landscape," M. King, January 1980, *USA Today Magazine.* Copyright ©1980 by the Society for the Advancement of Education. Reprinted by permission.

USA Weekend for "Bosses for the '90s: More Than Just a Paycheck," C. Clurman and P. Aburdene, 21 January 1990, *USA Weekend.* Copyright 1990 USA Weekend. Reprinted with permission.

The Washington Post for "Health Club . . . For Kids," S. Burling, 21 November 1991, p. D5; "Wedge of Americana: In Moscow Pizza Hut Opens Two Restaurants," 12 September 1990, p. B10; "Frying Down to Rio," J. Blount, 18 May 1994, p. F1; "McMilestone Restaurant Opens Doors in Dale City," J. Harris, 7 April 1988, p. D1; "How I Spent (and Spent and Spent) My Disney Vacation," B. Garfield, 7 July 1991, p. B5; "In Praise of McDonald's," R. Samuelson, 1 November 1989, p. A25; "No Service, No Smile, Little Sauce," L. Hockstader, 5 August 1991, p. A12; "Raising Fast Food's Speed Limit," M. Lev, 7 August 1991, p. D1; "Calling the Technology of Voice Mail into Question," M. Schrage, 19 October 1990, p. F3; "Companies Unveil 'Scanfone' Shopping Service," K. Swisher, 16 April 1992, p. B1; "Blockbuster Struggles with Merger Script," M. Potts, 9 December 1991, p. 24; "On the Inside at Parks à la Disney," L. Darling, 28 August 1978, p. A10; "Arches of Triumph," M. Clark, 5 June 1977; "The Credentials Epidemic," S. Gervasi, 30 August 1990; "Stanford President Sets Initiative on Teaching," K. Cooper, 3 March 1991, p. A12; "Wonder Bread, Any Way You Slice It," H. Mitchell, 22 March 1991, p. F2; "Lukas Has the Franchise on Almighty McDollar," A. Beyer, 8 August 1990, p. F1; "Computers Reach Out, Respond to Human Voice," G. Langer, 11 February 1990, p. H3; "'Personalized' Publishing: Confusing Information with Intimacy," M. Schrage, 23 November 1990, p. B13; "McDonald's Customers: Made-to-Order Audience," P. Farhi, 19 November 1991, p. B1; "Take a Message-Please!" R. Cohen, 5 August 1990, p. 5; "Who Put the Sunshine in the Sunshine Scent?" P. Carlson, 16 December 1990, p. 21; "McDonald's Makes a Play to Diversify," S. Levine, 30 August 1991, p. G1; "A Mall for America," K. Swisher, 30 June 1991, p. H1; "The Fast-Disappearing Family Meal," N. von Hoffman, 1978, p. C4; "The Machine We Love to Hate," V. Sussman, 14 June 1987, p. 33; "When Fast-Food Goes on a Diet," A. Ramirez, 19 March 1991, p. D1; "Hardee's to Introduce Recycled Plastic in Area," W. Brown, 22 March 1991, p. B1; "Chock Full o' Nuts Restaurants Are Dying Quietly," E. Maykuth, 16 September 1990, p. H16; "Fast Is Beautiful," P. Perl, 24 May, 1992; "Paris' Sex Change Operation," S. Waxman, 2 March 1992, p. B1, *The Washington Post.* Copyright © 1977/78/87/88/89/90/91/92 The Washington Post. Reprinted with permission.

Virginia Welch for "Big Brother Flies United," V. Welch, 5 March 1995, *The Washington Post.* Copyright 1995 Virginia Welch. Reprinted by permission.

Index